New York Essays

New York Essays

RESOURCES for the GENEALOGIST
in NEW YORK STATE Outside New York City

MARIAN S. HENRY

NEW ENGLAND HISTORIC GENEALOGICAL SOCIETY
BOSTON, MASSACHUSETTS

ISBN-13: 978-088082-210-7
ISBN-10: 0-88082-210-4

Library of Congress Control Number: 2007929213

Printed in the United States of America

Cover design by Ann Conneman

Cover images: Top, "Northeastern view of Geneva"; middle, "Southwest view of the central part of Canandaigua"; bottom, "Eastern part of Genesee-Street, Auburn." All are from John W. Barber, *Historical Collections of the State of New York* (New York: Clark, Austin & Co., 1851).

Published by
New England Historic Genealogical Society®
101 Newbury Street
Boston, MA 02116
www.NewEnglandAncestors.org

To my beloved David —
my best friend, my life's companion,
and my staunchest supporter.

CONTENTS

Contents

PREFACE

Most of the essays in this collection were first published electronically by the New England Historic Genealogical Society on its website *NewEnglandAncestors.org*. The first essay was posted on February 25, 2000. Other essays followed at irregular intervals over the next four years. During this time, each of three editors — Tom Kozachek, Rod Moody, and Michael J. Leclerc — left his mark on the style.

Two internet-based essays were deemed to have content too ephemeral to include here. Five essays that were never posted are published here for the first time. The essays are presented essentially as written with only minor alterations to update or correct. As such the collection is, inherently, more of a work in progress than a tightly unified narrative. In harmony with long tradition at NEHGS, I have tried to include both historical and genealogical subjects. Part I contains those essays primarily genealogical in focus. Essays of a more historical nature are collected in Part II. Each essay is, in fact, a blend of both, making the placement somewhat arbitrary.

The genealogy side contains the beginning of a New York state research genealogist's toolbox. The toolbox contains some standard items such as state census records (Chapter 10) and finding aids (Chapters 9 and 11). Special mention must be made of the Historical Documents Inventory (Chapter 1). This is a most remarkable resource that goes a long way to make up for other difficulties. Also of particular interest to those researching in early colonial New York is a discussion of the complexities of Dutch naming practices (Chapter 2).

Four essays are concerned with vital records and their substitutes. The widening of public access to the state vital records index is celebrated in Chapter 6. Even though official state records did not begin until 1880, three companion essays (Chapters 3–5) show that there is a lot of information available, if one simply knows where to look.

Two essays illustrate the experience and importance of visiting local repositories. The Ontario County archives (Chapter 7) contains the earliest records for western New York. The Magee House (Chapter 20) in Bath is a typical example of a county historical society. A visit to a similar institution in another county will differ only in the details.

On the history side you will find the "where" and "when" of population flow as the frontier swept across the state from east to west. This section begins with an initial overview of settlement (Chapter 16). After that you will find essays that discuss the transformation of the state in the years following the Revolutionary War. The majority of pioneers came from New England. Many of the families remained in New York for only a short time before continuing further west. As an aid to researchers, I have tried to mention, wherever possible, surnames of the earliest immigrants. The process of clearing the land involved an enormous amount of labor, but not much time from a historical perspective. A single lifetime sufficed. Settlement flowed through the Phelps-Gorham purchase (Chapter 17) into the "Genesee Country" (Chapter 18), then into the "Niagara Country" (Chapter 21) over the course of only about thirty years.

Part II is rounded out with several "local color" essays each of which contains smaller-scale pieces of history. Each focuses on a single group that made an interesting contribution to the settlement of the state. Three ethnic groups are represented – Palatines (Chapter 24), Welsh (Chapter 25), and French (Chapter 26). Several essays deal with an individual playing a starring role. John Brown and his children tried to promote settlement in the Adirondacks (Chapter 23). Jemima Wilkinson and her followers were pioneer settlers in Yates County (Chapter 27). John Humphrey Noyes founded the utopian Oneida Community (Chapter 28). The village of Prattsburg grew from wilderness to settled community during the lifetime of its most famous citizen, Narcissa Prentiss Whitman (Chapter 19). Finally, this book could not be complete without some mention of the impact of the Erie Canal (Chapter 22).

The final tool combines history and genealogy and is offered as an appendix. This is the genealogy of counties within the state, listing year of formation, county seat, and the parent county or counties from which the county was formed. Consider, for example, the town of Hector now in Schuyler County. County records from 1854 to the present are in Watkins Glen, the county seat. But, from 1817 to 1854 this land was part of Tompkins County and records are in Ithaca. From 1804 to 1817 the area was part of Seneca County, which had two county seats – Ovid and Waterloo. From 1799 to 1804 the area was in Cayuga County, county seat Auburn. Records from 1794 to 1799 are in Syracuse, Onodaga County. The first permanent settler arrived in 1791 when the area was part of Herkimer County.

One of the confusing aspects in historical writings in New York is the use of similar names to designate a different place. Thus, Niagara County is a political entity occupying the northwest corner of the state, but "The Niagara Country" meant the millions of acres of western New York which became the Holland Land Purchase. Subsections of counties are termed "towns" in New York, and correspond to "townships" in other states. (Township has a different meaning, explained in Chapter 8.) Within a town there is often a village, or city, which has the same name as the town. The distinction between the two is not always clear.

Marian S. Henry
Rochester, New York
May 2007

ACKNOWLEDGMENTS

Assistance and encouragement in the writing of these essays came from various people. I would particularly like to acknowledge the following: Ralph Crandall, director emeritus of NEHGS, who invited me to undertake this project; Anita Hartwig, guardian of the state vital records index in the Rochester (New York) Public Library; staff of the local history section of the Rundel Memorial Library in Rochester, now headed by Larry Naukham; Dr. Hans Finke, director, Ontario County Records and Archives Center, and his staff; Marion Springer of the Magee House in Bath; Geneva Historical Society archivist Karen Osburn; Ogden Farmers' Library staff; and Kate Mockler, Curator of Interpretation and Collections, Oneida Community Mansion House. Special thanks also go to Michael J. Leclerc and Penny Stratton of NEHGS for their assistance during the book's preparation.

PART I

RECORDS

How to Find Primary Sources in New York State: The Historical Documents Inventory

In our research we all recognize that a primary record is better than a secondary one. Primary records include not only the usual vital records and census records, but a vast array of other personal records. A paradox of doing genealogy well is that the very references one wants to use are the ones most difficult to find. Thousands of these items are available in public repositories such as libraries and museums. What we need is a comprehensive listing of the holdings of all of these repositories. New York State is almost unique[1] in having just such a finding aid, the Historical Documents Inventory, or HDI. This survey was undertaken by the New York Historical Resources Center at Cornell University. From 1978 to 1993 the Center inventoried all of the manuscripts and other archival material in all repositories within the state open to the public and published a Historical Resources Guide for each of New York's sixty-two counties. In this chapter we examine how this project came into existence, how to find these guides, and how to use them.

Primary documents are one-of-a-kind items. Although we sometimes work with copies, such as the familiar microfilms of census records, generally a single document was created — a letter, a journal, a certificate — and was later deposited in some repository. Each county in the state has numerous repositories of this kind, many of them small and somewhat obscure. As G. David Brumberg, Director, New York Historical Resources Center, explained, "The great variety of reposito-

---

[1] The state of Tennessee has also undertaken such an inventory.

ries, and the lack of a comprehensive finding aid, has made it extremely difficult for researchers to locate the primary source materials needed for the study of New York State's history. The New York Historical Resources Center began a state-wide survey of manuscripts and archives collections in repositories in 1978."[2] The inventory contains a description of each of the items held by more than 1,700 publicly accessible repositories. For the purposes of the Historical Documents Inventory, a historical records repository was defined broadly as "an institution or program making a deliberate organized effort to care for Historical Records."[3] The goal of the inventory was to "locate, identify, describe, and report all of the manuscripts and archives materials in New York State repositories."[4] Records included in the survey include "reports, letters, diaries, journals, ledgers, minutes, photographs, maps, drawings, blue prints, agreements, memoranda, deeds, case files, receipts, and other material."[5]

The project was sponsored by New York Assemblyman Edward C. Sullivan [D-Manhattan] and was carried out by the New York Historical Resources Center, housed in the Olin Library at Cornell University, Ithaca, New York, under the direction of G. David Brumberg. Fieldworkers were sent to each repository to collect the data for the survey. The introduction written for each county's published guide acknowledges those who did this work. The name of Patricia E. White is particularly prominent. Editing and indexing was supervised by Elaine Engst, the Assistant Director. Early guides were funded by the National Historical Publications and Records Commission, the New York State Council on the Arts, and Cornell University. Before about 1987, local foundations frequently shared in funding this project. For example, the guide to Erie County, published in 1983, received grants from the Buffalo Foundation, Graphic Controls Corporation, and the Peter C.

---

[2] *Guide to Historical Resources in Chautauqua County* (New York Historical Resources Center, Cornell University, Olin Library, Ithaca, N.Y., 1982).

[3] Arthur F. Sniffin, "The New York State Historical Documents Inventory: Hidden Treasures in New York State Repositories, S-112," in *In Your Ancestor's Image*, 1996 Conference Syllabus, Federation of Genealogical Societies (Austin, Tex.: FGS, 1996).

[4] Ibid.

[5] Ibid.

Cornell Trust. The Gebbie Foundation, located in Jamestown, Chautauqua County, helped with production of the guide to that county. Later guides were most frequently funded by the New York State Education Department with matching funds from Cornell University.

During the lifetime of the project, revised and updated guides were published for two counties, Chautauqua and Chenango. The guide to New York County is, as expected, the largest at seven volumes. The guide to Franklin County[6] is one of the smaller ones. It lists six repositories (see Table 1), and the entries occupy nineteen pages. The index covers forty-four pages.

TABLE 1
FRANKLIN COUNTY REPOSITORIES

Franklin County Historical and Museum Society Malone, NY	(NIC)NYFR52J-240	p. 1
Goff-Nelson Memorial Library Tupper Lake, NY	(NIC)NYFR896-280	p. 18
Paul Smith's College Paul Smiths, NY	(NIC)NYFR68W-640	p. 6
Robert Louis Stevenson Memorial Cottage Saranac Lake, NY	(NIC)NYFR790-690	p. 8
Saranac Lake Free Library Saranac Lake, NY	(NIC)NYFR790 720	p. 8
Trudeau Institute Saranac Lake, NY	(NIC)NYFR790 760	p. 15

When the work was completed, the project was handed off to the State Archives, and the Historical Resources Center at Cornell University was disbanded. The information is available online at the New York state archives website, *www.archives.nysed.gov/aindex.shtml.*

Each collection was given a unique identifying number as part of the RLIN system.[7] The initial designation (NIC) indicates that the data

---

[6] *Guide to Historical Resources in Franklin County* (New York Historical Resources Center, Cornell University, Olin Library, Ithaca, N.Y., 1987).

[7] The Research Libraries Information Network, the online national data base operated by the Research Libraries Group (RLG).

comes from Cornell University, and the letters NY stand for "New York." The next two letters represent the county. The next three digits identify the town or city within the county. The next three digits specify the individual repository. Within each repository, each document (or collection) is given a unique four-digit identifying number. This control number is followed by a description of the collection. For example, working from back to front, (NIC)NYFR52J-240-0020 refers to records of the O'Neil and Hale insurance firm (0020) held by the Franklin County Historical and Museum Society (240), in Malone (52J), Franklin County (FR), New York (NY). The full entry reads as follows:

(NIC)NYFR52J-240-0020
O'Neil and Hale (Malone, NY)
Records, 1891–1898
4 v.
Summary: Registers of Insurance Policies sold, 1891–1898.
Franklin County Historical and Museum Society,
Malone, NY.

As might be expected, collections of family papers are numerous. The amount of detail given in the description varies. The description of "Coatsworth Family photographs, 1895–1950," (NIC)NYER13Q-050-0010, reads, "114 Photographs of family members and residences." On the other hand, the description of the "Jacobson family collection," (NIC)NYWA331-120-0063, contains a generous amount of genealogical information:

The Jacobson family descends from Julius Jacobson and his wife, Rosa Weinstein. Their children included Jessica Jacobson Boss, Pauline Jacobson Newberger, and Byron J. Jacobson. Jessica was born on October 1884 in Corry, Erie County, Pa. She died in Glens Falls, N.Y. on April 13, 1968. Byron J. Jacobson, a Glens Falls business man, died at age 76 on April 2, 1956. Nathan J. Newberger, son of Pauline, was an attorney in Washington, D.C.

The collection "Genealogical Manuscripts, 1880(ca.)–1980(ca.)," (NIC)NYER13Q090-0029, would catch the eye of any genealogist. According to the description, the collection occupies 60 cubic feet and contains the records of the Buffalo Genealogical Society. There are maps and atlases. "Maps and Drawings, 1828–1975," (NIC)NYOD872-120-0009, is concerned with construction of the Erie Canal. "Niagara County records, 1808–1821," (NIC)NYER13Q!-060-0179 contains oaths of allegiance from that time period. "Land Records, 1801–1863," (NIC)HYGE07W-280-0010, contains some records from the Holland Land Company, registers of deeds, and the like, including deeds for the Phelps-Gorham Purchase, 1808. "Vital Statistics from Canandaigua Newspapers, 1960(ca.)–1980," (NIC)NYON147-880-0005, contains exactly what it says. Skillful use of the search engine will help to focus research if you are looking for something specific. For example, a search on "Cattaraugus County" yields 53 hits, but adding "AND land" to the search criterion reduces the yield to 14 hits. The HDI describes such a wide variety of material, you might not want to put any limits on your search. You might miss a treasure like "Hutchinson Central High School records, 1860–1961," (NIC)NYER13Q-060-0108, which contains class lists from 1860 to 1943 and related material.

The guides are, of course, to be found at the Olin and Uris Library, Cornell University, even though the New York Historical Resources

```
(NIC)NYOD872-610-0185
Town of Onondaga subject file, 1910-1980.
   3 cubic ft.
   Organization: Subject.
   Summary: Clippings, historical sketches, pamphlets research
notes and correspondence, and photographs for the Town of
Onondaga and the villages or settlements of Howlett Hill,
Navarino, Nedrow, Onondaga Hill, South Onondaga, Split Rock, and
Taunton, arranged by subjects, including news items, businesses,
associations, industries, and churches.
   Onondaga Historical Association, Syracuse, NY.

(NIC)NYOD872-610-0186
Town of Otisco subject file, 1856-1985.
   1 cubic ft.
   Organization: Subject.
   Summary: Clippings, historical sketches and research notes,
articles, pamphlets, maps, and photographs pertaining to the Town
of Otisco and the villages of Amber, Maple Grove, and Otisco
Valley, arranged by subjects, including general history,
churches, and reminiscences.
   Onondaga Historical Association, Syracuse, NY.
```

Excerpt from the *Guide to Historical Resources in Onandoga County, New Repositories, Volume III*, prepared by the New York Historical Resources Center. at Cornell University showing how entries are organized.

Center, which produced them, is no longer in existence. The guides are also commonly found in local public libraries throughout the state. But the easiest way to access this information, and certainly the only way to get the most up-to-date information, is to use the online catalog of the New York State Archives. From the Archives' home page, *www.archives.nysed.gov/aindex.shtml,* click "catalog." Enter the county name — for example, "Cattaraugus County" — as a search term, and choose "Historical Document Inventory" from the drop-down menu as the library to be searched.

The published guides contain a description of each repository with contact information, hours, etc., which is not available in the online search. To find out about the repository online, go to New York History Net.[8] The repository you are interested in will probably be listed. Click on the link to take you to its home page.

These guides were well received. In 1990 the Archivists Round Table of Metropolitan New York, a not-for-profit organization representing more than 330 archivists, librarians, and records managers in the New York metropolitan area, gave its annual Award for Outstanding Support of Archives to HDI's sponsor, Assemblyman Edward C. Sullivan.[9] In 1991 G. David Brumberg and Elaine Engst jointly received the Society of American Archivists' C.W.F. Coker Award[10] for their work on this project. The value of the HDI should by now be obvious. Using this finding aid, a genealogist can find descriptions of rare and valuable source material. If you have not yet used the HDI to solve a stubborn New York State genealogy puzzle, then you haven't looked everywhere. Take heart.

---

[8] *www.nyhistory.com/links/museums.htm*

[9] *www.nycarchisvists.org/awards2.html*

[10] Established in 1984, the Coker Award recognizes finding aids and other tools which "in some significant way, set national standards, represent a model for archival description, or otherwise have a substantial impact on descriptive practices." See *www.archivists.org/governance/handbook/section12-coker.asp.*

CHAPTER 2

Dutch Naming Practices
in Colonial New York

The earliest immigrants to New York were the Dutch, beginning with Henry Hudson's exploration up the Hudson River in 1609 and the subsequent founding of New Netherland. Although the English seized the territory in 1664, Dutch naming practices continued to be widespread well into the eighteenth century. This is important to genealogists working in this period because the Dutch did not use the system of surnames which we take for granted today. Instead they used a patronymic system in which the "last" name was derived from the father's given name. Pieter, the son of Jan, would be known as Pieter Jansen. Jan would name his daughter Catharina Jansdr. And Jan's own patronymic would derive from his father's given name, say, Jan Pieterzen (John, son of Peter). However, he might instead use a name indicative of his occupation, perhaps Jan Smit (John the smith) Or he might use a name indicating his place of origin, Jan van der Werken, or something more personal such as Jan de Klyn (Little John). The Dutch also employed an astounding number of nicknames, which at first glance look nothing like their roots. Grietje comes from Margaretha. Bartel, Mees, and Meus all come from Bartelmeus. In this chapter we explore the intricacies of Dutch naming customs and the difficulties they create for the genealogist. Understanding the rules is the first step in recognizing and avoiding the inevitable errors of the uninitiated.

PATRONYMIC AND DUTCH NAMING CUSTOMS FOR GIVEN NAMES

In a small community, such as a classroom or an office, a single name for each individual can suffice. When the number of individuals significantly exceeds the number of given names, an additional designation is required for clear identification. A common solution in many societies was the use of patronymics. In a patronymic ("father's name") system, a person bears both a given name and his father's name. Mystery fans will recognize Cadfael ap Rhys as their favorite Welsh monk/sleuth and readers of Russian literature will translate Chekhov's Ivan Ivanovich as John Johnson. In such a system, the last name can change with each generation. The patronymic system was still in use with the Dutch when they settled New Netherland. Since all the sons of a man named Jan would bear the patronymic Jansen (or Janse/Jansz/Jans . . .) and his daughters Jansdochter (or Jansdr/Jans . . .), moving forward in time is a bit easier than moving back. When the English took over, they found this non-English muddle too much. No longer familiar with patronymics, they could not easily deal with a man named Martin Adriaens whose father was named Adriaen Reyersen and whose son was named Rem Martense.[1] They insisted that all families adopt fixed surnames. However, compliance was slow, and the use of patronymics continued well into the eighteenth century.

Another key element in Dutch genealogy, besides the lack of surnames, is the naming pattern for children. Given names of children came from relatives — grandparents, parents, aunts, and uncles. The two oldest sons were usually named for their grandfathers, and the two eldest daughters were usually named for their grandmothers. Also, if a child died, the next child born of the same sex was usually given that name. As an illustration, Table 1 shows the Bible record of the children of Pieter Strycker and his wife Annetje Barends, married 29 May 1681.[2] Although eleven children are listed, four of them died young and the names were used again. Of the seven surviving children, four are named for grandparents, one for the father, and two for paternal uncles.

These two naming customs — using given names over and over, and using patronymics — means that in any Dutch community at any given time there often were two (or more) people with the same name. In Dutch genealogy, therefore, it is necessary to identify not only all your ancestors' siblings, but also all of his aunts and uncles — a family cluster.

---

[1] Rosalie Fellows Bailey, *Dutch Systems in Family Naming: New York–New Jersey*, Special Publications of the National Genealogical Society, No. 12 (Washington, D.C., 1954), p. 3.

[2] Kenn Stryker-Rodda, "New Netherland Naming Systems and Customs," *NYG&B Record*, 126 (1995): 40.

Table 1
BIBLE RECORD SHOWING
DUTCH NAMING PATTERNS FOR CHILDREN

NAME	BIRTH	DEATH	NAMED FOR
Lammetje	26 Mar 1682	9 Apr 1682	Paternal grandmother
Lammetje	16 Feb 1683	26 Jul 1690	Paternal grandmother
Jan	6 Aug 1684		Paternal grandfather
Barent	3 Sep 1686	3 Jul 1690	Maternal grandfather
Jacob	4 Aug 1688		Paternal uncle
Barent	14 Sep 1690		Maternal grandfather
Hendrick	3 Dec 1692	17 May 169?	Paternal uncle
Sytie	17 Dec 1694		Maternal grandmother
Pieter	12 Feb 1697		Father
Hendrick	18 Feb 1699		Paternal uncle
Lammetje	21 Dec 1700		Paternal grandmother

With so many duplicate names, it is more difficult to know, from an individual document, which person is involved. Thus it is even more important to obtain all the available records for each person. Records that link several family members, such as wills and baptismal records, are most useful. One additional rule may be helpful. In the event of a second marriage after the death of a spouse, the next child of appropriate sex was often named after the deceased.

Ignorance of Dutch naming customs and of the equivalence of these variants on given names has led to unfortunate errors in printed family histories. Kenn Stryker-Rodda[3] illustrates with an example from the family of Martin Cregier. The family had a daughter, Catharina. Several years later they had another daughter, Trijntje. Because Trijntje is a variant of Catherine (see below), the same name is being used again. You also recall the practice of naming the next child of the same sex for a child who died and conclude, correctly, that the first daughter died. Others, not fully conversant with Dutch names and naming

---

[3] Ibid., 37.

practices, kept both girls alive on paper and further complicated an already complex family group.

DIMINUTIVES AND ENGLISH EQUIVALENTS

There is a good deal of variability in given names. We are accustomed to this kind of variability in English names, of course. Hence, we readily recognize Rob, Robbie, Robin, Bob, and Bobbie as all being derived from Robert. In Dutch names we can recognize three types of variants: *verkortwoorden,* or shortened words; *verkleinwoorden,* or diminutives; and *verbasterdwoorden,* or illegitimate words.[4]

Names are shortened (*verkortwoorden*) by dropping a syllable or two. In English often the last syllable is dropped (Louis/Lou); Dutch names are usually shortened by dropping the first syllable. Matthys becomes Thys. Nicolaes, in general, becomes Claes, and St. Nicholas, in particular, becomes Santa Claus. Some confusion can result in going back from the shortened form to the original name. Just as Al might be short for either Albert or Alfred, Lena might come from either Magdalena or Helena.

Diminutives (*verkleinwoorden*) are formed by adding an ending -*ie*/-*je*. The ending is often added to an already shortened name (William/Will/Willie). Thus Cornelia is shortened to Nelia, and the diminutive is Neeltje. In a similar progression Katharina becomes Katrina and then Katrintje and finally Trijntje. Margaretha first forms the diminutive Margrietje, which is then shortened to Grietje — not to be confused with Geertje, a diminutive of Gertrude.

The occurrence of "illegitimate" variants (*verbasterdwoorden*), such as Polly from Mary, is infrequent in Dutch names. However, one should be aware of Krelis from Cornelis.

One source of diminutives and Dutch/English equivalents is Table 2 in Arthur Kelly's book *Names, Names, & More Names: Locating Your Dutch Ancestors in Colonial America* (Orem, Utah: Ancestry.com, 1999). The listings are Dutch/English (Table 2A) and English/Dutch (Table 2B). The English name Matthew has 57 Dutch

---

[4] Ibid., 37–38.

equivalents. Variations on Matthias lead to the shortened form Thys and its diminutive Tysje. But how does Debiss arise? One might speculate that Matthias leads to Hias, which leads to Heis, to Dies, to Debiss. Another useful source is John Neafus's article "English Names with Dutch Equivalents," published in *Proceedings of the New Jersey Historical Society,* new series, 9:374–81.

OTHER SUBSTITUTES FOR SURNAME

The patronymic was not the only means used to distinguish between people with the same given name. The Dutch also used occupation, place of origin, and/or personal characteristics. If a person changed his occupation during his lifetime, his name would reflect that. Place of origin may refer to city, area, feature, estate, manor house. If a person used all of his names, he might begin with some title, equivalent to present-day Mr./Mrs., followed by given name (in full or a shortened or diminutive form), patronymic, place of origin, occupation, and, finally, personal characteristic. Obviously not every person had all these names, and it was not customary to use all of these names on every document — but it is important to know what all the possibilities are for each of your ancestors.

Table 2 lists names for a few common occupations and personal characteristics, along with their English equivalents. Note that "de" is not French "of" but Dutch "the."

Table 2

NAME	OCCUPATION	NAME	CHARACTERISTIC
Smit/d	smith	Swart	black/swarthy
Koylert/Cuyler	archer	Vroom	pious/wise
Wantenaer	glovemaker	Krankheyt	invalid
Kuyper/Cooper	cooper	de Groot	big
Metselaer	mason	de Witt	white

With such fluidity in a man's name, a name index would be difficult to construct and to use. Consider a specific example: Nicholas whose father's given name was Jan. When he immigrated, the entry in the ship's list reads "Claes jansen vanpurmerent ramaker," which we can interpret as: shortened form of given name (Nicholas/Claes), patronymic, place of origin, occupation (ramaker, that is, wheelwright). His marriage record names him Claes Janszen van Purmerendt. At the baptism of his children he is Claes Janse/Jansen/Janszen. He switched his occupation from wheelwright to cooper and was buried as Claes Janszen Kuyper. To be complete, this individual would have to be listed in a name index under J, V, P, R, and K.

The slow and uneven shift to a hereditary family name, combined with this array of possible "last" names, has an interesting consequence for Dutch families. Some brothers and cousins settled on surnames a generation later than others, and they did not all choose the same surname. Using the previous example, a history of the descendants of Claes Jansen could easily contain branches of the family that settled at various times on surnames Van Purmerendt, Ramaker, and Kuyper/Cooper (all with various spellings) in addition to Jansen/Johnson.

AIDS TO DUTCH GENEALOGY

In addition to these naming customs, there are two other customs that give much-needed aid to the genealogist. The first is the last names of married women and the second is godparents.

Ancient Dutch church.

"Image of the old Dutch Reformed Church in Sleepy Hollow, New York," from *Historical Collections of the State of New York* by John W. Barber (New York: Clark, Austin & Co., 1851), p. 381.

Contrary to English custom, a woman did not change her name when she married. When she witnessed a legal document, had her children baptized, or stood as godmother to another child, she used what we would think of as her "maiden" name. If that name is her patronymic, we know her father's given name as well.

The names of godparents or sponsors in a baptismal record should be noted carefully. They will be close relatives, not just neighbors or family friends. Expect to find as godparents: grandparents, aunts and uncles, siblings and their spouses. Each baptismal record is a rich genealogical datum, linking five (or more) names: the child, the relative the child is named for, both parents, and two or more relatives as godparents. Here is a typical example of a baptismal record taken from records of the Dutch Reformed Church at Clarkstown, Rockland County, New York, transcribed by Gertrude A. Barber:[5]

> Antje, b. 22 Dec 1796, bp. 22 Jan 1797, parents Henderick
> de Ronde and Hilletje Noorstands, sponsors Abraham
> Gones and Effe de Clerck.

SOURCES

Since 1999 the first place to look when starting to research a family in colonial New York, particularly a Dutch family, is David Riker's five-volume work on persons in New Netherland to 1674.[6]

With such importance attached to baptismal records, access to Dutch Reformed church records during the colonial period gains in significance. A good place to start is the Vosburgh Collection.[7]

Arthur Kelly's *Names, Names, & More Names,* mentioned earlier, also contains a significant collection of data on individuals. Table I contains names extracted from 43 different sources. The first entry will serve as an illustrative example. "Aaten, Hendricks, Ship Lists,

---

[5] For more information on Gertrude Barber's work, see Chapter 3.

[6] David M. Riker, *Genealogical and Biographical Directory to Persons in New Netherland, from 1613 to 1674,* 4 vols. and supplement (Salem, Mass.: Higginson Book Co., 1999, 2004); 4 vols. also published as *New Netherland Vital Records, 1600s* on CD-ROM by Family Tree Maker (1999).

[7] For more information on the Vosburgh Collection, see Chapter 5.

1687" means the name Hendricks Aaten was found in Boyer's "Ship Passenger Lists, NY and NJ" and the original entry was made in 1687. Table 3 A&B lists Father/Mother and Mother/Father pairs. First entry reads "Abel and Anna, NY Ref, bp, 1662, 1664, 1667, 1669, 1671." NY Ref stands for New York [City] Dutch Reformed Church baptisms and marriages. Table 3 C&D similarly lists Groom/Bride then Bride/Groom given names, followed by a reference and the year of the original record.

Another source of church records is *Records of the Reformed Dutch Church of Albany, New York, 1683–1809,* excerpted from *Year Books of the Holland Society of New York,* (Baltimore: Genealogical Publishing Co., 1978). The Holland Society of New York was founded in 1885 to collect information respecting the settlement and history of New Netherland.

As a final reference, useful for general background information, see Alice P. Kenney, *Stubborn for Liberty: The Dutch in New York* (Syracuse: Published for the New York State American Revolution Bicentennial Commission, Syracuse University Press, 1975).

It should be clear by now that successful genealogy involving Dutch ancestors in the colonial period of New York requires careful, cautious work with great attention to detail. It is not to be undertaken lightly, especially by the inexperienced. If you rise to the challenge and succeed, your sense of accomplishment should be that much greater.

SUMMARY OF SOURCES

Rosalie Fellows Bailey, *Dutch Systems in Family Naming: New York–New Jersey,* Special Publications of the National Genealogical Society, No. 12 (Washington, D.C., 1954)

Arthur C. M. Kelly, *Names, Names, & More Names: Locating Your Dutch Ancestors in Colonial America* (Orem, Utah: Ancestry.com, 1999)

David M. Riker, *Genealogical and Biographical Directory to Persons in New Netherland, from 1613 to 1674,* 4 vols. and supplement (Salem, Mass.: Higginson Book Co., 1999, 2004); 4 vols. also published as *New Netherland Vital Records,* 1600s on CD-ROM by Family Tree Maker (1999)

Kenn Styker-Rodda, "New Netherland Naming Systems and Customs," *NYG&B Record,* 126 (1995): 35–45.

CHAPTER 3

New York State Vital Records: The Legacy of Gertrude Audrey Barber

T rying to find nineteenth-century vital records in upstate New York can be a frustrating experience. Fortunately, we have an ally in Gertrude Audrey Barber, who made it her life's work to transcribe vital records information from different sources in various counties in New York State. Beginning in the late 1920s and continuing for nearly 40 years, Barber painstakingly transcribed many kinds of nineteenth-century records useful to genealogists. Using original county court records, she prepared extracts of deeds and abstracts of wills. She made transcriptions of church records and visited cemeteries to copy gravestone inscriptions. She extracted marriage and death notices from local newspapers. In this article we look at how upstate New York researchers could benefit from the legacy left by Gertrude Barber. The type of information she transcribed for each county and the time period covered are listed below. Suggestions are included for accessing the information since these typewritten transcriptions were not published in book form. Little information is readily available about this woman who worked for so long for the benefit of New York State genealogy. Her obituary in the *New York Times* of December 17, 1974, reads simply: "Barber — Gertrude A., Genealogist, Widow of Williard Barber, died suddenly, Dec. 12, at age 83. Interment private."

An earlier version of this chapter was posted at *www.NewEnglandAncestors.org* April 23, 2004.

WILLS

Gertrude Barber prepared abstracts and/or an index of wills for the following counties: Cayuga, Chemung, Chenango, Columbia, Delaware, Dutchess, Greene, Monroe, Oneida, Otsego, Rockland, Schenectady, Schoharie, Sullivan, Tioga, Tompkins, Warren, and Washington. Many of these transcriptions are in several volumes and include surname indexes. A more complete listing is in the summary table at the end of this article. The description of her abstracts of wills for Columbia County, which was published in *The New York Genealogical and Biographical Record* (Vol. 67, 1936, page 190), will serve to illustrate what is contained in this collection:

> An indexed abstract of wills is always a most helpful publication for genealogists. It is the names mentioned in the will, rather than the names of the testators themselves, of which the searcher desires to be made aware. The author has here made the first of such compilations, concerning Columbia County, available to the public. The wills have been completely abstracted and thoroughly indexed. Fifty pages of the manuscript set forth the abstracts of the will and nearly as many pages are taken up with the valuable index. Genealogical libraries collecting manuscript material should have this one in their files.

CHURCH AND CEMETERY RECORDS

Barber's transcriptions of church records consist of extracts of birth, baptism, marriage, or death information. Individual churches are listed under each county in the table below. Although other counties are represented, Sullivan County predominates in her transcriptions of church records. (Those seeking early church records should see Chapter 5 concerning the Vosburgh Collection.)

Barber's efforts in copying tombstone inscriptions are especially valuable. As gravestones weather over time, these original records become increasingly illegible, and transcriptions are all we have left. Information was collected from cemeteries in Allegany, Cattaraugus, Chautauqua, Columbia, Erie, Orange, Otsego, Rockland, Schoharie, Sullivan, and Wyoming counties. Individual cemeteries are listed by county in the table. Some of these items are quite extensive, such as "Gravestone Inscriptions in Columbia County, New York." It occupies 12 volumes and was released in stages from 1935 to 1941. (The finding aid "The Association of Municipal Historians of New York State Name/Location Survey Project 1995–1997," the subject of Chapter 14, may be helpful in locating these cemeteries.)

NEWSPAPER EXTRACTS

Collections of vital records extracted from newspapers include such items as "Deaths and Marriages taken from Cayuga County, N.Y. newspapers, 1825–1834" and "Marriages and deaths taken from the *Delaware Gazette* at Delhi, Delaware County, N.Y." This newspaper was apparently published weekly. Issues with no marriages are entered with "none" rather than skipped, an indication of the author's care taken to produce complete, reliable results. Several more examples are included in the table. (An even more extensive collection of vital records extracted from early newspapers may be found in the work of Fred Q. Bowman, the subject of Chapter 4.)

ACCESSING THE COLLECTION

Barber's typewritten transcriptions were usually deposited in the library of the New York Genealogical and Biographical Society in New York City. Members of the "G&B" will find her work there. Most have been microfilmed and today are available at many major genealogical libraries.

NEHGS lists more than 30 items in its catalog, including some relating to downstate counties not included here. Her transcriptions of marriage (*www.newenglandancestors.org/research/Database/ NYPMarriages/default.asp*) and death (*www.newenglandancestors .org/research/Database/nypdeath/default.asp*) notices from the *New York Evening Post,* 1801–90, are among the searchable databases available on the Society's website.

The New York State Archives (*www.archives.nysed.gov/aindex .shtml*) at Albany lists 120 items authored by Gertrude Barber — a very complete collection. The Archives participates in the national interlibrary loan network, which allows researchers to borrow microfilm for use in their own public library. Similarly, the Family History Library catalog (at *www.familysearch.org*) lists 144 entries, including many microfilms that may be borrowed for use at local Family History Centers. The library is constantly adding to its collection, so check the catalog often for new materials. The online catalog of the Library of the National Society Daughters of the American Revolution (*www.dar.org/library/onlinlib.cfm*) in Washington, D.C., contains 39 entries.

Public libraries in upstate New York may hold some of this material. Results will vary. The public library for Monroe County, in Rochester, New York, lists 49 items authored by Gertrude Barber. However, the online catalog for all 50 of the public libraries in the Southern Tier Library system lists none.

Table 1 lists works related to 21 upstate counties including, when known, the time period covered for each item. For cemetery transcripts, the date of publication is given. The table, while extensive, is far from a complete record of the work of Mrs. Barber.

Table 1
TRANSCRIPTIONS COMPILED BY GERTRUDE BARBER
RELEVANT TO UPSTATE NEW YORK

COUNTY	TITLE
Allegany	Cemetery records of Allegany County, New York.
Cattaraugus	Cattaraugus County, N.Y., cemeteries.
	Cemetery near Yorkshire Corners, Cattaraugus County, New York and Maple Grove cemetery, town of Freedom, Cattaraugus County, New York.
	Gravestone inscriptions in Cattaraugus County, New York: including cemeteries in the towns of Freedom, Franklinville and Yorkshire.
	Gravestone inscriptions of Cadiz cemetery, town of Franklinville; Sugartown cemetery, town of Franklinville; Delevan cemetery, town of Yorkshire; Cattaraugus County, N.Y.
	Silome cemetery in the town of Freedom, Cattaraugus County, New York and Farmersville Center cemetery, in the town of Farmersville Center, Cattaraugus County, New York.

COUNTY	TITLE
Cayuga	Abstracts of wills of Cayuga County, New York, 1799–1842. Vols. 1–4. Includes indexes after each volume.
	Cayuga County, New York, deaths and marriages taken from Cayuga County, N.Y. newspapers, 1825–1834.
Chautauqua	Gravestone inscriptions of Chautauqua Cemetery, Chautauqua, N.Y., published 1932.
Chemung	Abstracts of wills of Chemung County, N.Y. from 1836–1850. Copied from the original records at the Surrogate's Office, Elmira, N.Y., 1941. Includes index.
Chenango	Index to wills of Chenango County, New York, from 1797–1875.
Columbia	Abstract of wills of Columbia County, New York, 1796–1851, 8 vols.
	Gravestone inscriptions in Columbia County, New York, published 1935–41, 12 vols.
Delaware	Abstracts of wills of Delaware County, N.Y., 1796–1875.
	1855 census of Delaware County, New York. Lists name, age, state or area of birth, and occupation, with index.
	Deaths, 1819–1879, copied from *Delhi Gazette*, published at Delhi, Delaware County, N.Y.
	Index of wills, Delaware County, New York, from 1797–1885.
	Letters of administration of Delaware County, New York: copied from the original records at the court house, Delhi, N. Y., v. 1 1797–1844, v. 2 1844–1863, v. 3 1863–1874, v. 4 1874–1875.
	Marriage and deaths taken from the *Delaware Gazette* at Delhi, Delaware County, N.Y., listed chronologically, with an index. Index does not include ministers' names.
Erie	Gravestone inscriptions from cemeteries in Erie County, New York, published 1930.
Monroe	Monroe County, New York abstracts of wills: copied from the original records at Rochester, New York, v. 1, 1821–1841, v. 2, 1841–1847.
Oneida	Abstracts of wills of Oneida County, N.Y., 1798–1848. v. 1, 1798–1822, v. 2, 1822–1832, v. 3, 1832–1839, v. 4, 1840–1843, v. 5, 1843–1847, v. 6, 1847–1848.

continued on next page

Table 1 *(cont.)*

COUNTY	TITLE
Oswego	Records of the Congregational Church at New Haven, Oswego County, N.Y. Includes baptisms, 1821–1850, deaths, 1817–1850, and members, 1817–1850.
Otsego	Abstracts of wills of Otsego County, New York, five volumes: 1794–1824, 1817–1829, 1829–1838, 1837–1845, 1845–1850.
	A collection of abstracts from Otsego County, New York, newspaper obituaries, 1808–1875.
	Deaths taken from the *Otsego Herald* and *Western Advertiser* and *Freeman's Journal,* Otsego County, N.Y., newspapers, 1795–1840.
	Index of wills of Otsego County, New York, from 1792–1850.
	Inscriptions from the Lake View Cemetery at Richfield Springs, Otsego County, N.Y., Published 1930. Names not arranged alphabetically, probably in order of location. With index.
	Marriages taken from the *Otsego Herald* and *Western Advertiser* and *Freeman's Journal,* Otsego County, N. Y., newspapers from 1795–1850.
	Record of births and baptisms, 1797–1827: kept by Daniel Nash, Christ Church, Cooperstown, Otsego County, N.Y.
	Tombstone inscriptions in the Catholic Cemetery at Richfield Springs, N.Y. and also in the Exeter Cemetery at Exeter, N.Y.: both located in Otsego County, N.Y. Published 1931.
Schenectady	Abstracts of wills of Schenectady County, N.Y.: copied from the original records at the court house, Schenectady, N.Y. Three volumes, each with index.
Schoharie	Abstracts of wills, letters of administration, letters of guardianship, of Schoharie County, New York, from 1795–1863.
	Schoharie County, New York, cemetery records, 7 vol., published 1932.
Sullivan	Sullivan Co., New York cemetery records: Wurtsboro, Bridgeville, Bethel, Hurd, Swan Lake, Brookside & Harris, Fallsburgh-Neversink. (no date)
	Sullivan County, New York, gravestone inscriptions, 10 vol., published 1929–1934.
	Bloomingburgh Cemetery, Bloomingburgh, Sullivan County, N.Y., published 1930.

The church record of the Kenoza Lake Charge of the Methodist Episcopal Church: Heard Settlement–Foster–Dale–Jeffersonville–Youngsville–Pike Pond, now known as Kenoza Lake; all in Sullivan County, N.Y.

Church records of various places in Sullivan County, New York.

Cemetery, Ferndale, N.Y., and Old Fallsburg (Palens) Cemetery, Fallsburg, N.Y. All located in Sullivan Co., N.Y.

Index of wills, Sullivan County, New York, 1876–1909.

Index to records of the Presbyterian Church, Monticello, Sullivan County, New York.

Records of consistory of the Union Tabernacle Reformed Church, Unionville, Sullivan County, N.Y.

Records of the Associated Reformed Church of Mongaup Valley, Sullivan County, N.Y.: membership records; baptisms, 1830–1919; marriages, 1831–1919. This Church was abandoned in 1927.

Records of the Barryville Congregational Church of Barryville, Sullivan County, New York, 1836–1927.

Records of the Dutch Reformed congregation of Mamakating, later known as the Dutch Reformed Church of Wurtsboro (Rome), Sullivan County, New York.

Records of the First Congregational Church in the town of Lumberland, Sullivan County, New York: formerly known as the First Presbyterian Congregational Church of Narrow Falls and also as the Narrow Falls and Middlebrook Church.

Records of the First Presbyterian Church at White Lake, Old Newburgh, Cochecton, Sullivan County, New York.

Records of the Free Methodist Church, Ferndale, Sullivan County, N.Y.

Records of the Methodist Episcopal and the Baptist Church of Sullivan County, New York.

Records of the Methodist Episcopal Church, Monticello, Sullivan County, N.Y.

Records of the Methodist Episcopal Church, Rock Hill, Sullivan County, N.Y.: baptisms, 1884–1892; marriages, 1883–1893; membership records.

Records of the Methodist Episcopal Church, Sandburgh, Sullivan County, N.Y.: baptisms, 1863–1880; marriages, 1863–1882; membership records.

continued on next page

Table 1 *(cont.)*

COUNTY	TITLE
	Records of the Presbyterian Church of Cochecton, Sullivan County, New York.
	Records of the Presbyterian Church, Monticello, Sullivan County, New York.
	Records of the Reformed Dutch Church, Grahamsville, Sullivan County N.Y.: baptisms, 1845–1905; membership records; marriages, 1844–1888.
	Records of the Reformed Protestant Dutch Church of Bloomingburg, Sullivan County, N.Y.
	Records of the White Lake Presbyterian Church, Bethel, Sullivan County, New York.
	Cemetery inscriptions, Sullivan County, New York, published 1929.
Tioga	Abstracts of wills of Tioga County, N.Y., from 1799–1847.
Tompkins	Abstracts of wills of Tompkins County, N.Y., from 1817–1833.
Warren	Abstracts of wills of Warren County, New York: book A, 1813–1850.
	Extracts of deeds of Warren County, NY from 1813–1825, copied from the original records at the Court House at Lake George, N.Y.
Washington	Abstracts of wills of Washington County, New York, v. 1, 1786–1806; v. 2, 1806–1814; v. 3, 1814–1825.
	Index of wills of Washington County, New York: from 1825–1890.
Wyoming	Gravestone inscriptions of Wyoming County, N.Y.: including cemeteries in Sheldon and Bennington, N.Y., published 1933.
	Gravestone inscriptions of Wyoming County, N.Y.: including cemeteries in Silver Springs, Hermitage and Genesee Falls, published 1932.
	Prospect Hill cemetery at Arcade, Wyoming Co., N.Y., published 1930.
	Tombstone inscriptions from cemeteries located in Wyoming County, New York. Includes index. Published 1931.

CHAPTER 4

Early Vital Records of New York State: The Work of Fred Q. Bowman

A s any genealogical researcher dealing with New York State can attest, early records tend to be scattered and not widely available. It is therefore with great pleasure that I introduce in this chapter the work of Fred Q. Bowman. During the last twenty years Mr. Bowman has compiled a number of volumes of vital records extracted from local newspapers, as well as a volume of early land records. The books described in this article are: *Landholders of Northeastern New York, 1739–1802; 10,000 Vital Records of Western New York, 1809–1850; 10,000 Vital Records of Central New York, 1813–1850; 10,000 Vital Records of Eastern New York, 1777–1834; 8,000 More Vital Records of Eastern New York State, 1804-1850; Directory to Collections of New York Vital Records, 1726 1989, with Rare Gazetteer* (with co-author Thomas J. Lynch); and *7,000 Hudson-Mohawk Valley (NY) Vital Records, 1808–1850* (also with Thomas J. Lynch). An additional volume on the 1855 census of Greene County is not included here. A review published in the *New York Genealogical and Biographical Record* notes: "Since New York had virtually no public vital records in this period, newspaper notices can be of immense value to genealogists, and the importance of Mr. Bowman's books is obvious."[1]

An earlier version of this chapter was posted at *www.NewEnglandAncestors.org* October 24, 2003.

[1] *New York Genealogical and Biographical Record*, Vol. 176 (1987), p. 176.

LANDHOLDERS OF NORTHEASTERN NEW YORK

Published in 1983, *Landholders of Northeastern New York, 1739-1802* covers early records for Franklin, Clinton, Essex, Warren, and Washington counties.[2] From 1739 to 1772 the entire region was part of Albany County. In 1772 a portion of the region was split out and became Charlotte County. In 1784, in a fit of patriotic fervor, the name was changed to Washington County. In 1788 Clinton County (containing present-day Franklin, Clinton, and Essex counties) was split from Washington (which also contained present-day Warren County). In 1799 Essex County was separated. The scope of the book ends in 1802. The organization of the book is described in its introduction.

This directory consists of two parts. The first part, pages 3–12, identifies approximately 600 original grantees whose land awards, 1739 through 1775, lay within northeastern New York. The second part, pages 13–209, identifies approximately 9,000 persons whose land transactions were completed between 1764 and 1802 within this same region.

Appendix A, pages 211–13, serves three purposes. It furnishes the dates of organization of all the towns formed in northeastern New York prior to 1803. It indicates the population of the towns of this region as of 1790 and 1800 and it lists by counties the numbers of deeds and mortgage agreements filed in this region from 1772 through 1802 inclusive.

Appendix B discusses the incompleteness in deed filings in northeastern New York within the time period of concern. It provides a list of approximately 250 landholders whose names do not appear elsewhere in the book.

Part 2, the major segment of this report, reflects the fact that at contract time relatively large numbers of participants lived in northeastern New York. However, residence towns are identified in all the settled regions of early-day New York as well as in ten additional

---

[2] Fred Q. Bowman, *Landholders of Northeastern New York, 1739-1802* (Baltimore: Genealogical Publishing Co., 1983).

states, the Northwest Territory, Upper and Lower Canada, England, Ireland, Scotland, France, and Germany. Hundreds of family relationships are defined or implied. Frequently, occupations of participants are posted. Occasionally, probate matters are highlighted. Source citations are given for all transactions reported.

Land transactions are entered alphabetically by surname and numbered sequentially. Note that there is frequently a considerable lapse between the signing of a land contract and when it was filed. In contrast, mortgage agreements were filed promptly. Bowman hypothesizes, "Presumably the new land owners, once they had pocketed their deeds, felt relatively secure. In contrast, the money-lenders, financially unsatisfied at the outset, were eager to file or to have their agents file their mortgage agreements."[3]

Each entry in the book begins with a number. If the number is underlined, it means that it is the "key" entry for the transaction, containing references to all the related entries. The sequence of each entry, taken from the original record, is: date, principal grantor and his/her location, location of the land in question, related entries of grantee(s) and any co-grantors, and finally, the code for the source book. The location of the land in question is underlined. Land deeds for Charlotte and Albany counties were filed in Washington County. Prior to 1772 (formation of Washington County) all records for land north of Kingston were filed in Albany. Bowman notes that "these relatively few [records held by Albany] pertaining to northeastern New York, difficult to cull from the massive set, have not been here pursued."[4]

It is not necessary to begin with the key entry. Any related entry will lead to it. As an example, I randomly chose entry 1337, which reads:

1337. 6/20/01 gor Chadwick, Eunice. See 1339

This entry states that Eunice Chadwick was involved in a land transaction in the role of grantor ("gor") on June 20, 1801, and further information is contained in entry 1339.

---

[3] Ibid., Appendix B.
4 Ibid., Introduction.

1339. 6/20/01 gor Chadwick, John (w. Eunice); Kingsbury, WAS. See 4843.

Entry 1339 is not underlined and so is not the key entry. From this entry we learn that Eunice Chadwick was the wife of John Chadwick of Kingsbury in Washington County ("WAS"). John Chadwick was also involved in this land transaction as a grantor and more information is in entry 4843.

4843 6/20/01 gor Mann, Solomon (w. Abigail); Cambridge, WAS; —, WAS: co-gors 1337, 1339, 2475, 2479; gee 1323 (F:242)

The underlined number tells us that this is the key entry. Solomon Mann and his wife Abigail of Cambridge, Washington County, are the principal grantors (because they are listed in the key entry). The land in question is underlined ("—, WAS") and is an unspecified location in Washington County. The co-grantors ("co-gors") are to be found in entries 1337, 1339, 2475, and 2479 while the grantee ("gee") is in entry 1323. The source of the information is Book F, page 242.

2475 6/20/01 gor Fisher, Elizabeth. See 2479.

2479 6/20/01 gor Fisher, John W. (w. Elizabeth); Cambridge, WAS. See 4843.

1323 6/20/01 gee Center, John S.; Cambridge, WAS. See 4843.

The supporting entries give us the names of the additional grantors, John W. Fisher of Cambridge, Washington County, and Elizabeth, his wife. The grantee is John S. Center, also of Cambridge.

Mortgage records are handled similarly. The mortgagor is listed in the key entry and mortgagee in the linked entry.

1915 3/20/02 mor Davis, James; —, —; Willsborough, ESS; mee 5777. (A:83)

5777 3/20/02 mee Platt, Nathaniel; —, —; See 1915.

We see from these entries that land in Willsborough, Essex County ("ESS") was mortgaged on March 20, 1802, as recorded in Book A, page 83. The mortgagor ("mor") was James Davis, and the mortgagee ("mee") was Nathaniel Platt. The entries do not identify the residences of either man.

Many entries state or imply family relationships such as the following examples relating to the estate of John Murray, deceased.

5244 12/1/97 — Murray, John, dec'd. See 4721.

4721 12/1/97 mor McNeal, Sarah; Argyle, WAS; Queensbury, WAS; co-mees 2265, and 5164. Co-mortgagees are "executor and executrix of the ... will ... of John Murray, deceased." (B:258)

2265 12/1/97 mee Eddy, John; —, —, See 4721.

5164 12/1/97 mee Morgan, Anstis; —, —, See 4721.

From these entries someone researching the family of this John Murray would learn that he died before December 1, 1797, and that on that day a mortgage was executed on land in Queensbury, Washington County. The mortgagor was Sarah McNeal of Argyle, Washington County. Co-mortgagees were John Eddy and Anstis Morgan, no residence listed, the executor and executrix of John Murray's estate. The transaction is to be found in Book B, page 258.

THE "10,000" TRILOGY — WESTERN, CENTRAL, AND EASTERN NEW YORK

We turn now to the "10,000" trilogy. Each volume contains over 10,000 vital records. In turn they treat western (published in 1985), central (1986), and eastern (1987) regions of the state. The introduction to the "eastern" volume specifies the organization of the counties within the trilogy.

"This is the final volume in a three-volume series of vital records drawn from early New York newspapers. The first volume, *10,000 Vital Records of Western New York, 1809–1850,* covered the section of the state from Geneva westward.[5] The second volume, *10,000 Vital Records of Central New York, 1813–1850,* covered the area lying between Geneva and Utica.[6] This third volume [10,000 Vital Records of Eastern New York, 1777–1834] focuses on the interior county of Otsego and on the 300-mile north-south strip comprising the eastern-most counties of Clinton, Essex, Saratoga, Rensselaer, Albany, Columbia, and "Old Dutchess," which latter, prior to 1812, included the territory of present-day Putnam.[7] Records in this volume are drawn from the marriage and death columns of newspapers published prior to 1835 in each of the above-named counties. Birth announcements were not published in these early papers. Fortunately, many of the marriage and death notices made mention of birth years, birthplaces, and parents' names.

The entries in each volume are alphabetical by surname and also numbered sequentially. Each entry ends with a code for the source. The first number specifies the newspaper, while the second identifies the month and day of the newspaper article. Usually the year of publication in the newspaper is the same as the year of the event. The tables here list these newspapers and the towns in which they were published, along with the dates searched. These dates do not necessarily correspond to the full dates of publication of each newspaper. Collections extant are sometimes incomplete and each volume has an arbitrary date range. The information in these tables should guide researchers to volumes with a location and time period that matches their needs.

---

[5] Fred Q. Bowman, *10,000 Vital Records of Western New York, 1809–1850* (Baltimore: Genealogical Publishing Co., 1985).

[6] Fred Q. Bowman, *10,000 Vital Records of Central New York, 1813–1850* (Baltimore: Genealogical Publishing Co., 1986).

[7] Fred Q. Bowman, *10,000 Vital Records of Eastern New York, 1777-1834* (Baltimore: Genealogical Publishing Co., 1987).

Table 1
NEWSPAPER SOURCES FOR 10,000
VITAL RECORDS OF WESTERN NEW YORK, 1809–50

NUMBER	TOWN	NEWSPAPER	DATES
1	Batavia	*Republican Advocate*	3/19/22–12/31/50
2	Bath	*Steuben Farmers Advocate*	1/5/31–12/31/50
3	Geneva	*Geneva Gazette**	6/21/09–12/31/27
4	Jamestown	*Jamestown Journal*	7/21/26–12/31/50

* As Geneva lies on the border between central and western New York, vital records that appeared in the Geneva Gazette between 1828 and 1850 are included in 10,000 Vital Records of Central New York, 1813–1850.

Table 2
NEWSPAPER SOURCES FOR 10,000
VITAL RECORDS OF CENTRAL NEW YORK, 1813–1850

NUMBER	TOWN	NEWSPAPER	DATES
1	Baldwinsville	*Onondaga Gazette*	1846–50
2	Binghamton	*Broome County Republican* (scattered issues)	1842–45
3	Chittenango	*Chittenango Herald*	1831 44
4	Corning	*Corning Weekly Journal* (scattered issues)	1840–43, 1847–50
5	Elmira	*Elmira Republican*	1847–50
6	Geneva	*Geneva Gazette**	1830–49
7	Norwich	*Norwich Journal* (scattered issues)	1816–30
8	Oxford	*Oxford Gazette*	1813–26
		Chenango Republican	1826–30
		Oxford Republican	1833–47
		Oxford Times	1845+
9	Utica	*Utica Western Recorder*	1824–34
		Utica Daily Gazette	1842–50

* Records from 1809 to 1829 in this newspaper are in the Western New York volume.

Table 3
NEWSPAPER SOURCES FOR 10,000 VITAL RECORDS OF
EASTERN NEW YORK, 1777–1834

NUMBER	TOWN	NEWSPAPER	DATES
1	Albany	*Daily Albany Argus**	1829–31
2	Ballston Spa	*Ballston Spa Gazette*	1821–25
3	Cooperstown	*Otsego Herald*	1795–20
		Freemen's Journal	1821–26
4	Essex County	*Essex County Times* (E'town)	1833–34
		Essex Republican (Essex)	1831–32
		Keeseville Argus	1833–34
		Keeseville Herald	1828–34
5	Fishkill	*New York Packet*	1777–83
6	Hudson	*The Balance*	1801–8
		The Northern Whig	1809–20
7	Plattsburgh	*Plattsburgh Republican*	1811–34
8	Poughkeepsie	*Poughkeepsie Journal*	1785–1833
9	Troy	*Lansingburgh Gazette*	1798–1803
		Troy Budget	1803–28

* For vital records from other Dutchess County newspapers between 1778 and 1825, see *Collections of the Dutchess County Historical Society,* Volume 4 (available in reprint from the Society in Poughkeepsie).

** "For Albany-area newspaper records prior to 1829 see Joseph Gavit, *American Deaths and Marriages, 1784–1829* (microfilm, 1976?) available at the State Library, Albany, and at the New York Genealogical and Biographical Society's library in New York City."

Each volume of the "10,000" trilogy includes an all-name index (except for ministers) in which reference is made to the entry number. There is also an appendix of ministers who officiated at the weddings. Marriages are entered alphabetically by groom's name only — the bride's name is found in the index. Thus, on page 19 of the volume of Eastern New York records:

662. Belden, Lawrence m 4/15/23 Louisa Gregory in
Dover; Rev. C. P. Wilson (8-4/16).

The "8" refers to the *Poughkeepsie Journal* (see above table) and "4/16" is the date of the notice in the newspaper. No year is given, so we are to assume that the notice appeared soon after the wedding. In the index, on page 330, is the bride's entry "Gregory, Louisa 662."

Then, as now, newspapers often focused on the unusual as the following entries from the eastern volume illustrate.

4025. Hay, Mary, 65, youngest dau of David, Esq, late of Fifeshire, Scotland, d 9/19/24 in Poughkeepsie, NY (David arrived in this country "about ninety years ago". He was son of Robert Hay of the noble fam of Hays in Fifeshire. His mother was a descendant of the Earl of Murray, Regent of Scotland during the minority of James the Sixth.) (8-0/6)

4018. Hawley, Stiles drowned 1/18/30 in the Kaskaakia River in Illinois (born in CT and visited NY state as agent of the American Sunday School Union) ("In the winter" he left Springfield, IL for Macon Co. Later only his horse was found.) (1-5/13)

4754. Johnson, Robert (or "the person calling himself that") d 1/5/07 in the Albany gaol – committed for an attempt to rob the house of Mr. Pye on the Albany road (R. J. died from a wound inflicted by Mr. Pye, "after being himself shot thro' the body. Mr. Pie is said to be out of danger.") (9-1/13)

6203. Nelson, Alva m Laura Wells in Woodbury, VT (This entry includes a long statement of the tangled family relationships existing among the bride, groom, and the two witnesses "yet there was no blood relation between the bride and bridegroom") (8-12/24/28) [Bowman's parenthetical]

7220. Richards, Gustavus U. of NYC m 7/31/33 Electra (sic) B. Wilder, dau of S. V. S. Wilder, Esq. of Bolton, NY in B; Rev.? W. Chickering (newspaper account contains details concerning unusual wedding festivities) (7-8/31)

MORE EASTERN RECORDS

Because of the large number of records available for eastern counties, the last volume of the "10,000" trilogy only included records up to 1834. In 1991 Bowman published *8,000 More Vital Records of Eastern New York State, 1804–1850*.[8] The format of this volume is slightly different. Related names, such as the name of a bride, are included in the body of the work instead of an index. An individual may not be listed under his own name, but may be included in the listing of a relative. The author suggests reading all entries for the surname in question. His example is a search for the wife of the Rev. David Brown. There is no listing for David Brown. However, a search of all the entries under Brown yields a death notice for "BROWN, Mary B., wf of Rev. David of Lockport ..."

The newspapers consulted in this work are listed in Table 4. With the exception of the *Daily Albany Argus,* this work contains records from a new set of eastern newspapers.

THE DIRECTORY

In 1995, working with co-author Thomas J. Lynch, Bowman published his *Directory to Collections of New York Vital Records, 1726–1989, with Rare Gazetteer*.[9] The Directory is divided into three sections. Part one contains collections of newspaper-based vital records and "in which of five large genealogical libraries each of these collections is available." These libraries are the New York State Library, the New York Genealogical and Biographical Society Library, the Brooklyn Historical Society Library, the Family History Library, and the National Society Daughters of the American Revolution Library. Part two is a gazetteer of 6,710 cities, villages, and hamlets showing where they are in present day towns. Part three lists the formation and origins of the sixty-two present counties of New York.

---

[8] Fred Q. Bowman, *8000 More Vital Records of Eastern New York State, 1804-1850* (Rhinebeck, N.Y.: Kinship, 1991).

[9] Fred Q. Bowman and Thomas J. Lynch, *Directory to Collections of New York Vital Records, 1726–1989, with Rare Gazetteer* (Bowie, Md.: Heritage Books, 1995).

Table 4
NEWSPAPER SOURCES FOR 8,000 MORE VITAL RECORDS
OF EASTERN NEW YORK STATE, 1804–1850

NUMBER	TOWN	NEWSPAPER	DATES
1	Ogdensburgh	*St. Lawrence Gazette*	1826–30
		Northern Lights	1831–33
		St. Lawrence Republican	1833–43
2	Malone	*Franklin Telegraph*	1820–29
		Frontier Palladium	1849–50
3	Albany	*Daily Albany Argus*	1832–34
4	Kinderhook	*Kinderhook Sentinel*	1836–50
5	Huntington	*Portico*	1826–27
		*Long Islander**	1839–50
6	Sag Harbor	*Suffolk Gazette*	1804–5
		The Corrector	1822–26

*"Collections from this newspaper 1839–1864 (Marian F. Stevens, compiler) and 1865–1881 (Robert L. Simpson, compiler) are available at the Huntington (NY) Historical Society Library."

HUDSON-MOHAWK VALLEY RECORDS

The most recent book considered here is *7,000 Hudson-Mohawk Valley (NY) Vital Records, 1808–1850,* also co-authored by Thomas Lynch.[10] The listings are arranged alphabetically by surname. As with *8,000 More Vital Records of Eastern New York State,* secondary entries are included in the main body of the book and refer to the main entry. Each main entry consists of an abstract of a newspaper account of a marriage or death. Here, for example, are two death notices:

BENNETT, Thomas, Esq., 79, d (date not given) at his home in Rome, a Revolutionary War soldier, born in Western Fairfield Co., Conn., 18 March 1761 (served

---

[10] Fred Q. Bowman and Thomas J. Lynch, *7000 Hudson-Mohawk Valley (NY) Vital Records, 1808–1850* (Baltimore: Genealogical Publishing Co., 1997)

during the War from age 16 in the militia, the continental army and the "Coast Guards"; after the War lived in Montgomery County, NY until a few years before his death. Joined the Congregational Church in Conn. in 1782 and the Presbyterian Church in NY) (1-11/10/40)

BUTTS, Amy (Mrs.), 86, mother of Deacon Daniel, d 11/11/48 in Rome (one of the earliest settlers of Rome and among the first members of the Congregational Church — she was the only survivor of the original 34 members of that church) (1-11/17)

Many of the entries mention family connections and events, such as the following:

CONINE, Mary, 86, relict of Peter, Jr. (dau. of Sybrant G. Van Schaick and sister of Col. Goshen Van Schaick, deceased, of the City of Albany) d 3/24/35 at Coxsackie at the home of her son-in-law, John L. Bronk, Esq. (6-3/31)

HATCH, Sibyl, 49, wf of Sylvanus, d 9/6/38 suddenly at the home of her husband in Rome (her first husband, Thomas Alrich, has died "a few years since") (1-9/15)

Not all of the events occurred in New York State. The Albany newspapers especially reported distant events.

BALL, Flamen, Esq., counselor at law and Master of Chancery, d (date not given) in Spartenburg District, South Carolina (a short and painful illness) (6-3/27/16)

DE BLAISEL, Le Marquis, Chamberlain to the Emporer [sic] of Austria, m 4/17/26 Maria Matilda Bingham, dau. of Hon. William Bingham of the United States (6-6/13)

Most newspapers at this time did not print birth announcements. However, death notices of children, such as this one for Azalia Hart, can provide approximate birth dates, and may be the only existing record of the child's existence.

> HART, Azalia Ernesteen, 1, dau. of William and Rachael Eliza, d 3/25/50 in Rochester (Mrs. Hart was formerly of Fort Plain) (4-3/28)

As noted previously, marriages in the "10,000" trilogy described above were entered by the surname of the groom. In this volume, an entry of the bride's name is in the main body of the book, not the index. Thus, information about the marriage of Sarah Felter and Richard Clark appears as follows.

> CLARK, Richard M. of NYC m 4/7/42 Sarah E. Felter, dau. of Theron, Esq. of Newburgh, in N.; Rev Charles A. Bleek (9-4/9)

As shown below, searching for the name of the bride will direct the reader to the groom's entry.

> FELTER, Sarah, — see CLARK, Richard M.

Table 5 (next page) lists the towns and newspapers from which these records were abstracted.

ACCESS TO THE BOOKS

These books are available at the NEHGS Research Library. They are available at the Family History Library (*www.familysearch.org*) in book form; they are not available in rentable microfilm form. Used copies of most of the books are often available for sale from Amazon.com and websites that sell used books. Check your local library. Those published by Genealogical Publishing Company are available at Ancestry.com.

Table 5
NEWSPAPER SOURCES FOR 7,000
HUDSON-MOHAWK VALLEY (NY) VITAL RECORDS, 1808–1850

NUMBER	TOWN	NEWSPAPER	DATES
1	Rome	*Rome Citizen*	7/7/40–12/31/50
2	Herkimer	*Herkimer Herald*	7/16/08–11/2/09
		Bunker Hill	11/30/09–2/1/10
3	Little Falls	*Mohawk Courier*	2/18/36–12/31/43
4	Fort Plain	*Montgomery Phoenix* and *Fort Plain Advertiser*	2/24/48–12/31/50
5	West Troy (in Watervliet)	*West Troy Advocate* and *Watervliet Advertiser*	10/4/37–12/30/50
6	Albany	*Albany Advertiser*	11/8/15–6/5/16
		Albany Gazette	1/1/26–12/31/26
		Daily Albany Argus	1/1/35–12/31/36
7	Catskill	*American Eagle*	1/11/09–5/8/11
8	Saugerties	*Ulster Telegraph*	12/30/48–12/31/49
9	Newburgh	*Newburgh Journal*	10/9/41–2/18/43
10	Carmel	*Putnam Democrat* and *Democrat Courier*	6/27/49–12/31/50
11	Peekskill	*Westchester Republican*	3/5/33–12/3/35 1/1/39–2/27/44
		Highland Democrat	12/7/41–12/1/42
12	Sing Sing (in Ossining)	*Hudson River Chronicle*	10/23/38–4/14/40

CHAPTER 5

The Vosburgh Collection of New York Church Records

New York State did not begin to collect vital records data until 1880, leaving genealogists seeking earlier records with incomplete, unpublished, and scattered substitutes. For this reason any reliable collection of early vital records is especially valuable. The Vosburgh Collection, containing over 100 volumes of transcriptions of Protestant church records, is such a resource. Commissioned by the Library of Congress and other institutions, the collection was compiled between 1913 and 1928. Royden Vosburgh, archivist and historian of the New York Genealogical and Biographical Society, transcribed many of the volumes and edited nearly all of them. In spite of its size, the Vosburgh Collection can not be considered a statewide database. The emphasis is on early congregations rather than on early records. The churches included are located almost exclusively in the valleys surrounding the Hudson and Mohawk rivers, sites of the earliest settlements in the state. Many of the transcriptions extend into the twentieth century, however. The collection has been microfilmed and is available in the NEHGS library, the library of the New York Genealogical and Biographical Society (NYG&B), and the New York State Library, as well as in some public libraries. Films are available at the Family History Library (and local Family History Centers).

Royden Woodward Vosburgh became the archivist and historian of the New York Genealogical and Biographical Society in 1913. The follow-

An earlier version of this chapter was posted at *www.NewEnglandAncestors.org* September 12, 2003.

ing biographical information was extracted from an obituary published in the *New York Genealogical and Biographical Record* in 1932.[1]

> Royden Woodward Vosburgh, a Life Member of the New
> York Genealogical and Biographical Society, died . . . on
> May 18, 1931. . . . Mr. Vosburgh was born Feb. 5, 1875, at
> Buffalo, New York, the son of William Henry Vosburgh
> and his wife Caroline Estelle Woodward. . . . He was edu-
> cated at the Brown and Nichols School in Cambridge,
> Massachusetts, and at Harvard University, 1893–1896. . . .
> In 1913 Mr. Vosburgh became the archivist of the New
> York Genealogical and Biographical Society, and devoted
> much of his time to make carefully prepared copies of the
> church records of the State of New York. His services
> enriched the Society with the records of 92 churches, occu-
> pying 101 volumes. . . . In the *Records* for Jan. 1918 (Vol.
> 49, pp. 11–16) and April, 1921 (Vol. 52, pp. 152–157) are
> listed the church records copied by Mr. Vosburgh. . . . Mr.
> Vosburgh was connected with the Staten Island Institute of
> Arts and Sciences, and edited for that Society nine volumes
> of Staten Island church and gravestone records.

The NEHGS library holds a copy of the thirteen-reel NYG&B film-ing of the collection. Its call number is F118/V67/1913. While there is no every-name index to the collection, the library has a copy of *A Guide to Vosburgh Church Records on Microfilm,* compiled by Robert M. Murphy (microtext REF F118/M86/1999). The majority of the records begin in the mid- to late eighteenth century. Some cover a relatively short time span, such as Round Top Lutheran Church of Pine Plains in Dutchess County (1760–88). Other records extend into the twentieth century, such as First Lutheran Church of Albany (1774–1901) or First Reformed Church of West Coxsackie in Greene County (1738–1918).

The catalogue entries at the Connecticut State Library for this filming are particularly complete. For example, the entry for the

---

[1] *New York Genealogical and Biographical Record,* Vol. 63 (1932), pp. 185–86.

Ancient Church, Mohawk.

"Representation of the ancient Dutch church in Caughnawaga, a stone structure believed to have been erected in 1763," from John W. Barber, *Historical Collections of the State of New York* (New York: Clark, Austin & Co., 1851), p. 147.

Reformed Dutch Church of Stone Arabia, in the town of Palatine, Montgomery County, contains the following description of the contents:

> *Contents* v. 1 : Baptisms and births, Oct. 14, 1739–Jan. 31, 1796. Marriages, Oct. 16, 1739–1795. Register of members, Jan. 13, 1739–1795. Elders and deacons, 1788–1796. Copy of the charter, 1791. Death register, 1787–1795. Seat owners, 1790. Seat regulations and transfer. — v. 2 : Births and baptisms, 1796–1824. Marriages, 1796–1821. Register of members, 1796–1830. Death register, 1796–1823. Miscellanea, dismissals, etc. Abstracts from the minutes of the consistory, 1789–1850. List of the church officers, 1743, 1788–1849. Subscription lists, 1821. — v. 3 : Births and baptisms, 1824–1911. Death register, 1851–1856. Marriages, 1844–1895. Register of members, 1826–1912. List of families, 1851. Deaths, 1872–1880. Minutes of consistory. The history of the Reformed Dutch Church of Stone Arabia, Gravestone inscriptions. Stone Arabia Reformed Burying Ground. Catalogue of books and documents

While it is true that the records of some of the churches in this collection were published elsewhere (with indexes), researchers are urged to consult the Vosburgh collection as well. Most of the published sources transcribe only the vital records; as the description above suggests, Vosburgh includes additional records. He carefully describes his sources and includes many notes, such as the following: "Note. three blank pages follow in the original record, after which comes the page inscribed: "RECORD OF BAPTISMS CONTINUED by Jno. J. Wack."[2] The following extract from the introduction to his "Abstracts from the minutes of the consistory" gives some idea of how extensive this additional material can be.

> Taken as a whole, this abstract with the notes gives every fact worthy of note concerning the history of this church for three score years. It contains all the documentary data relating to the building of, and the repairs made, to the present church edifice; the consecration of the church, its admission to the Classis of Albany;[3] and presents authoritatively for the first time, the facts concerning the suspension and deposition of Rev. John J. Wack (who was accused of repeated drunkenness and profanity). This latter phase of the church history is in itself a most interesting study, and it shows that the members of the Classis of Montgomery, by whose acts the Stone Arabia Church became independent for about ten years, were the same band of malcontents who finally organized the True Reformed Dutch Church. In short, what follows presents the primary sources of information from which the history of the church must be written.[4]

The version available at the Family History Library presents the same information in sixty-one reels instead of thirteen. FHL does not have a copy of Murphy's guide, but it does have an *Index to the*

---

[2] Vosburgh Collection, reel 12, item #1, p. 141.

[3] Classis: "In certain Presbyterian churches; an inferior judicatory consisting of the elders or pastors of the parishes or church of a district; a presbytery. Used in England under the Commonwealth; and subsequently in certain Reformed churches of the continent, and America. A district formed by the parishes so united." *Oxford English Dictionary*, 2nd ed., prepared by J. A. Simpson and E.S.C. Weiner (Oxford, England: Clarendon Press, 1989).

[4] Vosburgh Collection, reel 12, item #1, p. 153.

Vosburgh collection of the early church records of the state of New York (#1697744, item 27). Its catalog entries list the names of the churches included in each of the sixty-one reels.

Table 1 lists the relevant congregations, collected by county, together with the dates for which records were transcribed. From this a researcher should be able to evaluate the relevance of this collection to his or her work.

Table 1
CHURCHES FORMING THE VOSBURGH COLLECTION[5]

COUNTY	LOCATION	CONGREGATION	DATES
Albany	Albany	First Lutheran	1784–1900
	Albany	First Presbyterian	1785–1870
	Berne	Reformed Dutch Church of the Beaver Dam	1763–1877
	Berne	St. Paul's Evangelical Lutheran	1790–1875
	New Scotland	Presbyterian	1787–1893
Cayuga	Fleming	Reformed Protestant Dutch Church at the Owasco Outlet	1807–1886
	Owasco	Reformed Dutch	1799–1834
Columbia	Canaan	Congregational Church and Society of New Canaan	1740–1884
	Canaan	First Presbyterian	1830–1854
	Charham	Congregational Church of New Concord	1701 1851
	Claverack	St. Thomas Evangelical Lutheran	1760–1905
	Germantown	Christ's Evangelical Lutheran	1746–1859
	Ghent	Christ's Evangelical Lutheran	1801–1901
	Ghent	Reformed Dutch (known as Christ Church)	1775–1919
	Hillsdale	Reformed Dutch	1776–1849
	Kinderhook	Reformed Dutch	1716–1864
	Manorton (Livingston)	St. John's Evangelical Lutheran	1764–1848
	West Copake	Reformed Church of West Copake (formerly Reformed Church of Taghkanick)	1783–1856

continued on next page

---

[5] See *http://newyorkfamilyhistory.org/modules.php?name=Sections&op=viewarticle&artid=29.*

Table 1 *(cont.)*

COUNTY	LOCATION	CONGREGATION	DATES
Delaware	Harpersfield	Presbyterian Congregation	1787–1837
	Moresville (Roxbury)	Reformed Dutch	1836–1889
	Stamford	First Presbyterian	1834–1882
	Stamford	St. Peter's Episcopal Church in Hobart	1794–1907
Dutchess	Pine Plains	Round Top Lutheran	1760–1788
Fulton	Broadalbin	First Presbyterian	1799–1895
	Johnstown	Presbyterian	1785–1867
	Johnstown	St. John's Episcopal	1815–1862
	Mayfield	Reformed Dutch	1792–1821
	Perth	First Presbyterian Church of West Galway (formerly First Presbyterian Church in Galloway)	1793–1912
	Perth	United Presbyterian Church of Broadalbin	1821–1918
Greene	Catskill	Reformed Dutch	1732–1833
	Durham	First Presbyterian	1792–1857
	Durham	Reformed Dutch Church in Oak Hill	1794–1832
	Durham	Second Presbyterian	1816–1872
	Prattsville	Reformed Dutch	1798–1896
	West Coxsackie	First Reformed	1738–1918
Herkimer	German Flats	Reformed Protestant Dutch	1763–1848
	Herkimer	Reformed Protestant Dutch Church	1801–1848
Montgomery	Florida	United Presbyterian	1743–1861
	Florida	Reformed Protestant Dutch	1808–1918
	Fonda	Reformed (formerly Reformed Protestant Dutch Church of Caughnawaga)	1758–1858
	Glen	First Reformed Protestant Dutch (formerly First R.P.D. Church at Charleston)	1805–1882
	Minden	St. Paul's Lutheran (otherwise known as the Geisenberg Church, formerly at Hallsville)	1792–1836
	Minden	Reformed Dutch Church at Fort Plain (formerly Reformed Calvinist Church at Canajoharie)	1788–1850

COUNTY	LOCATION	CONGREGATION	DATES
	Palatine	Lutheran Trinity Church of Stone Arabia	1751–1866
	Palatine	Reformed Dutch	1739–1912
	St. Johnsville	St. John's Dutch Reformed	1788–1878
New York		Christ Protestant Episcopal	1793–1848
		Reformed Dutch Church at Greenwich [Greenwich Village]	1804–1859
		Madison Avenue Reformed (formerly Reformed Dutch Church in Sugar Loaf Street, and North West Reformed Dutch Church in Franklin Street)	1808–1850
		South Reformed Dutch Church ("in Garden Street" to 1835, "in Murray Street" 1837–48)	1812–53
Oneida	Clinton	Congregational Church (also known as the Society of Clinton)	1788–1846
	New Hartford	Presbyterian Church (formerly the First Religious Society in Whitestown)	1791–1887
	Paris	Congregational Church (also known as Paris Religious Society)	1795–1855
	Utica	First Presbyterian	1797–1852
	Whitestown	First Presbyterian Church of Whitesboro	1795–1898
Oswego	Oswego	First Presbyterian	1832–1870
Otsego	Cherry Valley	First Presbyterian	1799–1849
	Cooperstown	Presbyterian	1800–1869
	Springfield	First Baptist	1787–1852
Rensselaer	Brunswick	Gilead Evangelical	1777–1859
	East Greenbush	Reformed Protestant Dutch	1787–1910
	Hoosick	Reformed Dutch Church of Taishokeat Buskirk (formerly Buskirk's Bridge, or Tiossick)	1792–1873
	Lansingburgh	First Presbyterian	1804–1827 1833–1858
	Nassau	Reformed Dutch	1804–1878
	North Greenbush	Reformed Protestant Dutch Church of Wynantskill	1794–1889
	Schodack	Reformed Dutch Church of Schodack at Muitzeskill	1770–1832

continued on next page

Table 1 *(cont.)*

COUNTY	LOCATION	CONGREGATION	DATES
	Troy	First Presbyterian	1793–1864
	Troy	Second Street Presbyterian	1834–1911
	West Sandlake	First Evangelical Lutheran Church (formerly the Zion Evangelical Lutheran Church in Rensselaerwyck and Greenbush)	1785–1868
Richmond (Staten Island)	New Springville (in former Town of Northfield)	Asbury Methodist Episcopal (formerly M.E. Church in Town of Northfield)	1802–1809 1856–1881
	Port Richmond (Northfield)	Reformed Protestant Dutch Church on Staten Island	1790–1871
	Richmond (Northfield)	St. Andrew's Protestant Episcopal	1808–1875
	Rossville (Westfield)	St. Luke's Protestant Episcopal	1844–1877
	Tompkinsville (Castleton)	Reformed Protestant Dutch (in 1922 the Reformed Church of Brighton Heights)	1823–1871
	Tompkinsville (Castleton)	St. Paul's Protestant Episcopal	1833–1876
	West New Brighton (Castleton)	St. Mary's [Protestant Episcopal]	1849–1875
	Woodrow (Westfield)	Woodrow Methodist Episcopal	1798–1876
Rockland	Kakiat	Reformed Dutch	1774–1864
Saratoga	Ballston	First Presbyterian	1783–1865
	Charlton	Freehold Presbyterian	1800–1861
	Charlton	United Presbyterian Church at West Charlton	1794–1858
	Clifton Park	Reformed Dutch Church of Amity	1802–1856
	Schuylerville	Reformed Protestant Dutch Church of Saratoga	1789–1857
	Stillwater	First Congregational	1752–1849
	Stillwater	First Presbyterian	1791–1904
Schenectady	Duanesburgh	Reformed Protestant Dutch	1798–1804
	Niskayuna	Protestant Reformed Dutch	1783–1861

COUNTY	LOCATION	CONGREGATION	DATES
Schoharie	Blenheim	Reformed Dutch	1797–1831
	Cobleskill	Union Reformed Dutch	1827–1848
	Cobleskill	Zion's Evangelical Lutheran	1795–1871
	Gilboa	Reformed (formerly the Reformed Dutch Church in Dyse's Manor in Broome)	1801–1885
	Middleburgh	Reformed Dutch	1786–1865
	New Rhinebeck	German Reformed (later the Reformed Church of Lawyersville in Cobleskill)	1788–1882
	Schoharie	Reformed (formerly the High and Low Dutch Reformed Congregation)	1730–1892
	Schoharie	St. Paul's Evangelical Lutheran	1728–1882
Washington	Cambridge	First United Presbyterian Congregation	1794–1869
	Cambridge	Protestant Presbyterian Congregation	1791–1886
	Easton	Reformed Protestant Dutch	1803–1909
	Greenwich	Reformed Dutch (formerly Reformed Dutch Church of Union Village)	1809–1879
Bennington (Vermont)	Sandgate	Congregational	1782–1835 1860, 1867
Warren (New Jersey)	Johnsonburg	Hardwick Friends Meeting	1901–1922

CHAPTER 6

An Easier Way to Obtain
New York State Vital Records

Obtaining vital record information in upstate New York is difficult. There is no kinder way to state it. You will not find records published in books to be found on shelves of public libraries, and they are not available on the Internet. Using form DOH-1562, one may submit a request to the vital records section of New York State Department of Health (New York State Department of Health, Vital Records Section, Genealogy Unit, P.O. Box 2602, Albany, NY 12220-2602) for an uncertified copy of a birth, marriage, or death record. You can download this form from their website (*www.health.state.ny.us/nysdoh/consumer/vr.htm*). If an exact date for the event is not known, a search may be performed, but the researcher could pay dearly for this service. The minimum fee of $22 covers a search of one to three years. The maximum fee listed is $202 to search eighty-one to ninety years.

The fee is retained whether or not the record is found. In Albany, a single person processes all requests for certificates. I am told that this person is currently about two years behind. It used to be that the index to the vital records of upstate New York was available only at the New York State Archives in Albany and the National Archives Northeast Region in New York City. However, the job is now easier. A third copy of the index became available to the public in October 2000 at the main public library in Rochester, New York. While the information remains the same, the setting is much different. The

An earlier version of this chapter was posted at *www.NewEnglandAncestors.org* May 30, 2002.

index in Rochester is administered by friendly people dedicated to helping genealogists. It is also available at two additional locations: the Onondaga County Public Library, 447 South Salina Street, Syracuse, NY 13202; telephone (315) 435-1900; website *www.ocpl.lib.ny.us* and the Buffalo & Erie County Public Library, Grosvenor Room, 1 Lafayette Square, Buffalo, NY 14203; telephone (716) 858-8900; website *www.buffalolib.org.*

The index, which consists of thousands of microfiche, contains entries of births, marriages, and deaths for the entire state outside New York City or Brooklyn. It includes information from towns in Kings County before annexation by Brooklyn, and also portions of the counties of Westchester, Richmond, and Queens before they were annexed by New York City. It does not include births and deaths in Albany, Buffalo, and Yonkers before 1914 or marriages before 1908. These earlier records may be available through the local registrar of each county. While adopted babies are not included in the birth index, there is information about babies born in state facilities. New York State Archives information leaflet #2 (*www.archives.nysed .gov/a/researchroom/rr_family_vitalstats.shtml*) contains more complete information. Statewide registration of vital records began in 1880–81. Marriage and death records are restricted for fifty years, birth records for seventy-five years. These restrictions can be waived for direct descendants, but the index entries are not available after these dates. Data on living persons is restricted regardless.

The index is arranged by year. Within each year entries are arranged by surname or, in later years, by Soundex code. Each index entry contains name, date, place, and certificate number (an identifier assigned by the State Department of Health). For example, the first entry in the index of birth records reads:

1881, Abbott, Georgianna, 22 Sept., Unionville, #4045

This serves as an official statement by the State of New York that this event took place. Finding the entry in the index assures the researcher that the certificate exists, decreasing the probability of a "false negative." Searching for a record that is not found costs just as much as a copy of the certificate.

The information available for marriages varies with the time frame, as the following example shows. The first marriage entry listed for the year 1881 is for Julia D. Abbey. The entry contains the date and place, but no information about the groom. Without the groom's surname, there is no way to move from here to a death record, or the birth records of children. Clearly the information on the original certificate is required. There is an alternative to waiting for two years for a reply from Albany, however. Help comes in the form of a gazetteer/directory combination. This index entry lists Arkwright as the location where Julia Abbey's marriage was recorded. The gazetteer places Arkwright in Chautauqua County. The directory gives the address and phone number of the current Registrar of Vital Statistics in the town of Arkwright. It is likely that this person will be able to process a request significantly faster than that poor, overworked soul in Albany.

Later marriage records can yield more information, since there is a link to the spouse. These records also use the Soundex system, so the research methodology is slightly different. My example is the last

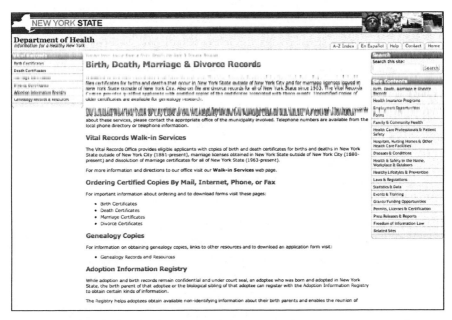

Website for the Vital Records Section of the New York State Department of Public Health (*www.health.state.ny.us/vital_records/*).

marriage record publicly available — the last entry under "Z" in 1951. The entry reads:

624, Zerkle, Joan M., Buffalo, Stee, 6 30, 24778

The three-digit number represents the Soundex code for the surname Zerkle (6-R, 2-K, 4-L). The location, Buffalo, is where the license was issued, but not necessarily where the marriage was performed. The next entry, Stee, is the first four letters of the spouse's surname, and following that is the month and day on which the marriage occurred. The final entry is the certificate number. With this information it is possible to find the groom.

The first four letters give a partial Soundex number of S3xx, but we do not know what other consonants might be in the full surname. The index is arranged by year, and then by Soundex code, so we start with the S300 entries for 1951 and search for "Zerk" in the spouse column. The image quality is good; the information is typewritten. This is not difficult. Here he is on the second fiche I try.

340, Steele, Richard E, Buffalo, Zerk, 6 30, 24778

Place, date, and — most important — certificate number match. Joan Zerkle became Mrs. Richard Steele.

CHAPTER 7

The Magee House: "Capital" of Genealogical Research in Steuben County, New York

N amed after Baron Von Steuben, of Revolutionary War fame, Steuben County was established March 18, 1796, from Ontario County. After its formation, portions were annexed to the neighboring counties of Allegany (1806), Livingston (1821), Yates (1823), and Schuyler (1854). Even at this reduced size Steuben County is larger in area than the state of Rhode Island. The largest industry is farming, followed by tourism. The county seat is Bath, founded in 1793.

The Magee House in Bath was built by John Magee in 1831. After he moved to Watkins, New York, in 1864, the house continued to be used as a residence, first by two generations of the Howell family, then by the Davenport family. In 1895 the building became the Davenport public library. In 1995 a new public library building was erected next door and the Magee House became the Steuben County History Center, containing both the Steuben County Historical Society and the County Historian's Office.

In this chapter I describe the genealogical information available at the Steuben County Historian's office and how to go about using it. The information includes census, probate, and vital records as well as genealogies of local families. There are a number of possible locations for the same information in this collection. For example, a birth date might be part of a census record or a marriage application. A death date might be part of a cemetery record or newspaper obituary. Death records may contain parents' names. This overlap helps to fill in the inevitable gaps in any one collection and provides some reassuring confirmation of data.

HOLDINGS OF THE MAGEE HOUSE

Probate Records

There is an every-name index of estate (probate or administration) proceedings from 1796 to 1900. This index lists case number, book, page, year of death, and town. I took as an example the name of Hanley from the town of Lindley. All of the people in the group had the same case number, book, etc., but only one had an asterisk, indicating that it was his will while the other names were merely mentioned.

NAME	I	CASE	BOOK	PAGE	YEAR	TOWN
Hanley, John	*	5094	10A	137	1890	Lindley

The more detailed information is available in a series of loose leaf notebooks arranged by case number. Looking under case number 5094, I found that John Hanley died 31 May 1890 in Lindley with the following information. Date of will/admin. 5 July 1890. Wife: Mary Hanley. Inventory of value $219.20.

HEIR MENTIONED IN WILL	RELATIONSHIP	CURRENT RESIDENCE
Martin Hanley	Brother	Weston Mills, NY
Catherine (Hanley) Gibbons	Sister	Ovid, NY
Thomas Hanley	Deceased son	
William Hanley	Son of Thomas	Australia

Executors: Mary Hanley, Frank Harris, Robert Huggins, Oliver Camp, S.M. Morgan.

These summaries do not provide any detailed information about how the estate is apportioned among the various heirs. If land is involved, the amount in acres is recorded along with the location. I was told that these records were filmed by the Family History Library in Salt Lake City.

Town Clerk Records

One of the most extensive collections here is an index of town clerk records from all over the county (with some minor exceptions). The time span of this collection is from the time of the earliest town clerk's records up to about 1950. The index contains no birth records, only marriage and death records, but these last often contain a birth date. The actual records remain with the individual town clerks. These printouts exist only in this office. The cooperation of the town clerks to assemble this database required the agreement that the printouts not be photocopied or microfilmed.

The information is available several ways, since the computer database can be sorted many different ways. The index is available sorted by surname as would be expected. Using my example above, I looked under Hanley in the death records for a listing of the death of John Hanley (not there) and for his son Thomas, named as deceased in his will (not there). I did find a listing for Mary Hanley who might have been John Hanley's wife. A search for the will of her father, Timothy Brown, might support this hypothesis.

NAME	BORN	DIED	FATHER	MOTHER	TOWN
Mary Hanley	1826	5 Jan 1916	Timothy Brown		Lindley

The index of town clerk records is also offered as a printout sorted by the name of the father or by the maiden name of the mother. In these listings married daughters are listed by their married name. For example, I find listed under the mother's maiden name, Susan Carey, the death record of her married daughter Mary Brennan. The index entry tells me that Mary Brennan, born 27 July 1871, died 17 July 1950, in Lindley, was the daughter of Susan Carey and Thomas Dunning. The same entry would be found in the listing sorted by the name of the father under Thomas Dunning. Other children of this same couple include Arthur Dunning, William H. Dunning, Frances Fairbanks, Jessie Northaway, and Edgar Dunning. When sorted in this fashion, family groups automatically come together, at least for those who stayed within the county.

Marriage records list the name (bride or groom), age, date of marriage, father, mother, spouse's surname, and town. There is one line each for bride and groom. Both entries are needed. Thus I read, for example, that Donald F. Gibbs, age 23, son of William and Catherine

(Gandro) Gibbs married ___ Doty on 18 May 1932 in Hornell City. Looking under the Doty surname, I find Eleanor M. Doty, age 19, dau. of George and Shirley (Van Nort) Doty married ___ Gibbs on 18 May 1932, in Hornell City. The date and town match, so I have the names of both bride and groom, their approximate birth dates, and both sets of parents.

Marriage information of sorts is also available in the listing of deaths by name of father or mother mentioned above. If the marriage record is missing look here. Suppose I am interested in Jane Burdick, but I know nothing of her marriage. There are three entries of death records with mother's name Jane Burdick. If the birth dates of the children are reasonable, then I would have these three possible husbands to investigate.

MOTHER	FATHER	CHILDREN	BORN	DIED	TOWN
Jane Burdick	Charles Babcock	George H. Babcock	7-2-1853	7-19-1933	Hornell City
Jane Burdick	Moses Hill	Chancy W. Hill	8-26-1869	1-26-1936	Lindley
Jane Burdick	Elijah Straight	Amos B. Straight	2-4-1866	1-09-1912	Hornell City

Cemetery Records and Newspaper Obituaries

Supplementing the town clerk death records, there are cemetery records and obituaries. I used the names of the bride's parents in the marriage example above and looked in the index to cemetery records. Both were listed.

NAME	PAGE	CEMETERY CODE	YEAR BIRTH	YEAR DEATH
George Leon Doty	63	HV6	1887	1938
Shirley Doty	64	HV6	1894	1968

The cemetery code, HV6, specifies a particular cemetery in Hornellsville. From that cemetery record, pages 63 and 64, I find the actual burial record.

NAME	BIRTH LOCATION	DATE	DEATH	LOT NO.
George Leon Doty	?	?	7 Mar 1938	437D
Shirley Doty	New York State	1894	13 Feb 1968	437D

There are more Doty graves in this cemetery, but none in the same lot.

The obituary collection has been compiled by the county historian's office. It consists of clippings of published newspaper obituaries. There is a computer printout of the index listed by surname. The index has no listing among the many Doty entries for George Leon Doty, but does have a listing for his wife Shirley. A newspaper clipping for her death is therefore a part of the collection.

NAME	CEMETERY CODE	AGE	YEAR BIRTH	YEAR DEATH
Shirley Doty	HV6	74	1894	1968

Because of the time involved in handling the records, the staff prefers to retrieve the actual newspaper clipping for photocopying not for reading.

Local Newspapers

In addition to the collection of newspaper obituaries, there is a microfilm collection of local newspapers. The records are not complete. There are significant gaps. However, in outline the collection is as follows:

NEWSPAPER	TIME SPAN
Addison Advertiser	1858–1927
Hammondsport Herald	1874–1931
Keuka Grape Belt	1939–41
Steuben Farmers Advocate	1852–1916
Steuben Courier	1843–1969
Bath Plaindealer	1883–1921
Hornellsville Weekly	1851–99
Wayland Reg. News	1903–68
Prattsburg News	1872–1920

Greenwood Times	1899–1919
Cohocton Valley Times Index	1898–1922
Canisteo Times	1880–1939

Census Records

The index of census records combines listings for federal, state, and county census returns, merged and sorted by surname. This is an every-name index. (Of course, for earlier census records only the head of household's name was recorded.) Actual records are in the County Clerk's office a few blocks away, but microfilm copies are here. Having all of the census records together gives a more complete picture of the evolution of each family over time and helps to compensate for omissions and errors in the records. For my example I return to the family of John Hanley of Lindley and choose the 1870 federal census.

NAME	YEAR	PAGE	TOWN	DISTRICT
John Hanley	1870	007	LN	

Other family members should be listed for this census on the same or following page. I find listed: Mary A., Bridget, Catherine, Eliza, Thomas, William. I note in passing that there is another John Hanley family on page 005 of the 1870 census. A study of these census records would go a long way toward building up a picture of the Hanley families of Steuben County.

Other Material

I find on the shelves several dozen published genealogies of local families and over 200 unpublished manuscripts of genealogies which have been compiled and donated to the Magee House. These manuscripts have not been microfilmed and are not, to the best of my knowledge, available anywhere else.

There are county histories, not only for Steuben County, but for other, neighboring counties in New York State. There are some county directories and Bath city directories. There is also a significant collection from nearby Tioga County in Pennsylvania because there was much traffic between the two counties.

The Magee House.

FINAL NOTES

John Magee, for whom the Magee house is named, was born near Easton, Pennsylvania, in 1794, son of Henry and Sarah (Mulhollon) Magee. His parents came from County Antrim, Ireland. His mother died 12 October 1805. In 1808 Henry Magee moved to Michigan with his children Rebecca, John, Hugh, Thomas J., and Mary. John Magee, with his father and brother Hugh, fought in the war of 1812 and was captured by the British on two different occasions before leaving the service in the spring of 1816. He came to Bath as a common laborer but quickly rose in prominence, becoming a constable in 1819, marshal in 1820, and high sheriff in 1821. In 1826 he was elected to Congress, serving two terms. In 1831 he married his second wife, Arabella Steuart, the mother of his ten children. She died in 1864. In 1831 he also became president of the newly formed Steuben County Bank in Bath. During this time the New York and Erie Railroad was built to Lake Erie and Mr. Magee became its president and chief executive officer. In 1851, with his son Duncan, he bought the Corning and Blossburg Railroad to move lumber and coal from Tioga County and from the mines at Blossburg. The coal interest was enlarged with the purchase of the coal lands at Fall

Brook and the organization of the Fall Brook Coal Company in 1859. Mr. Magee died in Watkins, New York 5 April 1868, and was buried in Glenwood Cemetery. Four children survived him: Duncan S., George J., Hebe P., and General George J. Magee.

The founder of the Davenport family in Bath was Col. Ira Davenport, born in Spencertown, Columbia County, New York on 20 September 1795. He married, in 1824, Lydia, the eldest daughter of Dugald Cameron. Their children were John, Ira, Christina, Fanny, Dugald, and Eliza. Colonel Davenport died in Bath on 2 May 1868. He was a very successful businessman and merchant. When a young man, he drove a wagonload of goods, three hundred miles to the frontier town of Canisteo (now Hornellsville), and built the first store in which he sold his goods. Within a short time he was operating stores in nine local communities. He moved to Bath in 1847. He founded The Davenport Home for Orphan Girls. Building began in 1861; the corporation was organized 1863; the orphanage opened in 1864. He donated sixty-five acres in Bath along with the building, and a generous endowment. Upon his death his sons John and Ira continued his business interests.

The Magee House, a handsome Federal-style red brick building located at the intersection of West Morris Street and Cameron Street is open to the public from 9 a.m. to 4 p.m. Monday through Friday. The phone number at this office is (607) 776-9631, ext. 3411. The website is *www.steubencony.org/hstorian.html*. Genealogists who visit the Magee House should seek the assistance of research assistant Marion Springer. Although she claims to be "just a volunteer," she is extremely knowledgeable about the holdings and efficiently guides people to relevant material. There is no charge for the use of these records, but there is a charge for making copies.

The new public library contains a few books which were duplicates in the Historical Society's collection, but generally leaves local history to the Historical Society. However, being open later in the evening, it would be a convenient location to continue to work on notes taken during the day at the Magee House. The Magee House is also only a few blocks away from Pultney Square and the County Clerk's office, which houses the county's land records.

CHAPTER 8

Earliest Records of
Western New York State

W hen conducting successful genealogical research, it is important that you know not only what sorts of records might prove useful for any given problem, but also where you might locate those records. For records at the county level, this requires keeping track of the changes in local government over time. Many of us have faced the situation in which our pioneer ancestors settled in a location before the modern county was created. Thus the earliest records for a location can be in a county seat quite far removed from the current one. A case in point is Ontario County in New York State. Present-day Ontario County covers an area of 640 square miles in central New York State — but when first formed in 1789, this venerable county encompassed an area of roughly 2,500 square miles! It covered all of New York State west of the preemption line — very roughly, a north–south line from Lake Ontario to the Pennsylvania line, passing through the northern end of Seneca Lake. The earliest records of this region, which currently comprises fourteen counties, are held in the Ontario County Records and Archives Center in Canandaigua.[1]

Ontario County maintained its initial size for less than twenty years. It was a time of intense land speculation, and hundreds of deeds in this time period track the land being sold, resold, and subdivided. Steuben County was formed from the southern portion of Ontario County in

---

An earlier version of this chapter was posted at *www.NewEnglandAncestors.org* March 15, 2002.

[1] I toured this facility in November 2001 and describe here what I found.

1796, and records for that county can be found in Bath. Territory to the west became Genesee County (county seat Batavia) in 1802. Genesee daughter counties include Allegany (1806); Cattaraugus, Niagara, and Chautauqua (all 1808); Orleans (1824); and Wyoming (1841). Livingston County (county seat Geneseo) was formed in 1821 from parts of both Ontario and Genesee counties. More territory to the south was lost with the creation of Yates County (county seat Pen Yan) in 1823. The present northern boundary was formed with the creation of Wayne County (county seat Lyons), also in 1823.

The Ontario County Records and Archives Center is located about three miles east of downtown Canandaigua, the county seat, in the town of Hopewell. (Canandaigua, pronounced can-an-DAY-gwa, is on the northern tip of Canandaigua Lake, less than ten miles south of exits 43 or 44 on the New York State Thruway.) The center receives material from all the county offices. Three full-time staff members work to convert the incoming records to microfilm. After filming, records are either returned to the county office or shredded, depending on the content. Original material to be archived is stored in acid-free folders and boxes in a climate-controlled chamber on floor-to-ceiling rolling shelves. Some of the records in the facility are closed to the public by court order or state law. Most of the records useful for genealogical research have been microfilmed. The following is a description of these records.

CENSUS RECORDS

Ontario County federal census records from 1790 to 1920 are available on microfilm. Indexes are available for 1790 to 1820, 1850, and 1860. State census records are available for 1845, 1855, 1865, 1875, 1892, 1905, 1915, and 1925. The indexes for 1850, 1855, 1860, 1865, 1870, 1875, 1892, and some indexes for 1905 are available online at the Archives Center website (*http://raims.com/censusmenu.html*).

LAND RECORDS

Deeds are available from 1789 (the inception of the county) to 1915 and include the original pioneer sales in the Phelps-Gorham Purchase. Mortgage records from 1789 to 1947 and assessment rolls from 1789 to 1993 are also available. Although the early records are not complete, they can be a useful complement to deeds and mortgages. Indexes to deeds (*http://raims.com/deedmenu.html*) from 1789 to 1845 are online.

COURT RECORDS

The indexing of county court records is a work in progress, though some are available to view in person and some are available online, as follows:

Naturalization records, 1803–1956, including declarations of intent, petitions for citizenship, and naturalization certificates. Available online: nineteenth-century naturalization records (*http://raims.com/naturalizations.html*) and twentieth-century naturalization records (*http://raims. com/nat20.html*).

Surrogate Court records,1789–1965, indexed by name, can include inventories and debts along with wills. Available online: indexes up to 1926 (*http://raims.com/surrogate.html*).

Guardianship records, 1789–1929, usually involving administering estates of minors.

Jury lists for the nineteenth century; indexes available online (*http://raims.com/jury.html*). In addition to establishing the residency of your ancestor, these lists also sometimes list occupation.

Southwest view of the central part of Canandaigua.

"Southwest view of the central part of Canandaigua," from John W. Barber, *Historical Collections of the State of New York* (New York: Clark, Austin & Co., 1851), p. 257.

Northeastern view of Geneva.

"Northeast view of Geneva," from *Historical Collections of the State of New York* by John W. Barber (1851), p. 260.

MILITARY RECORDS

Revolutionary War pension records and some early militia records are available. Draft lists are available for 1862, 1864, and 1917. A variety of Revolutionary and Civil War records are listed on the Center's website.

POOR HOUSE INDENTURES

Lists of children indentured to Ontario County families in the nineteenth and early twentieth century are available. The index, which is online (*http://raims.com/indenture.html*), includes child's name, guardian's name, year, and town.

VITAL RECORDS

Compared with New England and other well-documented regions, New York has very few vital records. The state did not require them until 1880. The vital records that do exist are usually held by the individual municipality rather than the county. The center does have some marriage records from 1908 to 1935, which are listed on the website (*http://raims.com/marriage.html*). You will not find alternative vital records sources such as newspapers or diaries here; you will need to consult historical societies for such documents.

HOW TO ACCESS THE RECORDS

Ontario County Records and Archives Center
3051 County Complex Drive
Canandaigua, New York, 14424
Tel: (585) 396-4376
Fax: (585) 396-4390
http://raims.com

The center is usually open for research from 9:00 a.m. to 4:30 p.m. weekdays, but call ahead to be sure regular hours are in effect. This is a "pencils and gloves" facility. Stacks are not open. You may bring a laptop computer, and even a flatbed scanner.

Research service is available for $40/hour (half-hour minimum). Direct inquiries to the Assistant Records Management Officer. Copying service is available. For further information, call or see the website at *http://raims.com/fees.html,* where you can download a request form. The only negative note: There are no public restrooms or public telephone in the building. The closest facilities are in a nearby building appropriately housing the Department of Human Services.

CHAPTER 9

Records of the Holland Land Company

In a separate chapter I discuss the role of the Holland Land Company in the settlement of western New York State (see Chapter 21, The Holland Purchase). This consortium of Dutch bankers in Amsterdam had purchased 3.3 million acres west of the Genesee River in 1792. When the company ceased operations in America in 1859, its records were transferred to the offices of Van Eeghen, one of the original members of the company. Each volume or folder was given an inventory item number. In 1964 the records were transferred to the Municipal Archives in Amsterdam. The entire collection was microfilmed in 1984.[1] This collection constitutes a local history of the area written by the participants — settlers, local land agents, bankers, and lawyers. In this chapter we explore information contained in this archive, access to the microfilms, and how to use the records.

The Holland Land Company was involved in many enterprises in America. Most of the 202 microfilm reels are filled with details of the stuff of everyday lives, but as they are not indexed, they are of little use to genealogists. The bulk of the records are made up of correspondence between the general agent in Philadelphia and the directors in Amsterdam, annual reports from local agents to the general agent, surveyors' reports, legal papers, maps, etc. Records may be written in Dutch, French, or English.

An earlier version of this chapter was posted at *www.NewEnglandAncestors.org* March 28, 2003.

[1] For more information on the microfilming project see Franciska Safran's "The Preservation of the Holland Land Company Records," *New York History,* LXIX (1988): 163.

When local agents sold land, the location of the land was specified relative to the grid of townships and ranges laid down by the original Ellicott survey described in Chapter 21. A range is a strip of land six miles wide running north-south. Ranges are numbered from one at the eastern border and run to the western border, reaching as high as fifteen in the southern part of the state. Ranges are subdivided into six-mile squares termed townships. Townships are numbered one at the Pennsylvania border and go north, reaching as high as sixteen along Lake Ontario. Each square is identified by a township and range number.[2] In reality, many of the townships were not six miles square. Surveyors had to work around the several Indian reservations not in the Holland Land Purchase as well as waterways and other natural features.

The microfilmed collection of the company's records is available at the Reed Library at SUNY Fredonia (*www.fredonia.edu/library/hlcguide.asp*), the New York State Library in Albany, and at the Family History Library in Salt Lake City. The microfilm reels are available through interlibrary loan and local Family History Centers. The Holland Land Company resource page (*www.hlc.wny.org/*) gives further details and a bibliography.

Although there is no overall index to the collection, bound volumes often have some summary of the contents either at the beginning or the end. The most useful items for a family historian are the land tables. The land tables take up only three full reels and two partial reels. They allow a researcher to connect a name with a location and a date. The general agent of the company compiled this information from annual reports of local agents. Each agent was required to send a list of all land transactions to the general agent. Each entry names the person, the location, the date, and the details of the transaction. Karen Livsey extracted these microfilmed records for her two-volume work titled *Western New York Land Transactions*.[3]

---

[2] Thus township 1 range 1 is in the southeast corner, currently in Allegany County. Township 1, range 15 is the southwest corner, bordering on Lake Erie and Pennsylvania. Township 16, range 1 is the northeast corner of the Holland Purchase.

[3] Karen E. Livsey, *Western New York Land Transactions*, Vol. I, 1804–1824, Vol. II, 1825–1835 (Baltimore: Genealogical Publishing Co., 1991, 1996).

The following example shows how to use this finding aid. In outline, one looks for a name in the index of the book, locates the appropriate extracts in the body of the book, uses the first table appended to this article to determine which microfilm reel contains the transaction information, and uses the second appended table to "translate" the township/range designation to a present-day county/town location.

Nehemiah Sayer is the first name in Volume I, so I chose that for our example. In the index to Volume I the name occurs five times, each time at the same location. See Table 1 for the corresponding extracts.

Table 1

NAME	DATE	LOT	S T R	D	REF-PAGE
Nehemiah Sayer	21 Sep 04	2	060501	s	484-0002
Nehemiah Sayer	21 Jun 03	2	060501	o	484-0016
Nehemiah Sayer	26 Jun 06	2	060501	s	484-00#8
Nehemiah Sayer	1 Feb 13	2	060501	s	490-0033
Nehemiah Sayer	4 May 13	2	060501	s	491-0032

Column "STR" lists section, township, and range, which specifies the location. Column "D" indicates the type of transaction. In this case, "o" means original contract issued, and "s" indicates subsequent transactions. The column "Ref-page" lists the inventory item number of the land table folder or volume and the page number within the volume. From this table of extracted entries we already know that Nehemiah Sayer originally contracted for lot 2 in section 6 of township 5, range 1 on June 21, 1803. The details of this transaction are to be found on page 16 of item #484. We do not know from this entry when he actually occupied the site. However, he had additional dealings with the local agent concerning this lot on September 21, 1804, June 26, 1806, February 1, 1813, and May 4, 1813. It is likely that these transactions involved additional payments. Deeds to the land were not issued until final payment was made.

From Table 2 below we find that item #484 is on reel 109 (FHL film number 1,414,983) and items 490 and 491 are both on reel 110

(FHL film number 1,414,984). From Table 2 we find that township 5, range 1 is in the town of Caneadea in Allegany County. This gives a fairly precise location to begin searching tax lists, church records, census records, and other sources. The table also indicates that the first contract in T5R1 was written in 1803, making Nehemiah Sayer one of the earliest settlers in the region. Allegany County was created in 1806 from Genesee County. We would therefore look for the Nehemiah Sayer household in Genesee County in the 1800 federal census and in Allegany County in the 1810 census.

Table 2
RELATIONSHIP BETWEEN INVENTORY NUMBER
AND REEL NUMBER AND FHL FILM NUMBER

Reel Num.	Inventory Num.	Year	FHL film Num.	Reel Num.	Inventory Num.	Year	FHL film Num.
109	484	1804-06	1,414,983	111	499	1821	1,414,985
109	485	1807	1,414,983	111	500	1822	1,414,985
109	486	1808	1,414,983	111	501	1823	1,414,985
109	487	1809	1,414,983	111	502	1824	1,414,985
110	488	1810	1,414,984	111	503	1825	1,414,985
110	489	1811	1,414,984	111	504	1826	1,414,985
110	490	1812	1,414,984	111	505	1827	1,414,985
110	491	1813	1,414,984	111	506	1828	1,414,985
110	492	1814	1,414,984	112	507	1829	1,414,986
110	493	1815	1,414,984	112	508	1830	1,414,986
110	494	1816	1,414,984	112	509	1831	1,414,986
110	495	1817	1,414,984	112	510	1832	1,414,986
110	496	1818	1,414,984	112	511	1833	1,414,986
110	497	1819	1,414,984	113	512	1834	1,414,487
111	498	1820	1,414,985	113	513	1835	1,414,487

Table 3
RELATIONSHIP OF TOWNSHIPS OF THE
HOLLAND PURCHASE AND TOWNS AND COUNTIES

County (year formed)	Township	Range	Present Town	1st Contract
Allegany (1806)	1	1	Bolivar	1821
Allegany (1806)	1	2	Genesee	1806
Cattaraugus (1808)	1	3	Portville	1806
Cattaraugus (1808)	1	4	Olean	
Cattaraugus (1808)	1	5	Burton	1823
Cattaraugus (1808)	1	6	Carrollton	1806
Cattaraugus (1808)	1	7	Little Valley	
Cattaraugus (1808)	1	8	South Valley	
Cattaraugus (1808)	1	9	South Valley	1809
Chautauqua (1808)	1	10	Carroll	
Chautauqua (1808)	1	11	Ellicott, Carroll, Busti	1808
Chautauqua (1808)	1	12	Busti, Harmony	1810
Chautauqua (1808)	1	13	Harmony	1811
Chautauqua (1808)	1	14	Clymer	
Chautauqua (1808)	1	15	French Creek	1812
Allegany (1806)	2	1	Wirt	1810
Allegany (1806)	2	2	Clarkesville	1821
Cattaraugus (1808)	2	3	Portville, Hinsdale	1813
Cattaraugus (1808)	2	4	Hinsdale, Olean	1806
Cattaraugus (1808)	2	5	Burton	1820
Cattaraugus (1808)	2	6	Carrollton, Great Valley	
Cattaraugus (1808)	2	7	Little Valley	
Cattaraugus (1808)	2	8	Cold Spring	1819
Cattaraugus (1808)	2	9	Randolph	1821
Chautauqua (1808)	2	10	Poland	1807
Chautauqua (1808)	2	11	Ellicott	1807
Chautauqua (1808)	2	12	Busti, Harmony, Ellery	1804
Chautauqua (1808)	2	13	Harmony	1807
Chautauqua (1808)	2	14	Sherman	
Chautauqua (1808)	2	15	Mina	1811

continued on next page

Table 3 *(cont.)*

County (year formed)	Township	Range	Present Town	1st Contract
Allegany (1806)	3	1	Friendship	1806
Allegany (1806)	3	2	Cuba	1806
Cattaraugus (1808)	3	3	Hinsdale, Rice	1807
Cattaraugus (1808)	3	4	Hinsdale, Rice	1813
Cattaraugus (1808)	3	5	Humphrey	1805
Cattaraugus (1808)	3	6	Great Valley	1811
Cattaraugus (1808)	3	7	Little Valley	1805
Cattaraugus (1808)	3	8	Napoli	1819
Cattaraugus (1808)	3	9	Connewango	1815
Chautauqua (1808)	3	10	Ellington	1815
Chautauqua (1808)	3	11	Gerry	1809
Chautauqua (1808)	3	12	Stockton, Ellery	1805
Chautauqua (1808)	3	13	Stockton, Ellery, Chautauqua	1805
Chautauqua (1808)	3	14	Chautauqua, Westfield	1810
Chautauqua (1808)	3	15	Ripley	1804
Allegany (1806)	4	1	Belfast	1804
Allegany (1806)	4	2	Belfast, New Hudson	1806
Cattaraugus (1808)	4	3	Lyndon	1806
Cattaraugus (1808)	4	4	Lyndon, Franklinville	1805
Cattaraugus (1808)	4	5	Franklinville	1805
Cattaraugus (1808)	4	6	Ellicottville	1813
Cattaraugus (1808)	4	7	Mansfield	1816
Cattaraugus (1808)	4	8	New Albion	1816
Cattaraugus (1808)	4	9	Leon	1818
Chautauqua (1808)	4	10	Cherry Creek	1815
Chautauqua (1808)	4	11	Charlotte	1809
Chautauqua (1808)	4	12	Stockton	1809
Chautauqua (1808)	4	13	Stockton, Portland, Chautauqua	1809
Chautauqua (1808)	4	14	Chautauqua, Westfield	1810
Allegany (1806)	5	1	Caneadea	1803
Allegany (1806)	5	2	Rushford	1808

County (year formed)	Township	Range	Present Town	1st Contract
Cattaraugus (1808)	5	3	Farmersville	1811
Cattaraugus (1808)	5	4	Farmersville	1805
Cattaraugus (1808)	5	5	Machias	1806
Cattaraugus (1808)	5	6	Ellicottville, Ashford	1816
Cattaraugus (1808)	5	7	Otto	
Cattaraugus (1808)	5	8	Otto, Persia	1820
Cattaraugus (1808)	5	9	Dayton	1810
Chautauqua (1808)	5	10	Villenova	1809
Chautauqua (1808)	5	11	Arkwright	1805
Chautauqua (1808)	5	12	Pomfret	1805
Chautauqua (1808)	5	13	Portland	1804
Allegany (1806)	6	1	Hume	1806
Allegany (1806)	6	2	Centreville	1808
Cattaraugus (1808)	6	3	Freedom	1810
Cattaraugus (1808)	6	4	Machias, Freedom	1809
Cattaraugus (1808)	6	5	Machias, Yorkshire	1810
Erie (1821)	6	5	Sardinia	1810
Cattaraugus (1808)	6	6	Ashford	1807
Erie (1821)	6	6	Sardinia, Concord	1807
Cattaraugus (1808)	6	7	Otto, Ashford	1809
Erie (1821)	6	7	Concord, Collins	1809
Cattaraugus (1808)	6	8	Otto, Persia	1816
Erie (1821)	6	8	Collins	1816
Cattaraugus (1808)	6	9	Perrysburg	1815
Chautauqua (1808)	6	10	Hanover	1805
Chautauqua (1808)	6	11	Hanover, Sheridan	1804
Chautauqua (1808)	6	12	Pomfret	1804
Wyoming (1841)	7	1	Pike	1805
Wyoming (1841)	7	2	Eagle	1808

continued on next page

Table 3 *(cont.)*

County (year formed)	Township	Range	Present Town	1st Contract
Wyoming (1841)	7	3	China	1808
Wyoming (1841)	7	4	China	1809
Cattaraugus (1808)	7	5	Yorkshire	1809
Erie (1821)	7	5	Sardinia	1809
Erie (1821)	7	6	Sardinia, Concord	1808
Erie (1821)	7	7	Concord, Collins	1809
Erie (1821)	7	8	Collins	1809
Wyoming (1841)	8	1	Gainesville	1805
Wyoming (1841)	8	2	Wethersfield	1809
Wyoming (1841)	8	3	Java	1809
Wyoming (1841)	8	4	Java	1811
Erie (1821)	8	5	Holland	1807
Erie (1821)	8	6	Colden	1819
Erie (1821)	8	7	Eden	1803
Erie (1821)	8	8	Eden	1806
Erie (1821)	8	9	Brandt, Evans	1805
Wyoming (1841)	9	1	Warsaw	1803
Wyoming (1841)	9	2	Orangeville	1803
Wyoming (1841)	9	3	Sheldon	
Wyoming (1841)	9	4	Sheldon	
Erie (1821)	9	5	Wales	1804
Erie (1821)	9	6	Aurora	1804
Erie (1821)	9	7	Boston, Hamburg	1804
Erie (1821)	9	8	Evans, Hamburg	1804
Wyoming (1841)	10	1	Middlebury	1802
Wyoming (1841)	10	2	Attica	1802
Wyoming (1841)	10	3	Bennington	1803
Wyoming (1841)	10	4	Bennington	1804
Genesee (1802)	11	1	Bethany	1803
Genesee (1802)	11	2	Alexander	1802
Genesee (1802)	11	3	Darien	1805
Genesee (1802)	11	4	Darien	1807

County (year formed)	Township	Range	Present Town	1st Contract
Erie (1821)	11	5	Alden	1808
Erie (1821)	11	6	Lancaster	1803
Erie (1821)	11	7	Black Rock, Amherst, Cheektowaga	1804
Erie (1821)	11	8	Buffalo City, Black Rock	1803
Genesee (1802)	12	1	Stafford, Batavia	1801
Genesee (1802)	12	2	Batavia	1801
Genesee (1802)	12	3	Pembroke	1803
Genesee (1802)	12	4	Pembroke	1804
Erie (1821)	12	5	Newstead	1801
Niagara (1808)	12	5	Royalton	1801
Erie (1821)	12	6	Clarence	1801
Erie (1821)	12	7	Tonawanda, Amherst	1804
Erie (1821)	12	8	Tonawanda	1805
Genesee (1802)	13	1	Elba	1803
Genesee (1802)	13	2	Elba, Oakfield	1801
Genesee (1802)	13	3	Alabama	1810
Genesee (1802)	13	4	Alabama	1804
Erie (1821)	13	5	Newstead	1805
Erie (1821)	13	6	Clarence	1810
Niagara (1808)	13	6	Royalton, Lockport	1810
Erie (1821)	13	7	Amherst	1806
Niagara (1808)	13	7	Pendleton	1806
Niagara (1808)	13	8	Wheatfield	1805
Niagara (1808)	13	9	Niagara	1804
Orleans (1824)	14	1	Barre	1812
Orleans (1824)	14	2	Barre	1805
Orleans (1824)	14	3	Shelby	1810
Orleans (1824)	14	4	Shelby	1803

continued on next page

Table 3 *(cont.)*

County (year formed)	Township	Range	Present Town	1st Contract
Niagara (1808)	14	5	Royalton	
Niagara (1808)	14	6	Royalton, Lockport	1802
Niagara (1808)	14	7	Lockport, Cambria	1803
Niagara (1808)	14	8	Lewiston, Cambria	1803
Niagara (1808)	14	9	Lewiston	1803
Orleans (1824)	15	1	Barre, Gaines	1808
Orleans (1824)	15	2	Barre, Ridgeway, Gaines	1809
Orleans (1824)	15	3	Ridgeway	1810
Orleans (1824)	15	4	Ridgeway	1810
Niagara (1808)	15	5	Hartland	1803
Niagara (1808)	15	6	Hartland, Newfane	1804
Niagara (1808)	15	7	Wilson, Newfane	1805
Niagara (1808)	15	8	Wilson, Porter	1810
Niagara (1808)	15	9	Porter	1803
Orleans (1824)	16	1	Carlton	1804
Orleans (1824)	16	2	Carlton	1803
Orleans (1824)	16	3	Yates	1810
Orleans (1824)	16	4	Yates	1815
Niagara (1808)	16	5	Somerset	1809
Niagara (1808)	16	6	Somerset, Newfane	

CHAPTER 10

New York State Cemeteries:
A Finding Aid

Compared with much of New England, finding vital records in New York State can be challenging. The state's vital records do not begin until 1881, but cemetery records can help to fill the gap. To aid researchers, the Association of Municipal Historians of New York State (AMHNYS) undertook a project in 1997 to survey all of the known cemeteries in the state. This inventory, compiled by municipal and county historians, was the first statewide community service project of AMHNYS. The result is a three-volume set titled *The Association of Municipal Historians of New York State Name/Location Survey Project 1995-1997* (Bowie, Md.: Heritage Books, 1999).

Historians were asked to fill out a survey form for each cemetery in their area. The survey asked for the name or names of the cemetery, the status (active, inactive, deserted, unknown), type (family, religious, incorporated, indigent, military, etc.), time frame (year of first and last known interments), location, contact person, and any notes. Family plots are noted as over or under ten, but it is not clear whether the "ten" refers to the number of surnames or the number of gravesites. Entries are listed alphabetically by county, by town within each county, and by cemetery name within each town. If you know your ancestor's location, this finding aid will tell you which cemeteries were active in that town or county at the time of death. Not all of the historians contacted returned the survey. Towns in upstate New York not included in this publication are listed in a table at the end of this article.

An earlier version of this chapter was posted at *NewEnglandAncestors.org* May 23, 2003.

The information content can vary widely from one entry to another. Less promising are the cemeteries named "abandoned" (10), "no name" (27), "deserted" (2), "unknown" (31), "unnamed" (34), or "name unknown" (4). For example, there is little to be learned from the two entries shown in Table 1.

Table 1

NAME	PLOWED UP	CASTLER FARM PLOT
Type	Family — under 10	Unknown
Stat[us]:	Unknown	Unknown
T[ime]F[rame]	Unknown	Unknown
Loc[ation]:	About 150 ft. west of 19 in field on what is now Dawsen Farm.	Unknown
Cont[act]:	Unknown.	Greene town historian or town clerk

One can only hope that at some earlier time the information was transcribed and may be found in some library or archive. The information returned for a Crossettanner Farm Cemetery, for example, lists the location as "DAR Records. 4 stones."

When browsing through the entries, it becomes apparent that there are many ways in which a cemetery can be destroyed. Here is a sampling:

- Farm barn burned 1910, stones were used in rebuilding foundation.
- Resident owns property for 30 years had no knowledge of cemetery.
- Existed under the junction canal, before construction of route 60.
- In/around 1822 bodies and markers were moved to Fulton street cemetery.
- Family members remember tombstones near fence, but they have long since been removed.
- Roads leading to it are over-grown.

- This cemetery has been plowed up, but was originally located on rte 26 just east of Taylor.
- No info on this cemetery has come up in research.
- Stones removed and relocated for railroad construction 1875–76.
- Historical marker of burials dedicated 9/20/82, stones laid flat and covered over in the driveway.
- Stones tumbled in and unreadable.
- In 1914 a road was built and the stone fence & monuments used in the road.
- No visible stones remaining. New construction in area has obliterated all traces.
- Nothing there today to show it was a cemetery.
- Destroyed during the building of new office buildings (1995).
- Only reached by overgrown abandoned roads, stones leaning against trees.

On a more positive note, we find evidence for a clear distinction between "inactive" and "deserted" as a status, as indicated by "Boy Scouts maintain the care of this burial grounds" and "Lions Club of Oxford maintains care of burial grounds."

Some of the entries provide specific genealogical information. Table 2 shows two of the best.

Table 2

NAME	BLESSING CEMETERY	KILLAWOB HILL ROAD BURIAL GROUND
Type:	Other	Other
Stat:	Deserted	Deserted
TF:	1852 1852	1878–unknown
Loc:	Salmon Creek Road, north of Red Bridge, at foot of East Hill, one grave, Homer Blessing.	441 Killawog Hill Road
Cont:	Lansing Town Historian	Lisle Town Historian
Note:	Died of small pox according to history. Death date Sept. 6, 1852.	Two stones Robert Pierce and Hannah, wife of, beside tree.

Many of the cemetery names are strong clues as to who might have been buried there. There are, of course, the family plots, for which you would simply look up your ancestor's surname in the index. (More about this peculiar index later.) Table 3 shows one instance, however, in which the cemetery name comes from the current location, but the responding historian has listed surnames in a note.

Table 3

NAME:	GREGOR FARM CEMETERY
Type:	Family — over 10
Stat:	Inactive
TF	1811 1887
Loc:	One mile south of Morris turnpike (route 13) on county rte 18 (River Road) located behind Everet Gregory residence.
Cont:	Pittsfield town Historian New Berlin.
Note:	Surnames: Matteson, McIntyre, Persons, Spafford.

There are also cemeteries named after religious groups, for example, Baptist Church Cemetery, Adath Israel Jewish Cemetery, Episcopal Church Cemetery, Asbury Methodist Church Cemetery, Catholic Cemetery, Congregational Church Cemetery, Dutch Reformed Cemetery, Evangelical Lutheran Cemetery, Presbyterian Church Cemetery, Friends (Quaker) Cemetery, German Evangelical Lutheran Cemetery, Reformed Church Cemetery, Universalist Church Cemetery. If you know the denomination your ancestors were affiliated with, these entries give you a starting point for cemeteries in your town or county associated with the proper church.

If your ancestors came into the area in the early stages of its settlement, you may look for them in "pioneer" cemeteries (22), "early" cemeteries (3), "old" cemeteries (200), "former" cemeteries (40), or "historic" cemeteries (3). Or look for the pioneers to bring a place name with them. One note states of the Ridgefield Cemetery, "these were settlers from a town in Conn. known as Ridgefield."

There are cemeteries attached to poor houses (one actually named "Potters Field") and to prisons. There is a Civil War cemetery, active from 1864 to 1865, with a section for Confederate prisoners of war. The Burden Mines cemetery "is for people who worked at the mines." A Black Cemetery is "a old Colored persons burial grounds."

There are some peculiar entries. It is stated twice in one entry that this is "not a Cemetery but a burying place." Two pet cemeteries have been included, one of which is described as "pet cemetery not known if a person is buried there." The other "Large Pet Cemetery" has had "8 human burials there" as of 1995. There is a cemetery currently on the grounds of a McGraw School, which was active from 1850 to 1854, that contains "about 6 graves of students from the college who died of smallpox." In some cases a site visit by a conscientious historian is hinted at. One location contains the parenthetical warning "poison ivy." Another entry ends with the words "about 200 ft. back in a bed of lilies."

Another peculiarity is the index. Apparently some of the returns were submitted in all capital letters. This was retained in the data entry. The index distinguishes these entries from the others. In the index all-cap entries are listed, in alphabetical order, before the mixed case entries. For example, entries for the letter K are as follows:

KALES HILL PIKE-HAWKINS
KEENEY SETTLEMENT CEMETERY
KEERYVILLE CEMETERY

. . .

KNOLL CEMETERY
KNOX CEMETERY
KNOX FAMILY CEMETERY
Kaley Family Plot
Kallmann Ground
Kanona Cemetery

. . .

Kyle Cemetery
Kysorville

The index is case sensitive. KNOX is not the same entry as Knox. BAPTIST is not the same as Baptist. You must look in both locations in the index.

The book's introduction provides the following information about this professional organization.

> The Association of Municipal Historians of New York State was founded in 1972 and is the professional organization for the New York State Municipal (City, Town and Village) Historians. The purposes are 1) to encourage local units of government to appoint official historians in compliance with Section 148 of New York State Educational Law; 2) to promote the training and establishment of professional standards for individuals appointed as local historians; and 3) to encourage local units of government to support the collection, preservation, interpretation and dissemination of the history of their communities and to support the work of appointed historians. Membership is open to county historians and through Associate level memberships to all interested in New York State local history. AMHNYS offers conferences including training sessions and workshops with the County Historians Association of New York State (CHANYS) and publishes the Historians Exchange, a bi-annual newsletter. AMHNYS has eight chapters or regions across the state; is a non-profit organization that works closely with the New York State Historian's Office. For further information, contact your local historian.

Historians of the following towns in upstate New York did not respond to the request to survey their cemeteries. If you are searching for burials in these towns, this finding aid will be of no use to you.

Table 4

ALBANY COUNTY

Berne	Bethlehem	Coeymans	Green Island
Guilderland	Knox	New Scotland	Rensselaerville
Westerlo			

ALLEGANY COUNTY

Belfast	Birdsall	Burns	Caneadea
Centerville	Clarksville	Friendship	Wellsville
West Almond	Wirt		

BROOME COUNTY

Fenton

CATTARAUGUS COUNTY

Allegany	Ashford	Carrollton	Coldspring
Conewango	Dayton	East Otto	Ellicottville
Farmersville	Franklinville	Freedom	Great Valley
Humphrey	Ischua	Leon	Little Valley
Machias	Mansfield	Napoli	New Albion
Otto	Perrysburg	Persia	Portville
Randolph	Red House	Salamanca (town)	Salamanca (city)
South Valley			

CHAUTAUQUA COUNTY

Arkwright	Busti	Carroll	Charlotte
Chautauqua	Cherry Creek	Clymer	Dunkirk (town)
Dunkirk (city)	Ellery	Ellicott	Ellington
French Creek	Hanover	Harmony	Jamestown
Kiantone	Mina	North Harmony	Poland
Pomfret	Portland	Ripley	Sheridan
Sherman	Stockton	Villenova	Westfield

CHENANGO COUNTY

New Berlin	North Norwich	Norwich (town)	Norwich (city)
Pharsalia	Pitcher	Plymouth	Preston
Smyrna			

continued on next page

Table 4 *(cont.)*

COLUMBIA COUNTY

Austerlitz	Canaan	Claverack	Gallatin
Hillsdale	New Lebanon	Stockport	Stuyvesant
Taghkanic			

ERIE COUNTY

Amherst	Boston	Brant	Buffalo
Clarence	Colden	Eden	Elma
Evans	Grand Island	Hamburg	Holland
Lackawanna	Lancaster	Marilla	North Collins
Orchard Park	Tonawanda (town)	Tonawanda (city)	Wales

GREENE COUNTY

Catskill	Williams	Durham	Halcott
Hunter	Jewett	Lexington	

HAMILTON COUNTY

Benson	Inlet

JEFFERSON COUNTY

Cape Vincent	Champion	Clayton	Ellisburg
Henderson	Hounsfield	LeRay	Lorraine
Pamelia	Philadelphia	Rodman	Worth

LEWIS COUNTY

Lowville	Lyonsdale	Martinsburg

LIVINGSTON COUNTY

Mount Morris

MADISON COUNTY

DeRuyter	Georgetown

MONROE COUNTY

East Rochester

ONEIDA COUNTY

Annsville	Augusta	Ava	Boonville
Bridgewater	Camden	Deerfield	Florence
Floyd	Forestport	Kirkland	Lee
Marcy	New Hartford	Rome	Sangerfield
Sherrill	Trenton	Utica	Vernon
Vienna	Western	Whitestown	

OSWEGO COUNTY

Minetto	Volney

OTSEGO COUNTY

Burlington	Plainfield

PUTNAM COUNTY

Putnam Valley	Southeast

ST. LAWRENCE COUNTY

De Peyster

SULLIVAN COUNTY

Bethel	Callicoon	Cochecton	Delaware
Fallsburg	Forestburgh	Lumberland	Mamakating
Neversink	Rockland	Thompson	

TOMPKINS COUNTY

Ulysses

CHAPTER 11

State Census Records
for New York

T he census is one of the first tools a beginning genealogist is introduced to and remains a workhorse for experienced researchers. The experienced genealogist searches all relevant census records, including state as well as federal censuses, recognizing that an aging parent or a child who died young may be recorded on only one census. Families moving into upper New York State in the early nineteenth century were often transient, passing through the state rapidly on a genealogical time scale. In this situation it is doubly important to check all possible censuses. There is a gap in the federal census record due to the loss of the 1890 census. The 1892 New York State census can help to fill that gap for your New York ancestors. In this chapter I discuss what state census records were created, how to get to these records, and what information can be gained from each state census.

WHAT RECORDS WERE CREATED

Census enumerations for New York State occurred every ten years from 1825 to 1875 and from 1905 to 1925. There is more information in the nineteenth-century records than one usually expects from a census. In addition to an enumeration of the population, the state was interested in information about farms and businesses, about churches and newspapers, and about marriages and deaths. If your ancestor lived in the state during this time and owned land, even a few acres, or a small business such as a gristmill or a cabinetmaking

---

An earlier version of this chapter was posted at *www.NewEnglandAncestors.org* January 3, 2003.

shop, then you may find how many acres he planted in buckwheat and how many sheep he owned, or how many people he employed and how much he paid them.

Only one census was taken between 1875 and 1905 — that of 1892. This census, dated February 16, 1892, was quite brief. It asked only name, sex, age, color, in what country born, citizen or alien, and occupation. This census gains in importance because of the loss in 1921 of the 1890 federal census.

The nineteenth century was a time of flux for the state. As settlers flooded in, new counties were established to provide local government. Thus your ancestor's location may change from one census to the next, not because he moved, but because a new county was formed. The following table lists upstate counties formed after the Revolutionary War. It lists the year the county was formed, the parent county/counties, and the first census in which the county is listed as a separate entity. The last column lists that part of the state census records which are incomplete or missing in the New York State Library in Albany.

Table 1
UPSTATE N.Y. COUNTIES
FORMED AFTER THE REVOLUTIONARY WAR

County	Year Formed	Parent County/Counties	First Census	NY State Library missing/incomplete
Allegany	1806	Genesee	1810	1825–45
Broome	1806	Tioga	1810	1825, 1845
Cattaraugus	1808	Genesee	1810	
Cayuga	1799	Onondaga	1800	1825–45, 1905
Chautauqua	1808	Genesee	1810	
Chemung	1798	Tioga	1800	1825–45, 1875
Chenango	1798	Herkimer, Tioga	1800	1825–45, 1892
Clinton	1788	Washington	1790	1825–75
Cortland	1808	Onondoga	1810	1845
Delaware	1797	Ulster, Otsego	1800	1825–45
Erie	1821	Niagara	1825	1825–45, 1875–92

88

County	Year Formed	Parent County/Counties	First Census	NY State Library missing/incomplete
Essex	1799	Clinton	1800	1825–45
Franklin	1808	Clinton	1810	1825–65, 1892
Fulton	1838	Montgomery	1840	1825–35, 1892
Genesee	1802	Ontario	1810	1825–65
Hamilton	1816	Montgomery	1820	1825–75
Herkimer	1791	Montgomery	1800	1825
Jefferson	1805	Oneida	1810	1825–65, 1892
Lewis	1805	Oneida	1810	1845
Livingston	1821	Genesee, Ontario	1825	1825–45, 1892–1905
Madison	1806	Chenango	1810	1825–45
Monroe	1821	Genesee, Ontario	1825	1825–45
Niagara	1808	Genesee	1810	1825–45, 1892
Oneida	1798	Herkimer	1800	1825–1905
Onondaga	1794	Herkimer	1800	1825–45
Ontario	1789	Montgomery	1790	1825–45, 1905
Orleans	1824	Genesee	1825	1825–45
Oswego	1816	Oneida, Onondaga	1820	1825–45, 1905
Otsego	1791	Montgomery	1800	1835–45
Saratoga	1791	Albany	1800	1825–45
Schenectady	1809	Albany	1810	1825
Schoharie	1795	Albany, Otsego	1800	1845
Schuyler	1854	Tompkins, Steuben, Chemung	1855	1825–45, 1892–1905
Seneca	1804	Cayuga	1810	1825–1905
St. Lawrence	1802	Clinton, Herkimer, Montgomery	1810	1845, 1865–92
Steuben	1796	Ontario	1800	none
Tioga	1791	Montgomery	1800	1845
Tompkins	1817	Cayuga, Seneca	1820	1845–55
Warren	1813	Washington	1820	1825–55
Wayne	1823	Ontario, Seneca	1825	1825–75
Wyoming	1841	Genesee	1845	1825–65, 1892–1905
Yates	1823	Ontario, Steuben	1825	1905

HOW TO ACCESS THE RECORDS

Original state census records were stored in each county clerk's office. Copies of these records were sent to Albany and are today held by the state library there. Public libraries with a local history or genealogy section frequently have microfilm copies for their county, and occasionally for neighboring counties. You should inquire about interlibrary loan of these microfilms. All of these collections are probably incomplete; earliest records will be hardest to find.

I searched the catalog of the Family History Library for 1825 New York census records and found only Washington and Cattaraugus counties. For the 1835 census only Cattaraugus County is listed. For a fairly current listing of what state (and federal) censuses for New York are available on microfilm, online, and in othe formats, see William Dollarhide, *New York State Censuses and Substitutes* (Bountiful, Utah: Heritage Creations, 2005). County web pages sometimes have census information. Schuyler County, for example, was formed in 1854. Nevertheless, the website offers 1825 census data for those parts of the county, which, at the time, were in neighboring counties. Ontario, one of the oldest upstate counties, offers indices for 1850–75 records online at the web page for the county archive. The archive holds records county records from 1845 to 1925. County historical societies may be another source of online information.

The remainder of this chapter details the wealth of information to be found in these records. After listing the questions asked on the various censuses, I present some examples to show how the state census can enhance the family information obtained from the federal census records. The most complete record in the state library is for Steuben County, so I chose that county for my examples. The original census records are held in the county clerk's office in Bath. The collection is not complete. Only a few towns are present for 1825, and 1845 is missing entirely. For my examples I have chosen the family of David McMaster, a farmer from Bath. In addition to David, (born 1796), the household contained his wife, Mary, (born 1815), her mother, Abby Humphries, (born 1782), and at least nine children born between 1829 and 1859.[1]

---

[1] This information was obtained from 1850, 1855, and 1870 census records.

QUESTIONS FOR 1825 AND 1835 STATE CENSUS

Information from the 1825 census is contained in thirty-six columns. Columns 1 to 13 do the basic job of a census — they count people. Columns 14 to 16 ask about marriage, birth, and death. Columns 17 to 21 are concerned with agriculture, and columns 22 to 36 with "domestic manufacturies." The 1835 census was slightly shorter.

Table 2
QUESTIONS FOR THE
1825 AND 1835 NEW YORK STATE CENSUS

1   The name of the head of each family

2   The number of male persons in the family (the name of whose head is in the first column), including its head, if male

3   The number of female persons in the same family, including its head, if female

4   The number of male persons in the same family subject to militia duty [i.e., age 18-45]

5   The whole number of male persons in the same family entitled by the constitution of this state to vote for all offices elective by the people

6   The number of male persons in the same family who are aliens not naturalized

7   The number of persons in the same family who are paupers

8   The number of persons in the same family who are persons of color not taxed

9   The number of persons of color in the same family who are taxed

10 The whole number of persons of color in the same family who are colored, taxed, and entitled by the constitution of this state to vote for all officers elective by the people (and not to be included in the ninth column)

11 The number of married female persons in the same family under the age of 45 years

12 The number of unmarried female persons in the same family between the ages of 16 and 45 years

13 The number of female persons in the same family, unmarried, under the age of 16 years

continued on next page

Table 2 *(cont.)*

14   The number of marriages occurring in the same family, where the female married resided, during the year preceding

15   Whole number of births in the same family during the year preceding

16   Whole number of deaths in the same family during the year preceding

17   The number of acres of improved land occupied by the same family

18   The number of neat cattle owned by the same family

19   The number of horses owned by the same family

20   The number of sheep owned by the same family

21   The number of hogs owned by the same family

22   The number of yards of fulled cloth manufactured in the domestic way in the same family, during the preceding year

23   The number of yards of flannel and other woolen cloths not fulled, manufactured in the domestic way in the same family, during the year preceding

24   The number of yards of linen, cotton, or other thin cloths, manufactured in the domestic way in the same family, during the year preceding

25*   Deaf and dumb, blind, idiots and lunatics [separated by age and "circumstances"]

25**   Whole number of Grist Mills owned by same family

26**   Whole number of Saw Mills owned by same family

27**   Whole number of Oil Mills owned by same family

28**   Whole number of Fulling Mills owned by same family

29**   Whole number of Carding machines owned by same family

30**   Whole number of Cotton Factories owned by same family

31**   Whole number of Woolen Factories owned by same family

32**   Whole number of Cotton and Woolen Factories owned by same family

33**   Whole number of Iron works owned by same family

34**   Whole number of Trip Hammers owned by same family

35**   Whole number of Distilleries owned by same family

36**   Whole number of Asheries owned by same family.

* Final question on 1835 census.

** These questions dropped on 1835 census.

1855 CENSUS QUESTIONS

The 1855 census is enormous. Like the 1850 federal census before it, this is the first state census to list by name every member of the household. Unlike the federal census, it also specifies the relationship of each person to the head of household. This census also asks how many years resident in this city or town, which can help you track your family's movements within the state.

The census information requires more than 150 columns. The population schedule occupies columns 1–21. The agriculture section of the second schedule is the largest section of the census, columns 22–101. This section is completed with questions about Domestic Manufactures, columns 102–108. Industry other than agriculture is in schedule III, columns 109–125. Schedule IV contains listings of marriages and deaths, columns 126–139. Schedule V lists churches and schools. Schedule VI lists newspapers and other periodicals. The questions in columns 1–139 are listed below by schedule.

Table 3
QUESTIONS FOR THE 1855 NEW YORK STATE CENSUS

A. POPULATION SCHEDULE (COLUMNS 1–21)

1   Dwellings numbered in the order of visitation

2   Of what material built

3   Value

4   Families numbered in the order of their visitation

5   Name of every person whose usual place of abode on the first day of June was in this family

6   Age

7   Sex

8   Color {whether black or mulatto}

9   Relation to the head of the family

10   In what county of this State or in what other State or Foreign Country born

11   Married

12   Widowed

continued on next page

Table 3 *(cont.)*

A. POPULATION SCHEDULE *(cont.)*

13   Years resident in this city or town

14   Profession, trade, or occupation

15   Native voters

16   Naturalized voters

17   Aliens

18   Persons of color not taxed

19   Persons over 21 years who cannot read and write

20   Owners of land

21   Deaf, Dumb, Blind, Insane, or Idiotic

B. AGRICULTURE (COLUMNS 22–101) AND DOMESTIC MANUFACTURES (COLUMNS 102–108)

	22	Name of the owner, agent, or manager of farm				
Acres	23	Improved	24	Unimproved		
Cash value	25	of Farm	26	of Stock	27	of Tools and Implements
Acres	28	plowed the year previous	29	in fallow the year previous	30	in pasture the year previous
Meadow	31	Acres	32	Tons of Hay	33	Bushels of grass seed
Spring wheat	34	Acres	35	Bushels harvested		
Winter Wheat	36	Acres sown	37	Bushels harvested		
Oats	38	Acres sown	39	Bushels harvested		
Rye	40	Acres sown	41	Bushels harvested		
Barley	42	Acres sown	43	Bushels harvested		
Buckwheat	44	Acres sown	45	Bushels harvested		
Corn	46	Acres sown	47	Bushels harvested		
Potatoes	48	Acres sown	49	Bushels harvested		
Peas	50	Acres sown	51	Bushels harvested		
Beans	52	Acres sown	53	Bushels harvested		
Turnips	54	Acres sown	55	Bushels harvested		

Flax	56	Acres sown	57	Tons of Lint	58	Bushels of Seed
Hemp	59	Acres sown	60	Tons of Hemp		
Hops	61	Acres planted	62	Pounds harvested		
Tobacco	63	Acres planted	64	Pounds harvested		
Apple orchards	65	Bushels of Apples	66	Barrels of Cider		
Market Gardens	67	Acres cultivated	68	Value of Products sold		
	69	Pounds of maple sugar made				
	70	Gallons of Maple Molasses made				
	71	Gallons of wine made				
	72	Pounds of honey collected				
	73	Pounds of wax collected				
	74	Silk Pounds of cocoons				
Unenumerated articles of farm produce	75	Kinds	76	Quantity	77	Value
Neat Cattle	78	Under one year old	79	Over one year, exclusive of working oxen and cows	80	Working oxen
	81	Cows	82	Number of cattle killed for beef	83	Whole number of cows milked
Butter	84	Number of cows	85	Pounds of butter		
Cheese	86	Number of cows	87	Pounds of cheese		
Cows milked for market	88	Number of cows	89	Gallons of milk sold		
	90	Horses				
	91	Mules				
Swine	92	under 6 months	93	over 6 months		
Sheep	94	Number of sheep	95	Number of fleeces	96	Pounds of wool

continued on next page

Table 3 *(cont.)*

B. AGRICULTURE AND DOMESTIC MANUFACTURIES *(cont.)*

Poultry	97	Value of Poultry sold	98	Value of Eggs sold		
Special Manures Used	99	Kinds	100	Quantity	101	Value
Domestic Manufactures	102	Yards of Fulled Cloth made	103	Yards of Flannel made		
	104	Yards of Linen made	105	Yards of Cotton and Mixed Cloth		
Other articles of Domestic Manufactures	106	Kinds	107	Quantity	108	Value

C. INDUSTRY OTHER THAN AGRICULTURE (COLUMNS 109–125)

	109	Name of Person or Company owning the Shop, Factory, Mine, Quarry, or other object of industry				
	110	Name of Business or Manufacture				
Capital Invested	111	in Real Estate	112	in Tools and Machinery		
Raw Materials	113	Quantity	114	Kind	115	Value
Annual Product	116	Quantity	117	Kind	118	Value
	119	Kind of Motive Power				
Persons Employed	Adults	120	Men	121	Women	
	Children under 18 years	122	Boys	123	Girls	
Wages exclusive of board	Average monthly wages	124	of men	125	of women	

D. MARRIAGES AND DEATHS (COLUMNS 126–139)

Marriages	Ages	126	of husband	127	of wife
Previous civil condition		128	of husband	129	of wife
		130	in what month married	131	Place of marriage, where different from present residence
Deaths		132	Age	133	Sex
		134	Color	135	Civil condition
		136	Time of death	137	Native Country
		138	Trade or occupation	139	Disease or Cause of Death

1865 AND 1875

The 1865 census contains some military service information. An added schedule lists the page and line of a person in the census and adds information such as their rank and the unit they are serving with. In the 1875 census the schedules appear in a different order, marriages and deaths coming before the agriculture and manufacturing sections. There is more detail in several entries.

The section on sheep, columns 141–148, is shown below as an example.

Table 4

141	Shorn in 1874
142	Shorn in 1875
143	Lambs raised in 1874
144	Lambs raised in 1875
145	Pounds of wool shorn in 1874
146	Pounds of wool shorn in 1875
147	Sheep slaughtered in 1874
148	Sheep killed by dogs in 1874

By the 1905 census, the number of questions had been drastically reduced to thirteen. Those same thirteen questions were used in the 1915 and 1925 censuses also, as shown in Table 5.

Table 5
QUESTIONS FOR 1905, 1915, AND 1925 CENSUS

Permanent Residence	1 Street			house number		
Name	2 Name of each person whose usual place of abode on June 1 was in this family					
Relation	3 relationship of each person to the head of the family					
Color, Sex and Age	4 color or race		5 sex		6 age at last birthday	
Nativity	7 If of foreign birth write name of the country					
Citizenship	8 Number of years in the United States		9 Citizen or alien		10 If naturalized when and where	
Occupation	11 Trade or profession		12 class [wages or not]			
Inmates of Institutions, Infants under one year of age	13 residence when admitted					

EXAMPLE: DAVID MCMASTER, FARMER

In the 1850 federal census we find David McMaster living in Bath with his (presumed) wife Mary, six (presumed) children, an older woman named Abby Humphries, and two other people who may be servants. The gap in ages of children, David M., age 20, and Adaline, age 6, suggests the possibility of several married daughters or children who died young. The 1855 state census identifies Mary as his wife, and Abby Humphries as Mary's mother, born in Connecticut. It also gives the county of birth for those born in New York State, and states how long they have lived in Bath. One son, Greg H. McMaster, is no longer in the household.[2] A daughter, Adaline

---

[2] He is not listed on his own in 1855, but there is a G. H. McMaster listed for Bath in the 1860 federal census.

McMaster, is no longer listed in the household. She would have been 11 years old, and so probably died rather than married. A son, James, has been added. Elizabeth Cummins, probably supplying domestic help in 1850 has gone, her place taken by Mary Heron.

Table 6

	Entry in 1850 Federal Census dwelling #300, family #314, Bath, Steuben Co.	Entry in 1855 NY State Census dwelling #122, family #133 2nd dist. Bath, Steuben Co.
Dwelling		frame house, $2000
David McMaster	46, M, County Judge, $5000, b. NY	51 M, b. Otsego, native, mar., 28 yrs in Bath, farmer, native voter, owner of land
Mary McMaster	35, F, b. NY	41, wife, b. Chemung, married, 34 yrs. in Bath
Greg H. McMaster	21, M, Lawyer, b. NY	[not listed in household]
David M. McMaster	20, M, Engineer, b. NY	24 M, son, b. Steuben, 24 yrs. in Bath, engineer, native voter
Adaline McMaster	6, F, b. NY, attended school	[not listed in household]
Mary McMaster	3, F, b. NY	9 F, daughter, Steuben, 9 yrs. in Bath
Clara McMaster	2, F, b. NY	7 F, daughter, Steuben, 7 yrs. in Bath
Edward McMaster (1850)	6/12, b. NY	5 M, son, b. Steuben, 5 yrs. in Bath
George E. McMaster (1855)		
James S. McMaster		3 M, son, b. Steuben, 3 yrs. in Bath
Abby Humphreys	68, F, b. Conn.	71, F, wife mother, b. Conn., wid., 30 yrs. in Bath, owner of land
Elizabeth Cummins	16, F, b. NY, attended school	[not listed in household]
Leander Thomas	15, M, black, b. NY, attended school.	19 M, black, servant, b. Steuben, 19 yrs. in Bath, colored not taxed
Mary A. Heron		17, F, servant, b. Steuben, 17 yrs in Bath

In addition to the population schedule, David McMaster is listed in the agriculture schedule since he owns land. This schedule gives the following description of his farm with milk cows, pigs, apple orchard, and bee hives. David McMaster, 92 acres improved, 2 acres unimproved, cash value of farm $5400, of stock $410, of tools and implements $130, 34 acres plowed previous year, none fallow, 24 acres in pasture, 14 acres of meadow, 15 tons of hay, no grass seed, no spring wheat, 20 acres sown to winter wheat yielding 236 bushels, 5 acres sown to oats yielding 60 bushels, no rye, 12 acres sown to barley yielding 300 bushels, 6 acres sown to buckwheat yielding 50 bushels, 10 acres sown to corn yielding 15 bushels, 1 acre sown to potatoes yielding 50 bushels, no peas, beans, turnips, flax, hemp, hops, or tobacco, 40 bushels of apples, no maple sugar, molasses, or wine, 100 pounds of honey, no wax or silk, 4 cattle over one year, no working oxen, 8 cows, 1 killed for beef, 8 cows milked yielding 1200 pounds of butter, 2 horses, no mules, 5 swine over 6 months, 15 sheep, 18 fleeces, 54 pounds of wool, no poultry sold, $60 value of eggs sold. I'm not sure how to get 18 fleeces off of 15 sheep; perhaps three of 18 original sheep were later slaughtered.

Although David's mother-in-law, Abby Humphries, is listed as an owner of land, I found no listing for her in agricultural schedules for any of the four districts of Bath. Perhaps she owned the farm jointly with her son-in-law. Or perhaps her land was managed by someone else and was listed under that name. The answer may lie in land records.

The first census in which the David McMaster household appears is the 1830 federal census.[3] From information in the 1850 and 1855 censuses about how long people were resident in Bath, we expect this 1830 household to contain David McMaster, 26, his wife Mary McMaster, 16, her mother Abby Humphries, 48, and their eldest son Greg McMaster, 1. What we find is 1M<5, 1M 30–40, 1F 20–30, 1F 40–50. The agreement is moderately successful.

The first state census listing the David McMaster household is 1835. This census describes the household as containing 3 males total, 3

---

[3] Bath, Steuben Co., p. 294.

females total, 1 male 18–45, 1 male voter, 1 married female under 45, no females 16–45, 1 female unmarried under 16, no marriages, 2 births one male and one female, 2 deaths one male and one female, 50 acres of improved land, 6 neat cattle, no horses, no sheep, 11 hogs.

We can account for the three males as the head of household and his two young sons. The three females we assign to Mary, her mother, and possibly a daughter, unmarried, under 16. The two births and deaths listed occurred during 1835 and may indicate babies, perhaps twins, who died young. We can also see that the farm is smaller — 50 acres of improved land instead of the 92 in 1855.

Even the somewhat skimpy information of the 1892 census can be useful. In this census I find three of the McMaster daughters, apparently unmarried, listed sequentially in Bath.[4]

Table 7

NAME	SEX	AGE	WHAT COUNTRY BORN	CITIZEN OR ALIEN	OCCUPATION
Mary McMaster	F	46	US	C	teacher
Clara McMaster	F	43	US	C	
Juliet McMaster	F	33	US	C	Stenographer

POSTSCRIPT

There is also more general information included in some state censuses that may not be found elsewhere.

In 1855 farm hands hired by the season or year earned $20 per month. Those hired for haying and harvest earned $1.50 per day. Women hired for household work $0.75 per day or $2 per week.[5] Wages in 1875 per month: blacksmith, $39; tailor, $35; cooper, $28; baker, $30; brick maker, $25; wagon maker, $25.

---

[4] Fourth district of Bath, Steuben Co., p. 003.

[5] This difference between daily and weekly wage makes more sense if the weekly wage includes room and board.

Farmers were apparently troubled by dogs attacking sheep flocks. Whether perceived or real, the matter merited a question in the 1875 census. In the 4th district of Bath I find that 8 sheep were reported killed by dogs; in comparison 45 sheep were slaughtered that year. Other data in the 2nd district are less easy to analyze. One farmer reported none of his 28 sheep killed by dogs, but he also slaughtered all 28. Apparently he was shifting to pig farming. Another farmer reported having no sheep, but 14 were killed by dogs. Is that why he had no sheep? Or did he sell or slaughter the rest?

CHAPTER 12

The Union Preserved: A Guide to Civil War Records in the New York State Archives

Since 1978 the New York State Archives has been accepting custody of Civil War records from various state government agencies. The resulting collection contains much material of value to historians and genealogists, if one is patient enough to navigate through the vast sea of paper and microfilm. Fortunately, a navigator is available in the form of a 172-page book titled *The Union Preserved*.[1] Subtitled *A Guide to Civil War Records in the New York State Archives,* this book is the tangible result of a project of the Archives Partnership Trust, a 501(c)3 public benefit corporation whose self-proclaimed purpose is "to describe and make available the Civil War-related records that are held by the New York State Archives." It was published jointly with Fordham University Press.

The bulk of the guide consists of descriptions of 111 series of records created by sixteen offices, boards, or bureaus. Series are grouped according to the agency that created the records; each section begins with an administrative history of that agency. The introductory essay to the book, "A State of War," written by Harold Holzer and Hans L. Trefousse, is a capsule history of the Civil War with various illustrations (including a preliminary copy of the Emancipation Proclamation). The first chapter, "Documenting New York's Role in the Civil War," by Daniel Lorello, is an overview of

---

An earlier version of this chapter was posted at *www.NewEnglandAncestors.org* November 29, 2002.

[1] Daniel Lorello, comp., *The Union Preserved: A Guide to Civil War Records in the New York State Archives,* ed. by Harold Holzer (New York: Fordham University Press, 1999).

how the records were created, preserved, and collected. The records are available at the New York State Archives' research facility in Albany:

New York State Archives
www.archives.nysed.gov/aindex.shtml
Cultural Education Center, Room 11D40
Albany, NY, 12230
Tel: (518) 474-8955.
Email: archref@mmail.nysed.gov

The vast majority of the record series contain little or no genealogical information. This material is useful to writers, historians, and scholars, but not to genealogists. In Appendix A of the guide, "Conducting Genealogical and Local History Research in Civil War Records in the New York State Archives," it says, "Three record series out of the many records described in this guide may be especially helpful to researchers seeking information on individual soldiers or sailors from New York who served in the Civil War" (p. 93). It is true that the three series, described below, contain genealogical information perhaps useful to a large number of genealogists, but there are other records with just as much information for a smaller subset. For example, if your ancestor was an officer in the 1st to 13th regiments of New York State Volunteers, you want Series A4152, "Roster of Officers of New York State Volunteer Regiments 1861–1862." Ranks include second lieutenant up to colonel and surgeon, assistant surgeon, chaplain, adjutant, and quartermaster. Or, if your ancestor served in the 51st regiment, you can look for Series A0087, "Records of the 51st Regiment, New York State Volunteers, 1861–1864," which include medical discharges, leaves of absence, payrolls, etc.

The only record series that contains extensive genealogical information is Series 13774, "Town and City Registers of Men Who Served in the Civil War," created by the Bureau of Military Statistics. The description in the guide (p. 57) reads as follows:

> These registers are printed forms issued by the bureau of
> Military Record and completed by the state's town and city

clerks pursuant to Chapter 690 of the Laws of 1865. The registers provide the individual's full name, residence, date and place of birth, present rank, regiment and company, dates of enlistment and muster, rank, length of enlistment, place of enlistment, race, amount of bounty paid by town or bounty if disbursed by supervisor, marital status, previous occupation, parents' names, and dates of any promotions, resignations, discharges or deaths.

The good news is that there is an index. The bad news is that data are missing for many major communities, such as New York City, Brooklyn, Buffalo, Rochester, and Utica.

An extremely large record series (1,363 volumes) to mine for information is Series 13775, "Civil War Muster Roll Abstracts of New York State Volunteers, United States Sharpshooters, and United States Colored Troops," created by the Bureau of Records of the War of the Rebellion. The description (pp. 65–66) is as follows:

Arrangement: By branch of service (artillery, cavalry, infantry) and therein numerically by unit number. Entries for each unit are arranged alphabetically by last name of officer or enlisted man. The abstracts are printed forms filled out during the late 1880s through the early 1900s from original military records. . . . For each individual the following information is included: date of enlistment, age (in years), place of enlistment and for how long, date mustered in, grade, company and regiment, date left organization, how, in what grade, explanation, and remarks."

The Archives has an unpublished seventeen-volume personal name index for this series. They are working an on online version of the index.

The third series selected by the guide as having general genealogical interest is Series A0389, "Registers of Officers and Enlisted Men Mustered into Federal Military or Naval Service During the Civil War," a six-volume set created, again, by the Bureau of Military Statistics. The description is as follows:

These folio-sized volumes provide both military and civil information on New York men mustered into federal military or naval service during the Civil War. Much of the information in the series was compiled from questionnaires distributed by the bureau to the soldiers themselves, friends, relatives, medical officers in charge of United States hospitals, and local officials . . . between 1683 and 1867. . . . [There are] three types of categories: New York Volunteers in service, New York Volunteers formerly in service, and New York volunteers deceased. . . . The first subseries . . . [consists of] three volumes that provide information on individuals who were still in federal service when the data was collected.

Information provided includes: county, town, village, or city (including ward number); name, age, and color; place of birth; marital status; trade or occupation; voter or alien; ability to read or write; regiment first entered; date originally entered service; length of first enlistment; first rank; promotions, transfers etc.; length of unexpired term till June 1, 1865; current regiment and rank; whether or not drafted; substitute or representative recruit; and remarks. . . . Second subseries . . . [consists of] two volumes very similar to the subseries described above. . . . The final subseries consists of one volume entitled "Deaths of Officers and Enlisted Men Which Have Occurred While in the Military or Naval Service of the United States or From Wounds or Disease Acquired in Said Service since April 1861, Reported by the Families to Which the Deceased Belonged at Home."

Unfortunately, there are no indexes.

The Bureau of Military Statistics, responsible for collecting and compiling Civil War records, was created on April 8, 1863, with an initial appropriation of $6,000. Bureau chief Lockwood Lyon Doty was required to "collect and preserve an authentic sketch of every person from this state who has volunteered into the service of the general government since April 15, 1861, and likewise a record of the service of the several regiments."[2] Doty, however, had a grander vision. In his first annual report, he declared his intention to collect "every fact relating to the rebellion, and especially to the part which New York has taken in the war, whether now recorded or printed, or still existing in memory."[3]

He developed a one-page, double-sided form that asked the following questions of the soldiers:

date and place of enlistment

regiment

company (or ship) and rank

promotions or transfers

previous military history in the militia or U.S. Regular Army, Navy, or European military organizations

battles or skirmishes participated in during the Civil War

descriptions of wounds received or illnesses contracted while in the service

date of discharge or death

date and place of birth

parents' names and nationalities

level of education

if married, wife's name and number of children

residence at date of enlistment

profession prior to enlistment

military experiences of relatives in either the Revolutionary War, War of 1812, or European wars

relatives presently in service including regiment and rank

if the individual was deceased and the form completed by an acquaintance, remarks concerning the individual's general character

---

[2] Lorello, p. 17.

[3] Ibid

Doty even asked that a photograph be attached to the form. And it was done. Unfortunately, subsequent political rivalry resulted in most of the material being discarded.

The Union Preserved is available from Fordham University Press (*www.fordhampress.com*) and from Amazon.com (*www.amazon .com/*).

Lockwood Lyon Doty (1827–73) wrote *A History of Livingston County, New York, from its earliest traditions, to its part in the war for our Union: with an account of the Seneca nation of Indians, and biographical sketches of earliest settlers and prominent public men.* The book was published posthumously in 1878.

Harold Holzer, an Abraham Lincoln and Civil War-illustration expert, is vice president for communications at the Metropolitan Museum of Art, and has authored, coauthored, and edited sixteen books, including *The Union Preserved*. Daniel Lorello is associate archivist at the New York State Archives. Hans Trefousse, a Civil War scholar, is the author of two books about Andrew Johnson, and *The Radical Republicans: Lincoln's Vanguard for Racial Justice*, among others.

Detail from title page of *The Union Preserved.*

CHAPTER 13

A Genealogist's Use
of Eyewitness Accounts
# of History

G enealogists are part-time historians. We have to be in order to understand, for example, how political and economic events drove migration patterns. Historians paint with a broad brush, trying to give us an objective, accurate view of events. Genealogists are also part-time snoops. Like the village gossip, we are interested in the everyday events in the lives of our ancestors. The popularity of reconstructed villages such as Williamsburg and Sturbridge Village attest to our interest in how they dressed, how they cooked their food, how they heated their homes, how they entertained themselves. For this we want eyewitness accounts. We're want people writing in the first person about their own lives, about what they saw and what they thought about it. In this chapter we look at the kind of information we can expect from eyewitness accounts of life in New York State in the eighteenth and nineteenth centuries and how that enriches our understanding of our ancestors.

LATE EIGHTEENTH CENTURY

Our first example involves personal letters from the Bronck[1] family, living in the Catskill area of New York State during the Revolutionary War. Personal letters[2] will reflect the world of any ancestor who lived at the same time and place. This published collection does not

---

[1] This family gave its name to the borough of the Bronx in New York City.

[2] Good sources for letters are manuscript collections of historical and genealogical societies in the area where your ancestor lived. If personal papers were passed down to succeeding generations, these papers could have been deposited outside of New York State in a repository along the family's migration route.

speak of battles, since this area was not directly involved in the fighting. Rather the letters give us a bystander's point of view, mentioning rooting out Tories, procuring supplies for the army, and the shortages of household staples. This excerpt was written shortly after the war by Leonard Gansevoort, Jr. of Albany to his cousin Leonard Bronk at Coxsackie.[3]

Albany 12th Feby. 1783

Dr. Sir

The Bearer of this Letter will deliver you a Frock for your little one I wish she may live to wear it out entirely

You told me that Boskerk would bring me Hay He has not yet don it I wish you would take the Trouble to let him know that I expect him and if he does not bring it, I shall most assuredly bear hard upon him, as I do not intend to be trifled with any longer.

Polly begins to grow uneasy whenever she looks at her little Store of Butter If you can help her without putting yourself to Inconvenience (which I would not by any means you should do) you will greatly oblige her

I suppose you have heard before now of the Western Expedition I for my Part do not like it as I am afraid it will irritate the Indians and bring them again upon our Backs next Summer However small Folks like you and me must acquiesce and say amen

I wish you and your wife Health We are well God bless you

Your Friend
L. G. Junr.

---

[3] Raymond Beecher, ed., *Letters from a Revolution, 1775–1783; a selection from the Bronck Family papers at the Greene County Historical Society* (Coxsackie, N.Y.: Greene County Historical Society, 1973), p. 46.

EARLY NINETEENTH CENTURY

An interesting subset of letters was written by foreign travelers, many of whom visited New York State. As Roger Haydon states: "New York State was for the early nineteenth century the very image of the United States. The 1820 census recorded New York's taking over from Virginia the title of country's most populous state, which position it would retain until the Korean War. In land mass it was only a few hundred square miles smaller than England itself. And between 1815 and 1845 its development, based on the building and operation of the Erie Canal, was stunning in its scale and complexity. Virtually all foreign travelers visited New York State and described it in their books."[4]

Our first example from this genre is Frances Wright, a well-to-do Scotswoman who visited New York from 1818 to 1820. Upon her return to Britain she turned twenty-eight of her letters into a book titled *Views of Society and Manners in America; in a Series of Letters from That Country to a Friend in England, during the Years 1818, 1819, and 1820.*[5] Letters IX to XIII inclusive are about upstate New York. Three excerpts follow. In Letter IX, July 1819, she gives us this sorry description of Albany at a time when there was talk of moving the state capital inland: "We have just made the passage up the magnificent Hudson (160 miles) from New York to this city, which has indeed but very through that no unimportant title to so grand a name, in being the capital of the state. It is probable however, that the government will soon have to travel in search of the centre of the republic in like manner with that of Pennsylvania."[6]

Albany indeed seems to stand as in expectation of her falling honors, for though there are some well-finished streets and many commodious and elegant private dwellings, the general appearance of

---

[4] Roger Haydon (ed.), *Upstate Travels : British Views of Nineteenth-Century New York*, 1st ed. (Syracuse, N.Y., 1982), p. x.

[5] Frances Wright, *Views of Society and Manners in America: in a series of letters from that country to a friend in England, during the years 1818, 1819, and 1820*, 2d ed. (London, 1822).

[6] In 1812 Harrisburg had been made the new state capital of Pennsylvania.

the town is old and shabby." In Letter X, she describes the arduous travel common in the region before the opening of the Erie Canal.

> Our second day's journey was long and fatiguing, but withal very interesting, the weather delightful and the scenery pleasing. The road bore everywhere heavy marks of the flagellations inflicted by the recent storms. It seemed often as if not only the rain but the lightning had torn up the ground and scooped out the soil, now on this side and now on that, into which holes, first the right wheel of our vehicle, and anon the left making a sudden plump, did all but spill us out on the highway. To do justice to ourselves, we bore the bruises that were in this manner most plentifully inflicted with very tolerable stoicism and unbroken good humour. . . . The importance of Utica will soon be increased by the opening of the great canal, destined here to join the Mohawk. We swerved the next day from our direct route for the purpose of looking at this work, now in considerable progress, and which, in his consequences, is truly grand, affording a water highway from the heart of

PLAN OF THE FALLS. — *A*, hotel; *BB*, steep bank; *c*, brink of the precipice; *e*, Goat Island; *hh*, perpendicular rock; *d*, rapids; *m*, platform; *f*, spiral staircase by which you descend; *g*, ferry; *k*, ascent to the American side of the Falls.

"Plan of the Falls," showing detail of Niagara Falls, from *A Pictorial Geography of the World* by S. G. Goodrich (1841), p. 235.

this great continent to the ocean. . . . It is thought that four or five years will now fully complete this work. The most troublesome opposition it has encountered is in the vast Onondaga Swamp, and not a few of the workmen have fallen a sacrifice to its pestilential atmosphere.

Finally, in Letter XIII she describes Niagara Falls audible at night from an inn seven miles away. "In the night, when all was still, I heard the first rumbling of the cataract. Wakeful from overfatigue, rather than from any discomfort in the lodging, I rose more than once to listen to a sound which the dullest ears could not catch for the first time without emotion. Opening the window, the low, hoarse thunder distinctly broke the silence of the night. When at intervals, it swelled more full and deep, you will believe that I held my breath to listen."

Tourists have always written about the landscape, the food, the difficulties of travel, and peculiar native customs and these tourists are no exception. However this description of a thunderstorm on Seneca Lake at Geneva by Alexander Mackay about 1848 stands the test of time rather well.[7]

On the evening of my arrival I took a small boat and went out upon the lake. . . . The air was still, but the western sky looked ugly and lurid. As it gradually blackened, a fitful light every now and then faintly illuminated the dark bosoms of the massive clouds, which had now made themselves visible in that direction. As they stole higher and higher up the clear blue heavens, the illumination became more frequent and more brilliant, and nothing was not wanting but the muttering of the thunder to complete the usual indications of a coming storm. I was then some distance up the lake, and made as speedily for town as possible. When I reached it, innumerable lights were gleaming from its windows upon the yet placid lake, whose dark, still surface was occasionally lit up for miles by the lightning

---

[7] Alexander Mackay, in *Upstate Travels,* p. 191.

which now coruscated vividly above it. The first growl of the distant thunder broke upon my ear as I stepped ashore; and, pleased with my escape, I hurried without loss of time to the hotel. In a few minutes afterwards the progressing storm burst over the town, and the dusty streets soon ran with torrents of water. The effect upon the lake was magnificent. It was only visible when the lightning, which now fell fast on all sides, accompanied by awful crashes of thunder, gleamed upon its surface, and seemed to plunge, flash after flash, into its now agitated bosom. You could not only thus distinguish the dark leaden waters, with their foaming white crests, but the shore on the opposite side for a considerable distance inland, and on either hand. The whole would be brilliantly lighted up for a moment or two, after which it would relapse into darkness, to be rendered visible again by the next succession of flashes, which fell from the black and overcharged heavens. In half an hour it was all over, when the scene displayed itself in a new aspect, veiled in the pale lustre of the moon.

View of Albany.

"View of Albany," from *A Pictorial Geography of the World* by S.G. Goodrich (1841), p. 243.

---

[8] Andrew Reed, in *Upstate Travels,* p. 66.

Occasionally one finds a traveler with more esoteric interests. Andrew Reed, traveling through Albany in 1835, was sufficiently interested in education to describe the curriculum of the Female Academy. If your ancestor taught or studied here, you would have a good description of their experiences. He lists all of the text books, describes the students' typical day, and graduation ceremonies.[8] "There are two examinations in the year. At the close of the examination in February, the names of those who have distinguished themselves are announced; at the July examination, premiums are given, and gild medals are awarded to those who excel in mathematics and original composition. Besides this, those who have gone through the whole course with approbation, are eligible to receive a diploma bearing the seal of the institution. This is its highest honour; and it is sought by those, especially, who are qualifying to become teachers."

British travelers sometimes paid for their way by giving lectures. James Silk Buckingham (1786–1855) was in Albany in July of 1838 giving a series of lectures on Egypt and describes the Fourth of July festivities.[9]

> The day-break was announced by a discharge of cannon; and at sunrise, a salute of 13 guns was fired, in honour of the 13 original States that united in the Declaration of Independence. This was followed by the ringing of the bells of all the churches; so that as early as five o'clock, the whole city was awake, and in motion. At ten o'clock, the procession (formed to march through the town, on their way to the first reformed Dutch church, where the "exercises," as all proceedings of public meetings are here called, were to take place,) was put in motion; . . . the bands of music, of which there were several, were all good, and one very superior; the various companies and societies, all habited in some peculiar costume, or distinguished by some peculiar badge, looked remarkably well; and the populace, who thronged the foot-pavement on each side of the street, while the procession filled the centre, were as well dressed,

---

[9] James Silk Buckingham, in *Upstate Travels*, p. 72.

as orderly, and as evidently interested in the proceedings of the day, as the best friend of the republic could desire. . . . the part of the procession which touched us most, and made unbidden tears, not of joy or sorrow but of mere exuberance of sympathy and feeling, start involuntarily into our eyes, was the sight of the veteran heroes of the revolution, as they passed us in the open carriages that contained them. As sixty-two years have passed away since the Declaration of Independence, the number of those who actually fought in the war of the revolution is now very small, and they are, of course, every year diminishing; so that in a few years more they will all have descended to the tomb. . . .

Our next eyewitness is not a tourist but a businessman. Edwin Scrantom was an auctioneer at the firm of Sibley & Scrantom in Rochester, New York. This advertisement in the local newspaper[10] marks the transition of the business into his hands.

New Auctioneer

April 1, 1841. — In consequence of the declining health of Mr. Sibley, and at his suggestion, as well as that of my own friends, the undersigned has conformed with the law relative to Auctioneers, and has constituted himself an Auctioneer for the city of Rochester, and county of Monroe. He will, therefore, from, and after the first day of April, sell Goods, Wares, Merchandize, Lots, or any other property in this city or the adjacent towns and villages, at Auction, in his own name, and will continue the Auction Business of Sibley & Scrantom as usual. No dissolution of the firm of Sibley & Scrantom is contemplated in this arrangement. EDWIN SCRANTOM

Edwin Scrantom's diary,[11] begun in 1837, is a mix of local events,

---

[10] *Rochester Daily Democrat,* March, 31, 1841, p. 2.

[11] Edwin Scrantom, *Edwin Scrantom's Diary, Vol. I* (Rochester, N.Y.: Rochester Public Library, 1936).

business concerns, and opinions clearly not intended for publication. Reading through these pages we see the bustle of a city created by the Erie Canal through the eyes of a hard-working, if slightly sanctimonious businessman. A few excerpts follow.

> *May 6, 1837* I am glad that Saturday night is come-my weary limbs cry out for rest, and every chord responds, Amen. Labour ceases and we now rest for the Sabbath. How important that we spend the Sabbath abstracted from all Earthly thoughts and persuits. Roswin Kingsberry killed by lightning near Brockport — a little boy killed in a school house on the Lyell Road 2 1/2 miles from this City.

> *Friday, May 19, 1837* Legislature adjournes the 16th of May. L. Sibley returned yesterday. . . . The Nation is Bankrupt, and our Rulers corrupt beyond all that we have ever dreamed of. The present President Martin VanBuren, obtained this office thru intrigue and corruption. The Vice President Richard M. Johnson, is the infamously, famous author of the report in Congress against keeping the Sabbath. But it is hoped that they have destroyed themselves and that their places will soon be supplied by Honest Men.

> *Saturday Aug. 26, 1837* Began to take lessons of John Ph. Beck in German (I shall want new jaws to get through with it, I fear.)

> *Monday Oct 1, 1838* L.W.S. called suddenly away to Utica as a witness. This bad, bad for us.

> *Oct 14, 1838* L.W.S. returned from Utica after being gone 12 days. H. Ely gained the suit and made us a present of $50.00. I qualified myself as auctioneer and held an auction of furniture, employing Wm S. Hull. We sold $800.00 worth of furniture.

---

[12] *Rochester Daily Democrat*, December 7, 1838, p. 2.

Newspapers are also a good source for details of everyday life, and the smaller the community the more local news you will find. The advertisements can serve as a partial substitute for a missing city directory. Here is a small item, published in December 1838,[12] describing western land opening to settlers: "More Lands. — The Miamies have just ceded to the United States some two hundred thousand acres of the choicest lands in the Wabash Valley of Indiana, by treaty. The lands are located on the Wabash, Mississinewa, Aboitee, and Eel Rivers, and cost the Government a little less than two dollars per acre." The historian's present-day overview of migration patterns was built up by individual people coming across specific information like this and making individual decisions.

CIVIL WAR

If your New York ancestor fought in the Civil War, you have many sources to check to get information about his military record. The personal side of his experiences will not be present in these official records, but in letters or a journal. The censorship that we are familiar with today regarding military matters did not exist during the Civil War. A high percentage of the soldiers were literate and their letters went home unedited.

Our first example is Daniel Morse Holt, M.D. He was born in Herkimer, New York, the son and tenth child of David and Elizabeth Holt. He volunteered as surgeon at age 43, joining the 121st New York Volunteers. He resigned in ill health in October 1864 and died of tuberculosis October 15, 1868. His letters to his wife, Mary Louisa Willard, describe in gritty detail the life of Civil War surgeon.[13] The first excerpt was written not long after his arrival, the second eight months later when the effects of his tuberculosis were becoming apparent.

---

[13] Daniel M. Holt, James M. Greiner, Janet L. Coryell, and James R. Smither, eds. *A Surgeon's Civil War: The Letters and Diary of Daniel M. Holt, M.D.* (Kent, Ohio: Kent State University Press, 1994).

Camp in field near
Bakersville, Md.
October 2, 1862

My dear Wife:—

Another welcome letter from home was received to-day. A thousand thanks for your kind remembrance. I thought I would write while I have a few moments leisure, not knowing when another opportunity may present itself. A few days ago I wrote you giving the general outlines of daily life, and what was true of yesterday is true also for to-day. At early dawn, we rise, wash and prepare to eat breakfast; that over, Surgeons Call is sounded and from one hundred and fifty to two hundred patients present themselves for treatment. The time required to attend all this consumes two or three hours and then the *Hospital* has to be visited and those sick in quarters:- that means, those who are too unwell to come up to call, but who are not sick enough to go into the barn which we have taken possession of for a hospital. We have to make from twenty-five to thirty of these calls daily, seeing that the medicines prescribed are faithfully given and that the condition of the men is comfortable, &c. — the diet of the sick in bed is also to be looked to — Sanitary condition of the camp musts be attended to, and a general supervision of the health of the men made and reported. You may think that we have hardly time for all this, and indeed you think correctly, but it has to be done daily, and sometimes we have to see a patient several times a day. After all, the treatment the poor fellows have to accept is very little and sometimes I think amounts to almost nothing, but it is all we can give. I would have it different if I could, but my hands are tied in more ways than one. . . .

Camp in field near
White Oak Church, Va.
May 31st, 1863.

My dear Wife:—

   This must be a short letter. It is written for two purposes
— one to keep your spirits up and another to keep *mine*
up. With the wounds and accidents of the regiment come
increase of labor on my part. The hospital is full to over-
flowing and many in quarters are about as badly off. As to
myself I am pretty well used up. Something akin to chronic
diarrhoea just for pastime is running me, while the plague
of scrofula has broken out with threats to render me use-
less. I need relaxation and respite from the constant strain
upon my system. I fear I shall come thoroughly unwell
unless I can in someway be relieved from so much care and
hardship. It is work, work, work, from dawn to dark and
no thanks from anyone. Good bye; from poor old worn out

Daniel

While Dr. Holt's writings were contemporaneous with events, the
next example is a journal written later in life by a soldier who survived the war and returned to a long and prosperous life.[14] Rice C.
Bull was born June 9, 1842, in Hartford, Washington County, New
York. In his words, "On August 13th, 1862 I worked with my father
in the oat field until noon gathering the grain; that afternoon I went
to Fort Ann and signed the papers that bound me to army service for
three years, unless sooner discharged. I became a member of Company D, 123rd Regiment, New York Volunteer Infantry."[15] After the
war, in 1866, he moved to Troy, New York, where he became a
banker and civic leader. He had kept a diary and written letters during the war. After his retirement in 1919 he wrote his memoirs from
them. He died 19 May 1930, three weeks before his 88th birthday.

---

[14] Rice C. Bull, K. Jack Bauer, ed., *Soldiering: The Civil War Diary of Rice C. Bull,
123rd New York Volunteer Infantry* (Novato, Calif.: Presidio Press, 1986).

[15] Ibid., p. 3.

These memoirs give us an enlisted man's view of the Civil War. In this excerpt[16] he describes a "dog tent" — a "pup tent" in today's parlance.

> As soon as our company streets were laid out by our officers each man was issued a tent cloth, and with these strips of cloth were directed to construct shelter tents: "dog tents" was the name given them. Usually three men would occupy a tent as the three cloths could be so arranged as to enclose, when finished, the three sides of a tent, in which they could lie. These tents were to be used chiefly for sleeping, as one could barely sit erect at the highest place in the center. They were far from comfortable living quarters. Yet they were the only kind of shelter we would have in the field during our term of service. For three years this thin cloth tent would be our cover from wind storm and cold. The tents were kept erect by driving a stake at each end, the stakes extending about three feet above the ground, and about six feet apart. They were connected at the top by a light pole over which was placed two of the tent cloths, buttoned together and stretched as much as possible at the sides. The third cloth covered the back of the tent. The head of our bed was at the back where we used our knapsacks for pillows. For our beds we would first spread our rubber blankets, on top of which we placed one woolen blanket, for covering we used the two other blankets.

LATE NINETEENTH CENTURY

In addition to combing manuscript collections for diaries, letters, and other personal papers, we can catch a glimpse of the times by looking through old city directories. A brief glance through the 1870 city directory for Rochester finds business categories common then, scarce today, such as hoop skirts, livery stables, tinsmith, blacksmith, carriage maker. We also find other snippets of information. Public

---

[16] Ibid., p. 10.

transportation — street cars — ran every twenty minutes from 6:30 a.m. to 10:40 p.m., except every ten minutes between 9 a.m. and 8 p.m. The fare was five cents, but a package of eleven tickets could be had for fifty cents. Among the societies active at the time were the Athletic Base Ball Club, Clerks' Mutual Aid Association, Ladies' Hebrew Benevolent Society, and the Monroe County Homoeopathic Society. Clearly sports, insurance, and medicine differed quite a bit from today. At this time we also see the introduction of the modern postal system. There is a table showing the location of "Iron boxes for the reception of letters, pre-paid by stamps, according to law."[17] In the absence of email and fax, letters were a major mode of communication. "Letters are collected from these boxes daily between 6 A. M. and 6:30 P. M.; in the business portions of the city, five times; in the intermediate portions, three times, and in the outer portions, twice."[18] We also find the notice that the city streets have been declared postal routes by the postmaster general, making it illegal for competing firms to use them to deliver the mail.

After 1880 newspapers begin to carry advertisements for a new invention — the bicycle. The following excerpt about three bicycling races held in Utica on July 4, 1892[19] was newsworthy in a way we do not experience today. The winning times, much slower than today's standards, suggests that early racing bikes were heavy machines built to accommodate rough roads.

Interesting Bicycle Races in Which Wheels Were the Prizes

Utica, July 4. — In the ten-mile Green race to-day thirteen men started. W. U. Helfert of Utica, won in 56 minutes; A. H. Davis, Utica, second; James A. England, Utica, third; Emil J. George, Utica, fourth.

Twelve wheelmen started in the fifteen mile handicap. K. B. Weatherbee, of Richfield Springs, won the race in

---

[17] Rochester [N.Y.] City Directory of 1870, p. 292.

[18] Ibid.

[19] *Democrat and Chronicle,* July 5, 1892, p. 1.

52 minutes; A. E. Weed of Syracuse second; James D. McTaggart, of Rochester, third; and P. C. Hammes and A. F. Ferris of Utica, tied for fourth place.

There were nine starters in the twenty-mile handicap. Dan Buss, of Tonawanda, won in one hour and eighteen minutes, G. E. Hancock, of Syracuse second; one minute later, Benjamin Cleveland, of Tonawanda third, and William Hardelben, of Tonawanda fourth.

The first prize in each race was a high grade wheel and the other prizes were correspondingly valuable.

The late nineteenth century also saw the introduction of the typewriter, which changed business practices of the time the way the personal computer did a century later. This newspaper advertisement of 1892,[20] while extolling the virtues of the Smith Premier typewriter, also gives us a picture of newsmen sending their copy to the AP via telegraph.

"Improvement the Order of the Age."
The Smith Premier Typewriter !
The SMITH PREMIER Typewriter leads them
all. Be progressive, and purchase a writing
machine that has many improvements.
Our new brush device cleans all of the type
in a few seconds without soiling the hands.
The SMITH PREMIER Typewriter has been
adopted to the exclusion of all other writing
machines by the Associated Press of the State
of New York to be used in their telegraphic
service to take dispatches direct from the wire.
Write for descriptive catalogue.
Rochester Office, 407 Powers Block.
The Smith Premier Typewriter Company,
Syracuse, New York, U.S.A.

[20] Ibid., p. 6.

CONCLUSION

The amount of eyewitness material available to construct the personal history of a favorite ancestor is both scarce and abundant at the same time. Scarce because our ancestors did not commonly leave diaries or journals. Those diaries which were written were often discarded. Those that have survived may be in a small, obscure repository far from where they were written. Scarce because the newspapers of the time did not often write stories specifically about our ancestors. But first-hand accounts of the times and places our ancestors lived in are abundant. We may not have newspaper stories about our ancestor, but we can read the same newspaper he read. We may not have a portrait or photograph of our ancestor, but we can find out what kinds of clothes he probably wore. You may find other sources useful as well. State census records will describe his farm, if he was a farmer, or list his wage if he was a carpenter. County histories sometimes contain interviews with the region's oldest citizens, preserving their personal account of pioneer times. Writing a biography of a favorite ancestor requires an ingenuity in finding and using source material to go beyond our initial hunt for names and dates.

CHAPTER 14

Bounty Lands in the Military Tract in Post–Revolutionary War New York State

Revolutionary War bounty land payments are a useful resource for genealogists. A grant of bounty land documents Revolutionary War service for a soldier who may not have applied for a pension. In Dr. Pangloss's "best of all possible worlds," this bounty land would serve to locate the soldier after the war. Dr. Pangloss, however, did not live in New York.

Whereas it is true that the federal government in 1776 had promised land to soldiers to maintain strength in the army, and that New York State added even larger bounties in 1783, the state's legal process was seriously flawed and involved numerous lengthy delays. The vast majority of soldiers did not trust the government and sold their rights to the land well before the state granted warrants to it. Only a very few of the soldiers actually settled on the acres allotted to them. In this chapter we look into the fiasco that was New York veterans' experience with bounty lands. We look first at the actions of the state legislature and then at the experiences of three individual soldiers.

THE NEW YORK STATE LEGISLATURE

The succession of snafus that constituted the state's payment of bounty lands is detailed in C. Edith Hall's extensive and carefully researched monograph, *Early History of Military Tract*.[1] As the table

---

An earlier version of this chapter was posted at *www.NewEnglandAncestors.org* July 5, 2002.

[1] C. Edith Hall, *Early History of Military Tract* (Baldwinsville, N.Y.: p.p., no date).

below illustrates, the state passed numerous acts, often separated by several years, to accomplish this land distribution. The whole procedure lasted twenty years.

YEAR	ACTION
1783	Land grants were authorized
1783	The land itself was designated
1786	A different tract was designated
1788	Original tract was decided on
1789	Balloting procedure was defined
1790	Survey of 25 townships was authorized
1790/91	Two additional townships were authorized and surveyed
1794	A twenty-eighth township was authorized and surveyed
1797	A commission was established to finally resolve conflicting land claims
1803	The commission completed its work when all land disputes were settled

The Beginning

The New York State Legislature, in an act dated March 27, 1783, granted:

> To a Major-General, 5,500 acres of land; to a Brigadier-General, 4,250 acres; to a Colonel, 2,500 acres; to a Lieutenant-Colonel, 2,250 acres; to a Major, 2,000 acres; to a Captain or Regimental Surgeon, 1,000 acres; to a Chaplain, 2,000 acres; to each Subaltern or Surgeon's Mate, 1,000 acres; and to each private or non-commissioned officer, 500 acres.

The short-term purpose of this legislation was to bolster enlistment to keep a military presence along the frontier. The long-term purpose was to place veterans on the frontier as a buffer against Indian attacks. The legislation was modeled on a bill passed by Congress, on September 16, 1776. In the federal legislation a private soldier was granted 100 acres; higher ranks were granted progressively more land, up to 500 acres to a colonel. In New York State, the land bounties were combined, giving each qualified private a total of 600 acres.

First Setback

On July 25, 1783, the state legislature specified 1.8 million acres of land to be set aside for this so-called Military Tract. This land, the lush Finger Lakes region in the center of the state, included all the present counties of Onondaga, Cayuga, Cortland, and Seneca, as well as parts of the counties of Oswego, Wayne, Schuyler, and Tompkins. Unbelievably, the specified region contained Indian land recognized previously in treaties by both the federal and state governments. Not until three years later — on May 5, 1786 — did the state propose to offer alternative land in Clinton, Essex, and Franklin counties. This area, in the extreme northeastern portion of the state, is part of the current Adirondack Park. As it was not well suited for farming, the plan was rejected and the region became known as the "Old Military Tract." Hall explains:

> Since the close of the war, land speculators had been
> engaged in purchasing from the veterans the rights to
> bounty lands, and, as the lands designated in this act were
> not considered to be as fertile as those around the finger
> lakes, objections were raised to the substitution of this
> northern section. In view of this opposition, it was decided
> to wait until the Indian title to the territory originally set
> apart as bounty lands should be extinguished before pro-
> ceeding with the distribution.

It should be noted that the opposition came not from veterans but from land speculators who had, by this time, acquired most of the rights to the bounty lands. Another two years passed before treaties with the Onondaga and Cayuga tribes released the original Military Tract land in 1788.

Land Distribution

In an act dated February 28, 1789, the legislature described the balloting procedure.

> . . . [T]he said commissioners shall cause the names of each
> of the officers, non-commissioned officers, and privates, . . .
> to be written upon separate ballots or tickets, . . . the bal-
> lots or tickets to be rolled up and put into a box, and then

cause one hundred ballots or tickets to be made and numbered from one to one hundred, which said ballots or tickets shall also be rolled up and put in a separate box for township No. 1, and as many ballots or tickets numbered and rolled up for township No. 2, . . . they shall appoint one or more persons who shall first draw a ticket from the box in which the names are put, and then a ticket from the numbers of township No. 1 . . . shall proceed in the same manner to draw the lots in the other townships until the whole drawing is completed, and the lots in each township drawn next after the ticket marked with the name of the person entitled to such lands . . . the said commissioners shall make a full and fair account in a book . . .

On July 3, 1790, the survey of the authorized twenty-five townships was completed and the board began issuing letters patent. Table 1 lists the names of the original townships.

Table 1
NAMES ASSIGNED TO THE ORIGINAL 25 TOWNSHIPS OF THE MILITARY TRACT

1	Lysander	14	Tully
2	Hannibal	15	Fabius
3	Cato	16	Ovid
4	Brutus	17	Milton
5	Camillus	18	Locke
6	Cicero	19	Homer
7	Manlius	20	Solon
8	Aurelius	21	Hector
9	Marcellus	22	Ulysses
10	Pompey	23	Dryden
11	Romulus	24	Virgil
12	Scipio	25	Cincinnatus
13	Sempronius		

One must keep in mind the distinction between a township and a town. A township was never a political entity. It was a square tract of land containing 60,000 acres surveyed into 600-acre lots (remember that each private soldier was entitled to a total of 600 acres, 500 from the state and 100 from the federal government). The only purpose of a township was to distribute bounty land to soldiers. A town, on the other hand, is a political subdivision of a county, and a form of local government. The twenty-eight townships of the Military Tract were originally formed into eleven towns. Thus the original town of Homer comprised the townships of Homer, Solon, Virgil, and Cincinnatus. Similarly, the original town of Lysander comprised the townships of Lysander, Hannibal, and Cicero. Some lands reserved to the Onondaga and Cayuga tribes when the Military Tract was first established were acquired later. These lands were not part of the townships but were incorporated into the towns.

Second Setback

Even though the Indian claims to the original Military Tract had been extinguished, the survey was still flawed. It was not until the end of July 1790 that the state noticed that the Military Tract, as it had been surveyed, overlapped the tract to the south known as Boston Ten Towns. As Hall explains:

> The board immediately checked the awards already made, and found that there were four lots in Township No. 23, fifteen in township No. 24 and three in Township No. 25, which had been balloted for, and which were affected by this new difficulty. They also found that there were one lot in Township No. 23, five lots in Township No. 24, and one lot in township No. 25, not as yet awarded to claimants, which were also affected.[2]

In other words, the state had been giving away land it did not own. To provide additional land to make up for this, two new townships were surveyed (completed January 29, 1791). Number 26 was named Junius and number 27 was named Galen.

---

[2] Ibid.

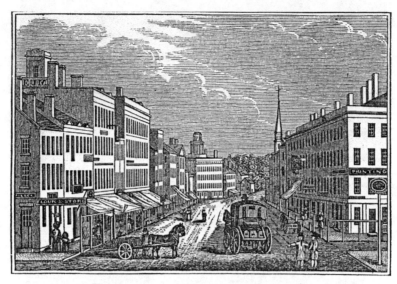

Eastern part of Genesee-street, Auburn.

"Eastern part of Genesee-street, Auburn" (the town of Auburn was formed from the original township of Aurelius in 1823), from *Historical Collections of the State of New York* by John W. Barber (New York: Clark, Austin & Co.,1851), p. 60.

Third Setback

The preemption line, which served as the boundary between the Military Tract and the Phelps-Gorham Purchase to the west, had been surveyed in 1788. When the land was sold to Robert Morris in 1790, one of the provisions of the sale was that the line be resurveyed. The resurvey of the preemption line shifted the western boundary of the Military Tract eastward, reducing the size of several townships. On September 11, 1794, the twenty-eighth and final township, named Sterling, was authorized to make up territory lost in this shift of the preemption line.

The Final Decision

In January 1794, the legislature attempted to clear up conflicting land claims by requiring that all deeds and conveyances be sent to Albany. According to Hall, "the title to these lands became a scandal." Some soldiers had been tricked into selling their claims and other soldiers did a bit of defrauding themselves, selling their claim more than once. In 1797, in answer to a petition, a commission was established to make a final decision on conflicting land claims. The commission completed its work in 1803. By the time the state had completed its goal of establishing a frontier settlement of veterans, the frontier had overtaken the Military Tract and moved on. By 1803 lands in central and western New York State were settled. Lewis and Clark were organizing their expedition into the new frontier — the Louisiana Purchase.

THE SOLDIERS

Conrad Bush

In the entire town of Pompey, the only Revolutionary War soldier to settle on the land awarded to him was Conrad Bush, who drew lot 47.[3] Georg Conrad Bush was born in Germany;[4] his tombstone inscription indicates that he was born in 1753. He arrived in Philadelphia on October 9, 1775, on the ship *King of Prussia*.[5] I did not find a naturalization record for him in Philadelphia.[6] In his Index to Revolutionary War Service Records, Virgil D. White lists the following:[7]

Bush, Conratt, srv in Yates' Regt of NY Mil

Bush, Conrod, srv as a Pvt in Rawlings' Regt of Cont troops

Bush, Conrod, srv as a Pvt & Matross[8] in 2nd Arty Regt of Cont Troops

---

[3] Sylvia Shoebridge, *Pompey: Our Town in Profile* (Pompey, N.Y.: Township of Pompey, 1976), Vol. 1, pp. 42–43.

[4] Rev. W. M. Beauchamp, *Revolutionary Soldiers Resident or Dying in Onondaga County, N.Y. with Supplementary List of Possible Veterans Based on a Pension List of Franklin H. Chase, Syracuse, N. Y.*, Publications of the Onondaga Historical Association, Vol. I, No. 2, April 1912, MCMXIII, Syracuse, N.Y., pp. 170–711.

[5] Ralph Beaver Strassburger, *Pennsylvania German Pioneers: A Publication of the Original Lists of Arrivals in the Port of Philadelphia from 1727 to 1808*, ed. by William John Hinke, (Norristown, Pa.: Pennsylvania German Society, 1934), Vol. I, p. 762, List 324 C.

[6] P. William Filby, ed., *Philadelphia Naturalization records*, (Detroit: Gale Research Co., 1982).

[7] Virgil D. White, *Index to Revolutionary War Service Records* (Waynesboro, Tenn.: The National Historical Publishing Company, 1995) Vol. I, p. 384.

[8] A matross is a kind of gunner's mate.

The name Conrad Bush is not common in the area, so it is likely that these all records refer to the same individual. The first entry is sufficient to entitle him to the state bounty land.

After the war, Conrad Bush settled first in Mamakating Town in Ulster County, with his wife, Mary Watson. The 1790 federal census lists George Coonradt Bush (1 M >16, 1 M <16, 3 F). Later census records list him at his farm in Pompey, although the name of the location changed as local governments evolved. Census indexes track his movements over the next twenty years: in 1800, a Coonrad Bush was in Ontario County; in 1810, a Conrad Bush was in Onondaga County; and in 1820, Conrod Bush appeared in Onondaga County, Pompey. As with his service record, his German accent shines through in the spellings in these census records.

Conrad Bush applied for a pension. The entry reads "Bush, Conrad, Cont., N.Y. res., S46424; BLWt. 6870-100. Iss. 7/11/1791 No papers."[9] His wife died in 1848; Conrad died in 1854. The burial location is "Bush, Conradt, Sand Knoll, his farm, Pompey NY."[10] The tombstone inscriptions of the couple read:[11]

> Conrad Bush / Died Dec. 19 1854 / Ae. 101 yrs. 1 mo. / & 20 days.

> Mary / wife of Conrad Bush / Died Dec 3, 1848 / Ae. 81 yrs, 11 mos. & 15 days.

John Shepard

Similarly, in the town of Cicero, the only man who occupied his own bounty land was John Shepard. He was the first justice of the peace in the town in 1804.[12]

---

[9] *Index of Revolutionary War Pension Applications in the National Archives*, Special Publication No. 40 (Washington, D.C.: National Genealogical Society, 1976), p. 82.

[10] Patricia Law Hatcher, *Abstract of Graves of Revolutionary Patriots* (Dallas: Pioneer Heritage Press, 1987), Vol. 1, p. 139.

[11] Beauchamp, *Revolutionary Soldiers Resident or Dying in Onondaga County, N.Y.*, pp. 170–71.

[12] W. W. Clayton, *History of Onondaga County, New York* (Syracuse, N.Y.: D. Mason and Co., 1878), p. 338.

According to Rev. W. M. Beauchamp, Capt. John Shepard enlisted in 1777 in Capt. James Young's company.[13] He left the army in the fall of 1781 from ill health and did not serve again. Beauchamp also claims a strong tie with Stamford, Connecticut, saying

> He was ordained in North Stamford Congregational church, Conn., June 27, 1787, and was dismissed June 11, 1794. Several deeds describe him as of Stamford as late as '96, and in some he is styled "Reverend." On June 7, 1783, he married Mrs. Melisent Edsall, widow of Nehemiah Finor, by whom he had four children. After leaving Stamford he lived in Orange Co., N. Y., which was partly peopled from that part of Westchester which Stamford claimed.

In addition, Beauchamp lists the following cemetery inscriptions:

> Rev. John Shepard, / Born / May 25, / 1757. / Died Jan 29, 1822

> Soldier of the Cross. / Well done, Rest from / thy loved employ.

> Millicent Edsall / Wife of / Rev. John Shepard / Died Nov, 12, 1805 / Aged 50 years

Beauchamp may be mistaken. Consider the following:

- A collection of biographies of Stamford's Revolutionary War soldiers does not contain an entry for John Shepard/ Shepherd.[14]

---

[13] Beauchamp, *Revolutionary Soldiers Resident or Dying in Onondaga County, N.Y.*, pp. 18–19.

[14] Edith M. Wicks and Virginia H. Olson, comps., *Stamford's Soldiers: Genealogical Biographies of Revolutionary War Patriots from Stamford, Connecticut*, ed. by Paul W. Prindle (Stamford, Conn.: Stamford Genealogical Society, 1976).

- The only Capt. John Shepard listed in White's index served from Massachusetts. The entry reads: "Shepard, John, srv as Capt in Porter's Regt of MA Mil."[15]
- The Pension List of 1820 contains the following entry: "John Shepard, captain, Massachusetts."[16]

However, service for New York State is a requirement for obtaining the bounty land. Of the fourteen "John Shepard" entries in White, there is one for a New York regiment: "Shepard, John, srv as Pvt in Hasbrouck's Regt of NY Mil."[17] The index of Revolutionary War pension applications contains the following entry: "Shepard, John, Cont., N.Y., S42292."[18] Patricia Law Hatcher confirms the burial place in her *Abstract of Graves of Revolutionary Patriots:* "Shepard, John, Shepard Point, Oneida Lake, nr Syracuse, Bremerton NY."[19]

Benjamin Epton

The experience of Private Benjamin Epton was significantly different. There is probably a tale for another time behind this brief outline. White lists his service record as follows:[20]

Epton, Benjamin, srv as a Pvt in the 2nd NY Regt

Epton, Benjamin, srv as a Pvt in the 4th NY Regt

Epton, Benjamin, srv in the 11th Regt of Cont Troops

Again, this source offers no evidence as to whether this refers to a single individual. However, the following discharge paper confirms the first entry.

---

[15] White, *Rev. War Service Records,* Vol. IV, p. 2442.

[16] U.S. War Department, *The Pension List of 1820* (Washington, D.C.: Gales & Seaton, 1820; repr. Baltimore: Genealogical Publishing Co., 1991), p. 451.

[17] White, *Rev. War Service Records* p. 2442.

[18] *Index of Revolutionary War Pension Applications in the National Archives,* p. 504.

[19] Hatcher, *Abstract of Graves of Revolutionary Patriots,* Vol. 4, p. 27.

[20] White, *Rev. War Service Records,* Vol. II, p. 873.

By his Excellency GEORGE WASHINGTON, Esquire, General and Commander in Chief of the forces of the United States of America. These are to certify that the bearer hereof, BENJAMIN EPTON, private in the second N. York Regiment, having faithfully served the United States six years and six months and being enlisted for the war only, is hereby discharged from the American Army. . . . The within certificate shall not avail the bearer as a discharge until the ratification of the definite Treaty of peace, previous to which time and until proclamation thereof shall be made, he is to be considered as being on furlough — George Washington."[21]

In 1790, Benjamin Epton received his grant to lot 7 in the town of Camillus.

The People of the State of New York, by the Grace of God, free and independent. To all to whom these presents shall come, Greeting: Know ye, that in pursuance of an act of our legislature, passed the sixth day of April, one thousand seven hundred and ninety, entitled, an act to carry into effect the concurrent resolutions and acts of the legislature for granting certain lands promised to be given and bounty lands, and for other purposes therein mentioned, We have given, granted and confirmed, and by these presents do give, grant and confirm unto Benjamin Epton, all that certain tract or lot of land situate, lying and being in the County of Montgomery, and in the township of Camillus known . . . by Lot number seven, containing six hundred acres, together with all and singular the rights, hereditaments and appurtenances, . . . On condition never the less that within the term of seven years to be computed from the first day of January next ensuing the date hereof, there shall be one actual settlement made on the said tract or lot of land hereby granted, otherwise, these, our letters patent, and the estate hereby granted, shall cease, determine and

---

[21] Recorded in Hall, *Early History of Military Tract*.

become void. . . . this sixth day of July, in the year of our Lord, one thousand seven hundred and ninety, and in the fifteenth year of our independence.[22]

About six years previously, however, on November 10, 1784, Benjamin Epton seems to have sold his land to John Suffern — but apparently Suffern did not or could not prove his claim.

> THIS INDENTURE made the tenth day of November one thousand seven hundred and eighty-four, between BEN-JAMIN EPTON, a privet soldier in the Second New York Regiment, of the first part, and John Suffern, of the New Antrinn of Orange County, Esqr. of the other part, WIT-NESSETH that the said Benjamin Epton, . . . hath sold . . . my right, title, claim, interest and demand from Congress or the United States to One Hundred Acres of land due me as a bounty as well as all my right, title, claim and demand from the State of New York to six hundred acres of land due me as a bounty and I do by these presents sell, release, convey, confirm and forever quit-claim unto John Suffern aforesaid all and every my above deeded rights, to have and to hold the same as his won and his heirs right against me and my heirs forever, and I do hereby empower the Surveyor-General of the United States and of his State to convey whatever lands are due me for my services as afore-said to convey the same unto John Suffern or to his lawful representatives and their heirs forever. In witness whereof I have hereunto set my hand and fixed my seal the day above written. Benjamin his mark Epton. Sealed and delivered in the presents of Jonas Secor, Jonat Youngs.

Epton appears to have successfully sold his land to Charles Weissenfel, on November 12, 1784.

> I, BENJAMIN EPTON, do acknowledge to have sold unto Mr. Charles F. Weissenfel all my rights of land due me from the State of New York and the publick for my services as a

---

[22] Ibid.

soldier in the 2d New York Regiment in the service of the
United States, for which I subscribe my name as a security
to the said Weissenfel on the back of this discharge as witness my hand and seal this 12th day of Novr. 1784.
Witness John Satten, Benjamin Epton, his mark.

Apparently the second claim was validated. The entry for his pension application reads: "Epton, Benjamin, N.Y., BLWts. 7095 &
7901-100-Pvt. Iss. 12/10/1789 to C.F. Weissenfels, ass. No
papers."[23] Benjamin Epton is not listed in New York State in any
federal census index from 1790 to 1820.

---

[23] *Index of Revolutionary War Pension Applications,* p. 175.

CHAPTER 15

County Historians for
the State of New York

D o you have an obscure ancestor who's hiding in the mists of time? Or do you want to know more about your ancestor's life than just a few dates? Interested in the local history of a faraway township? Perhaps it's time to consider consulting a county historian. An expert in local history, the historian possesses records that may not be widely available in larger collections.

New York State has required the appointment of historians as part of local government since 1919. The appointments and the job descriptions are local, varying from one location to another, but in general county and municipal historians oversee the historical files of their communities, educate the public and the schools, promote historic preservation, oversee historic sites, and run historical commemorations. They work closely with researchers, libraries, historical societies, genealogical societies, and every segment of the general public.[1]

The county historian will tell you what records are available. For example, the county historian's office (*www.rootsweb.com/ ~nywyomin/*) in Wyoming, New York, has over four file cabinets of genealogical queries and more than seventy genealogies. The

---

An earlier version of this chapter was posted at *www.NewEnglandAncestors.org* September 7, 2000.

[1] County Historians Association of New York State in cooperation with the New York State Education Department, Division of Historical Services. *1997 Directory of New York State County and Municipal Historians, County Historians Association of New York State* (Albany, N.Y.: County Historians Association of New York State, 1997).

marriage records of Clinton County are accessible only for the years 1908 to 1936 and are kept in the County Clerk's Office (*www.clintoncountygov.com/Departments/CC/CCHome.htm*). The documents in a county historian's office might include genealogies, census records, local histories, newspapers, wills, cemetery records, church records, vital records, tax lists, maps, and photographs.

A county historian's response to genealogical queries varies from one county to the next, but the majority do not do genealogical research. The Wayne County historian, for example, will search the office records; at the time of publication, fees are $20 per hour, with a $10 minimum charge. (There is generally no charge for people who go to the office to do their own searching or for residents of the county.) Your query must be concise and specific. There is an online form (available at *www.co.wayne.ny.us/Departments/historian/historian.htm*). Other county historians, however, such as the one for Sullivan County, do not do genealogical research and may not even have access to genealogical records. Usually, however, the county historian will be able to put you in touch with local historians who will do research and will be able to supply you with information if you know exactly what you want.

If you request information from a county historian, be sure to include all pertinent facts, but be concise. Supply a surname and dates as best you know them; your relationship to this person is not relevant. Be very clear about what you want. Stick to one item at a time. Include a stamped, self-addressed envelope (big enough to hold the anticipated reply). The office may be open only part-time and may be understaffed. Please be patient, kind, and courteous. The office does not have a large budget, so don't expect a return long-distance telephone call, but you should get an email response.

Table 1 lists county historians for New York. This information was obtained from the Association of Public Historians of New York State (*www.aphnys.org*). Visit their website for the most current contact information.

Table 1
COUNTY HISTORIANS FOR THE STATE OF NEW YORK

County	County Historian	Contact Information
Albany	John N. Travis	112 State St., Room 800, Albany, NY 12209
Allegany	Craig R. Braack	7 Court St., Belmont, NY 14813
Bronx	Dr. Lloyd Ultan	3309 Bainbridge Ave., Bronx, NY 10467
Broome	Gerald R. Smith	185 Court St., Binghamton, NY 13901
Cattaraugus	Carol A. Ruth	P.O. Box 32, Machias, NY 14101
Cayuga	Sheila S. Tucker	Historic Post Office, 3rd fl., 157 Genesee St., Auburn, NY 13021
Chautauqua	Michelle Henry	P.O. Box 170, Mayville, NY 14757
Chemung	James Arthur Kieffer	1011 Lincoln St., Elmira, NY 14901
Chenango	Dale C. Storms	Museum, 45 Rexford St., Norwich, NY 13815
Clinton	Addie L. Shields	137 Margaret St., Plattsburgh, NY 12901
Columbia	Mary Howell	490 County Rte. 10, Germantown, NY 12526
Cortland	Jeremy Boylan	46 Greenbush St., Suite 101, Cortland, NY 13045
Delaware	Patrick H. Grimes	P.O. Box 105, Bovina Center, NY 13740
Dutchess	Stan Mersand	170 Washington St., Poughkeepsie, NY 12601
Erie	William H. Siener	264 Middlesex, Buffalo, NY 14216
Essex	Margaret Gibbs	Court St., Elizabethtown, NY 12932
Franklin	Terry DeCarr (Society Trustee)	Franklin County Historical & Museum Society, 51 Milwaukee St., P.O. Box 388, Malone, NY 12953
Fulton	Peter C. Betz	Office of the County Historian, Fulton County Office Bldg., 228 W. Main St., Johnston, NY 12095
Genesee	Susan L. Conklin	3 W. Main St., Batavia, NY 14020
Greene	Raymond Beecher Charles B. Swain, Minorities	138 Beecher Rd., Coxsackie, NY 12051 R.D. #1, Box 76, Athens, NY 12015
Hamilton	Paul Wilbur	County Office Bldg., Rte. 8, Lake Pleasant, NY 12108
Herkimer	James M. Greiner	318 Margaret St., Herkimer, NY 13350
Jefferson	Jim Ranger	175 Arsenal St., Watertown, NY 13601
Kings		

continued on next page

Table 1 *(cont.)*

County	County Historian	Contact Information
Lewis	Lisa Becker	7552 South State St., P.O. Box 446, Lowville, NY 13367
Livingston	Amie Alden	5 Murray Hill Dr., Mt. Morris, NY 14510
Madison	Sarah Davies	County Bldg., North Court St., Wampsville, NY 13163
Monroe	Carolyn S. Vacca	Rundel Library, 115 South Ave., Rochester, NY 14604
Montgomery	Kelly A. Yacobucci Farquhar	History & Archives, Old Courthouse, P.O. Box 1500, Fonda, NY 12068
Nassau	Edward J.Smits	14 Wavy Lane, Wantagh, NY 11793
New York	Michael Miscione	1 Centre St., 19th fl., New York, NY 10007
Niagara	Catherine L. Emerson	Civil Defense Bldg., 139 Niagara St., Lockport, NY 14094
Oneida	Don White	1608 Genesee St., Utica, NY 13502
Onondaga	Vacant	31 Montgomery, Syracuse, NY 13202
Ontario	Dr. Preston E. Pierce	209 Davidson Ave., Canandaigua, NY 14424
Orange	Theodore Sly	1841 Court House, 101 Main St., Goshen, NY 10924
Orleans	C. W. Lattin	34 E. Park St., Albion, NY 14411
Oswego		
Otsego	Nancy Milavec	R.R.2, Box 297, Worcester, NY 12197
Putnam	Allan J. Warnecke	68 Marvin Ave., Brewster, NY 10509
Queens	Stanley Cogan	35–37 211th St., Bayside, NY 11361
Rensselaer	Vacant	Rensselaer County Historical Society, 59 Second St., Troy, NY 12180
Richmond		
Rockland	Thomas F. X. Casey	12 Ashwood Lane, Garnerville, NY10923
Saratoga	Kristina Saddlemire Reese	Bldg. #1, 40 McMaster St., Ballston Spa, NY 12020
Schenectady	Don Rittner	c /o County Manager's Office, County Office Bldg., 6th fl., Schenectady, NY 12305
Schoharie	Harold Zoch	P.O. Box 449, Middleburgh, NY 12122

County	County Historian	Contact Information
Schuyler	Barbara Bell	3460 County Rd., 28, Watkins Glen, NY 14891
Seneca	Walter Gable	Seneca County Office Bldg., 1 DiPronio Dr., Waterloo, NY 13165
St. Lawrence	Trent A. Trulock	Silas Wright House, P.O. Box 8, Canton, NY 13617
Steuben	Twila O'Dell	3 East Pulteney Sq., Bath, NY 14810
Suffolk	J. Lance Mallamo	180 Little Neck Rd., Box 0605, Centerport, NY 11721
Sullivan	John Conway	P.O. Box 185, Barryville, NY 12919
Tioga	Emma Sedore	P.O. Box 307, 16 Court St., Owego, NY 13827
Tompkins	Carol Kammen	125 E Court St, Ithaca, NY 14850
Ulster	Karlyn Knaust Elia	11 Main St., Saugerties, NY 12477
Warren		Warren County Municipal Center, 1340 State Rte. 9, Lake George, NY 12845
Washington	Deborah R. Beahan	Washington County Municipal Center, 383 Broadway, Fort Edward, NY 12828
Wayne	Peter K. Evans	9 Pearl St., P.O. Box 131, Lyons, NY 14489
Westchester	Vacant	Westchester Historical Archives, 2199 Saw Mill River Rd., Elmsford, NY 10523
Wyoming	Doris Bannister	26 Linwood Ave., Suite 1, Warsaw, NY 14569
Yates	Frances Dumas	110 Court St., Penn Yan, NY 14527

If the records available from the county historian's office do not bear fruit, don't give up. Perhaps the state historian can help. Visit *www.nysm.nysed.gov/services/srvstate.html* for more information. There is more local history available from town and village historians. Their addresses are available from the county historian's office. County websites often list names of, and contact information for, municipal historians. Another possibility is a county or municipal historical society. Some larger public libraries have a librarian who specializes in local history. All these people will be able to suggest records that may prove useful in your search for your ancestors.

CHAPTER 16

New York State Council of Genealogical Organizations (NYSCOGO)

T he New York State Council of Genealogical Organizations (NYSCOGO) is an umbrella organization for genealogical groups in New York State that may be of some assistance to genealogists doing research in the state. NYSCOGO (pronounced nice-CO-go) provides a statewide voice for genealogical interests, a means of communication among researchers, education via workshops and seminars, and helpful publications. NYSCOGO was founded in 1991 to accomplish the following stated goals:[1]

- To promote interest in genealogy
- To increase communication among researchers and genealogists
- To provide a forum for local and statewide discussion of the care, use, preservation, and accessibility of records related to genealogy
- To utilize various educational means to further knowledge regarding genealogy

To improve accessibility of state records related to genealogy, a NYSCOGO representative sits on the advisory board of the State Archives and Records Administration (SARA). Unlike the situation in the various New England states, vital records in New York State are not readily available. Until 2000, the index to the state's vital

---

An earlier version of this chapter was posted at *www.NewEnglandAncestors.org* October 4, 2002.

[1] Presented verbatim from the membership brochure.

records was only available to the public at two locations — the New York State Archives in Albany and the National Archives Northeast Region in New York City. Owing in part to this organization's advocacy, a copy of the index to the state's vital records was added to the public library in Rochester as well.[2] This is a concrete example of how a small organization can help make a big difference. As this index becomes available at more sites, researchers will be able to confirm quickly that an event has been recorded. Sometimes a researcher is looking for only one specific piece of information, and finding it easily will eliminate months of waiting.

The council has an active publications committee, which aims to produce publications that link researchers with sources.[3] They try not to compete with or rework existing guides, but instead choose an area in which the guide is missing. The data collection and writing are done entirely by NYSCOGO members. In 1996, NSYCOGO published its *Guide to Naturalization Records of New York State*. Updated in 2001, this 44-page finding aid contains a listing of sites within the state that hold naturalization records. Listings are arranged by county, beginning with the year 1790, and a description of the holdings of each site is included. The publication is available through member organizations as well as from NYSCOGO itself. You may obtain a copy by sending a check for $10, plus $3 for shipping and handling, to NYSCOGO at P.O. Box 2593, Syracuse, NY 13220-2593.

A guide to Native American records is currently in preparation. Similar to the previous publication, it will describe available sources of Native American data of use to genealogists. It will cover all sixty-two counties, including New York City. Work on this publication contains the added twist that tribal reservations usually have their own historians. Sensitive to this, NYSCOGO is considering limiting the guide to sources outside the reservation and providing contact information for reservation officials for further details.

---

[2] See Chapter 6 for additional information about vital records.

[3] The committee was formerly chaired by Ruth Metzler and is now chaired by Joyce Cook.

**N.Y. STATE COUNCIL OF
GENEALOGICAL ORGANIZATIONS**

P.O. Box 2593
Syracuse, New York 13220-2593

Welcome!

To the home page of the New York State Council of Genealogical Organizations. NYSCOGO was formed in 1991 to facilitate communication between genealogical and historical groups. NYSCOGO provides a forum for local and state-wide action and interest in the genealogical field.

Membership

Any genealogical organization in New York State is eligible for membership, which entitles the naming of two delegates who serve as the link between NYSCOGO and the individual society. "Genealogical organization" is defined as any organization that considers itself to have a genealogical function, including, but not limited to, genealogical, lineage and historical societies, libraries or archives with local history and genealogical collections.

Website for the New York State Council of Genealogical Organizations (*www.rootsweb.com/~nyscogo/*).

The council's quarterly member newsletter, *The Lifeline,* contains information about upcoming events and local society programs, and includes a calendar of events submitted by member organizations. The calendar also includes notices of meetings and conferences for larger organizations, such as the Federation of Genealogical Societies and the National Genealogical Society. In addition, *The Lifeline* publishes other items of news from member organizations such as the debut of the Niagara County Genealogical Society website; a project by the Jefferson County Genealogical Society to inventory holdings of libraries, museums, etc. in their county; a project by the Western New York Genealogical Society to copy nineteenth-century records in their eight-county region; and the twenty-fifth anniversary celebration of the Northeastern New York Genealogical Society.

Readers will also find original articles of general interest to genealogists. The winter issue of 2000–1 (Vol. 8, No. 32) contains an article by newsletter editor Joyce H. Cook titled "State Archives' New

Website an Award-Winner!" In this article we learn that the New York State Archives website, *www.archives.nysed.gov,* had received an Ancestry Family History Favorite Award from Ancestry.com. Details about the content of the website and instruction on how to navigate through it are clearly discussed. The summer 2001 issue (Vol. 9, No. 2) leads with an article by June Partridge Zintz, the council's treasurer, titled "New Equipment in the FHL in Salt Lake City." In this article members are informed, among other changes, of a new capability at the Family History Library — the ability to enhance microfilmed images and transfer the image onto CD-ROM for use at home.

NYSCOGO has a speakers' bureau of individuals willing to give presentations in their area of expertise. The list of speakers and topics is a resource available to member organizations for use in planning their individual meetings. NYSCOGO holds two meetings each year, one in the spring and another in the fall. These daylong meetings are open to the public. The location and topics vary, but the site is usually at or close to an archive or library. Members can combine a personal research trip with the meeting. Occasionally the meetings are held in conjunction with other society meetings.

NYSCOGO members include genealogical societies, historical societies, archives, family lineage groups, and libraries, as well as interested individuals. Ten years after it was founded, NYSCOGO membership was evenly split between individual members and organizational members — over thirty of each. Organizations designate two members to act as delegates to attend meetings and to transmit NYSCOGO information to their societies. Dues are $10 for individuals and $25 for organizations.

PART II

PEOPLE AND PLACES

CHAPTER 17

The Settlement of
New York State

EUROPEAN SETTLERS

The story of the settlement of New York State opens with Henry Hudson's exploration up the Hudson River in 1609. The next two centuries saw the frontier move westward and northward. The movement was not steady, but rather episodic, shaped by political events in North America and in Europe.

The Dutch period lasted from 1609 to 1664. Land policy was based on the European model. That is, landed gentry owned large tracts of land, granted to them as "patents" by the Dutch rulers. They in turn leased the land to tenant farmers. Despite this model for farming, the economy relied not on agriculture, but on trade, specifically the very profitable fur trade. Dutch settlements, often fortified, expanded north along the Hudson River and then west along the Mohawk River.

The period of Dutch settlement ended in 1664 when the English seized the territory. Charles II made a grant to his brother, the Duke of York and Albany, of all the territory claimed by the Dutch, and he commissioned the duke to take possession. Fort New Amsterdam surrendered in August of that year and Fort Orange shortly thereafter. In honor of the king's brother, the names New Amsterdam and Orange were changed to New York and Albany. Dutch landowners were able to keep their property; they themselves simply became subjects of the English crown. The English continued the policy of granting huge tracts of land to political favorites.

An earlier version of this chapter was posted at *www.NewEnglandAncestors.org* March 28, 2000.

While England slowly expanded her presence westward and north-ward, France moved southward out of Canada. England and France were to fight four wars in North America, each linked to European conflicts. The European wars were sparked by European politics, but in North America the competition was for the fur trade. Both the French and the English wanted the Iroquois as allies in the trade. The French established Fort Frontenac north of Lake Ontario in 1673 and Fort Niagara between Lakes Ontario and Erie in 1687. They aimed to take possession of the Hudson Valley (to have a bet-ter outlet to the sea), to deprive the Iroquois of English guns, to end English rivalry in the west, and to take control of the fur trade. During this time, from 1689 to 1763, expansion proceeded slowly during times of peace and faltered during times of war as frontier settlements were destroyed.

EMIGRATION DURING THE EUROPEAN WARS

King William's War (1689–97) was the first of the four wars. The conflict was part of a larger European struggle between the Grand Alliance (Austria, England, Netherlands, Savoy, Spain) and France. In 1690 the French and Indians attacked and destroyed the frontier outpost of Schenectady. Trade and settlement naturally declined. The Peace of Ryswick, which ended the war, failed to resolve the con-flicts, and war resumed in 1701. In Europe, Queen Anne's War (1701–13) was known as the War of the Spanish Succession. While the major battles took place outside New York, there was a decline in people entering the colony to settle.

During this time, the ill-starred immigration of Palatine families into New York began. (For more information on the Palatines, see Chapter 24.) These German settlers had left homes in the Palatinate region, on the Rhine River, after the devastation attending the wars of Louis XIV in the second half of the seventeenth century. Queen Anne, who had given them food and shelter in England, advanced the money to pay their emigration expenses. Late in 1709, four thousand set sail. Officials in New York expected these families to produce naval sup-plies (pitch and tar), but the Palatines wanted their own farms and believed that Queen Anne had promised them land. In the winter of 1712–13, after much heated debate, fifty stubborn Palatine families left the Hudson Valley and cleared a way through the wood to the Schoharie Valley (southwest of Schenectady). The following spring, many of the Palatines joined them, even though legally they were squatters. After attacking the sheriff, who tried to move them, and getting no support from government officials in London, they migrated south to Conestoga, Pennsylvania. Thirty families departed New York in the summer of 1723, fifty in 1725, and more in 1729.

The Scotch-Irish settlement of the state proved more successful. In 1740 a well-to-do Scotsman, John Lindsay, came with his family and servants to Cherry Valley, south of the Mohawk River and slightly west of the earlier Palatine settlement. In the next year he was joined by a group of thirty Scotch-Irish, including the families of David Ramsey, William Galt, William Dickson, and James Campbell, all from Londonderry, New Hampshire, led by Rev. Samuel Dunlop. Within a short time, sixty more families arrived and the settlement boasted a gristmill, sawmill, church, and school.

The Treaty of Utrecht that terminated Queen Anne's War was not successful at forging a lasting peace. King George's War (1744–48) followed, known in Europe as the War of the Austrian Succession. The Treaty of Aix-la-Chapelle provided an interval of peace until the beginning of the final conflict, the French and Indian War (1754–63), known as the Seven Years War in Europe, where it did last that long. This war proved decisive, and in the end the French withdrew. The Treaty of Paris in 1763 ended French control in Canada and all its territories east of the Mississippi River (except New Orleans).[1] In all of these conflicts the majority of the actual fighting took place outside New York. Nevertheless, Indian raids on the frontier and the state of war in general had a negative effect on trade and discouraged new settlements. After each treaty trade would pick up and a wave of new settlers would sweep westward.

---

[1] After the French Revolution, some efforts were made to establish permanent settlements of French colonists in what later became Lewis County. They located a hamlet on the lake shore, and others at Long Falls (Carthage), High Falls (Lyons Falls), and on the site of the present village of Castorland. The experiment failed, however. Unfit for the hardships of pioneer life, the French refugees abandoned their desolate homes and moved to more populated towns or returned to their native country.

With each outbreak of war and its inevitable Indian raids on the frontier, the wave would recede.

BRITISH CONSOLIDATION

Following the victory over France, Britain sought to improve her relationship with the Indians, who were not pleased with constant expansion of white settlement. Britain sought to establish a western limit to white settlement. The slightly vague Proclamation Line, issued on 7 October 1763, defined this boundary as lands lying west of the drainage of the Susquehanna River. In 1763 this was west of the frontier in New York, and its vagueness was of no consequence. Five years later, in October 1768, the more definite Fort Stanwix treaty line was agreed upon. Fort Stanwix was located at the "Carrying Place," the portage between Wood Creek and the Mohawk River, site of the present-day city of Rome. This line followed the east branch of the Susquehanna River to Owego, southeast to the Delaware River, along that to the junction of the Unadilla River and the Susquehanna River, along the Unadilla River to its head, to Wood Creek west to Fort Stanwix.

POST-REVOLUTIONARY SETTLEMENT

After the Revolutionary War, land policy changed fundamentally. In place of patent grants, large tracts of land were purchased by land speculators with a view to selling parcels to individual settlers. These speculators provided a valuable function in preparing the frontier by surveying the land and building roads. Many of them, however, including the famous financier Robert Morris, went bankrupt. In less than fifty years after the Revolutionary War, huge areas of the state made the transition from frontier to settled agriculture. Several important purchases include, from east to west, the Military Tract, the Phelps-Gorham Purchase, the Holland Purchase, and, in the northeast, Macomb's Purchase.

The northeastern part of the state was the last to be settled. The region was virtually unbroken wilderness in 1783 except for a few settlements along Lake Champlain. Most of the region lying between Lake Champlain on the east, Lake Ontario on the west, the St. Lawrence River on the north, and the southern slopes of the Adirondacks remained wilderness until late in the nineteenth century. The rugged topography, the stony soils, the shortness of the growing season and the lack of roads discouraged settlers, who preferred central and western New York. The St. Lawrence and Black River valleys did attract several thousand settlers, largely from Vermont, between 1783 and 1825. Pioneers coming from eastern and central New York to break ground in the northern wilderness generally followed two possible routes. Many chose to follow the Mohawk River, Wood Creek, Oneida Lake, and Oswego River route to Lake Ontario, and thence down the St. Lawrence to the mouth of the river that led to the desired location. Leaving the Mohawk at Utica or Rome, they could follow blazed trails overland to the Black River at High Falls (Lyons Falls). The second route to the new country followed the Lake Champlain waterway to the Chateaugay River and westward. It was mainly traveled in the winter, when sleighs could cross the frozen Lake Champlain and traverse the rough path that had been cut through in 1798. This was the route over which great numbers came from Vermont and other parts of New England.

THE MILITARY TRACT

When the French and Indian War ended in 1763, New York State veterans began to demand fulfillment of promises made by the government of New York and the United States, that every soldier would be granted 600 acres as a bounty. (For more information about the military tract, see Chapter 14.) For this purpose, the legislature in 1782 had set aside a tract of land approximately bounded on the north by Lake Ontario, the Oswego and Oneida Rivers, and Oneida Lake; on the west by Seneca Lake; on the south by a line drawn through the most southerly inclination of Seneca Lake; and on the east by the Oneida and Tuscarora Country (present eastern boundaries of Onondaga and Cortland Counties). This included the modern counties of Seneca, Cayuga, Onondaga, nearly all of Cortland, and portions of Wayne, Oswego, Schuyler, and Tompkins.

Unfortunately, some of this territory was west of the Fort Stanwix treaty line and thus conflicted with Indian rights. In 1786 the state passed a law forbidding the soldiers to take possession of their allotments. Since the possibility of extinguishing the Indian title seemed remote, twelve townships in the north were appropriated to satisfy

1805 Map of New York from *General Atlas* by Arrowsmith and Lewis (Philadelphia: John Conrad, 1804).

the soldiers. This tract, known as "The Old Military Tract," was in the extreme northern part of the state, where there were no Indian claimants to hinder settlement. Veterans also had no interest in the land, which was poor for farming.

Treaties with the Onondagas (1788) and the Cayugas (1789) made it possible for the state to open up the Military Tract to the long-suffering soldiers. It was laid out into twenty-eight townships, containing approximately 60,000 acres each, and subdivided into 100 lots. The townships were given classical designations, such as Cicero, Brutus, Scipio, Homer, and Virgil. A soldier who accepted the 100 acres the United States granted outside the state could claim only 500 in New York and had to surrender the 100 acres in the southeastern corner of each lot, which later became known as the "State's Hundred." Provision was made for the reservation of a lot of 400 acres in each township for the support of the gospel, and two lots of 200 acres for schools.

THE PHELPS-GORHAM PURCHASE[2]

By treaty with the Indians, signed 8 July 1788, Nathaniel Gorham, Oliver Phelps, and their associates purchased a tract of land bounded on the north by Lake Ontario, on the south by the Pennsylvania border, on the east by the preemption line, and on the west by a line running north from the Pennsylvania border to the shore of Lake Ontario. Most parcels in this tract, except those around the river, were uniform six-mile squares. The original Phelps-Gorham Purchase of 1789, transferred to Robert Morris in 1791, opened up 2.5 million acres in central New York. The majority of settlers came from Massachusetts, Vermont, Connecticut, and Pennsylvania. In less than a year Morris's London agents had sold the tract, at more than double the price, to three Englishmen, Sir William Pulteney, William Hornby, and Patrick Colquhoun.

THE HOLLAND PURCHASE[3]

The Holland Purchase comprised 2.5 million acres west of the Genesee River. Three years before the close of the century, one settler was living at the mouth of the Cattaraugus Creek on Lake Erie. Near the Pennsylvania border, in the southwestern part of the present county of Cattaraugus was a Friends' Mission established in 1798. Later the Friends purchased 300 acres from the Holland Land Company and built mills that supplied lumber and ground corn for both the Indians and themselves. Surveying, supervised by Joseph Ellicott, began in 1798. The east line of the territory, known as the Transit Line, started at the Pennsylvania–New York border, twelve miles west of the Phelps-Gorham Purchase, then due north to almost the center of the town of Stafford in Genesee County, west two or three miles, and due north to Lake Ontario. This large tract of undeveloped property was divided into ranges, and townships six miles square. Ellicott began selling land in the Holland Purchase in 1800. Handbills were distributed in the east that emphasized the advantages of a finely watered country, valuable timbers, good soil, and

---

[2] For more information about the Phelps-Gorham purchase, see Chapter 17.

[3] For information about the Holland Purchase, see Chapter 21.

choice of level or hilly land. In the early years, sales were greater in the eastern part because of easy access to settlements in the Genesee country, where provisions were obtainable.

In 1812 the Holland Purchase in the Genesee Country included about 25,000 inhabitants, but frontier conditions prevailed nearly everywhere west of the Genesee River. It has been estimated that the average extent of improvements upon the farms did not exceed fifteen acres. Except for the framed residences at Batavia and Buffalo, most of the houses were made of logs. A considerable number of the inhabitants were poor but made a scanty subsistence. Many had spent their savings to move to the Holland Purchase.

THE MACOMB PURCHASE

Alexander Macomb, a native of Ireland, received his first patent of 1,920,000 acres in 1792, the largest grant ever made by the state to an individual. It embraced the whole of present-day Lewis County, part of Oswego, and almost all of St. Lawrence, Franklin, and Jefferson counties. At intervals he acquired additional patents until 1798, when he had doubled his holdings. He divided his holdings into six tracts. Tracts IV, V, and VI fell under the supervision of William Constable, who took over complete control after Macomb became insolvent. Constable sold smaller tracts to John Brown of Providence, who divided his tract into townships named Frugality, Industry, and Temperance.[4] The labels, while politically correct in that Yankee culture, did nothing to improve the soil or the climate. Grants II and III of the Macomb Purchase were more slowly and sparsely settled, partly because of the sandy soil, which made them unsuitable for agricultural purposes, and partly because of their remoteness from the natural routes of entrance into northern New York.

By 1825 the settlement of New York was virtually complete. The growing network of turnpikes and canals meant that settlers moving into pockets of uninhabited territory were linked to established communities. True frontier conditions no longer existed.

---

[4] For more information about the Brown Tract, see Chapter 23.

SOURCES

F. S. Eastman, *A History of the State of New York* (New York: Augustus K. White, 1833).

David M. Ellis, James A. Frost, Harold C. Syrett, Harry J. Carman, *A History of New York State* (Ithaca, N.Y.: Cornell University Press, 1967).

Dixon Ryan Fox, *Yankees and Yorkers* (New York: New York University Press, 1940).

Francis Whiting Halsey, *The Old New York Frontier* (New York: Charles Scribner's Sons, 1901).

Ruth L. Higgins, *Expansion in New York* (Columbus, Ohio: Ohio State University, 1931).

CHAPTER 18

The Phelps-Gorham Purchase

T he opening of western New York State to settlement after the Revolutionary War was impeded because ownership of the land was contested — this region, the "Genesee Country," was long claimed by both Massachusetts and New York. General John Sullivan, who led his army on an expedition to subdue the Indians in 1779, had explored the region. When his soldiers returned to Massachusetts, Connecticut, New Hampshire, and eastern New York, they brought back a favorable opinion of the land. The conflicting claims of ownership prevented legal purchase, though. Resolution of the dispute became more urgent. When the matter was finally resolved, in 1787, the right to sell a 2.6 million-acre tract lying between the so-called Preemption Line on the east and the Genesee River on the west eventually devolved to Oliver Phelps and Nathaniel Gorham, prominent Massachusetts businessmen, and their company of investors. This company suffered financial reverses and in 1790, after less than two years, transferred all unsold holdings to Robert Morris. Nevertheless, Phelps and Gorham had sold approximately half of their original purchase, and the settlement of the Genesee Country was well underway.

THE STATES' CLAIMS

A confusing collection of contradictory royal charters from James I, Charles I, and Charles II, mixed with a succession of treaties with the Dutch and with the Indians, made the legal situation intractable.

An earlier version of this chapter was posted at *www.NewEnglandAncestors.org* February 25, 2000.

Massachusetts asserted priority of charter on the disputed claims. All the land on the eastern coast from the 34th to the 45th parallel was granted by James I in 1606 to the London Company and the Virginia Company. The colonists of Plymouth, Massachusetts, had gotten their charter from the Virginia Company, but they settled in land belonging to the London Company. So in 1620 James I granted land from the 40th to the 48th parallel from sea to sea to the council in Plymouth, England, which issued a sub-grant in 1621 to the colonists. In 1628 the same council issued another sub-grant, also running from sea to sea, to the Boston Company. Both charters expressly excepted "all lands actually possessed and inhabited by an other Christian prince or state." This became a point of debate.

New York based its right to the region on Henry Hudson's claim of New Netherland for Holland in 1609, which predates the 1620 and 1628 grants of Massachusetts. The western boundary was based on Indian treaties.[1] New York pointed out that all of the Indian treaties had been obtained through the efforts of officials of New York, deeds were witnessed by New York officials, no other colony was mentioned in the treaties, and New York paid treaty expenses. In 1640 Charles II granted New Netherland to his brother, the Duke of York and Albany, later James II. New York claimed that when England took over the Dutch holdings in 1640, New York succeeded to the Dutch claim. Massachusetts agreed with this but claimed that the Dutch had not actually settled territory west of the Mohawk, and so that territory was not subject to the exemption stated in the 1620 and 1628 grants. Massachusetts also argued that the grant of Charles II did not define a western boundary and that the Indians had not ceded anything directly to New York.

RESOLUTION OF THE DISPUTE

The states' positions were entrenched, and no mutually acceptable agreement appeared likely. In May 1784 Massachusetts appealed to

---

[1] Note that the western boundary had been decided with the conclusion of the Revolutionary War. New York ceded to the United States all lands west of Lake Ontario on 1 March 1781. In 1785 Massachusetts also ceded its claim to the same area. Connecticut did not agree until 1800 and even so kept a portion in Ohio known as the Western Reserve.

the federal government, at that time the Continental Congress, self-styled final arbiter of disputes between states. Massachusetts asked Congress to appoint commissioners, whose decision would be final. Instead, Congress directed that the states appoint their own commissioners and have them appear before Congress to argue the case. When the commissioners appeared before Congress the following December, they were instructed to agree upon judges to hear the case. This was done by the following June. But the judges backed out before the case could be heard, and Congress agreed to postpone the case. The two state legislatures empowered their commissioners to settle the matter. After two and a half years of congressional inaction, the commissioners settled the dispute in two weeks at Hartford in December 1786.[2] Massachusetts surrendered its claim to the government, sovereignty, and jurisdiction of the entire state. New York conceded to Massachusetts the right of preemption to the soil (subject to Indian title) for that part of the state lying west of the Preemption Line.[3] That meant that Massachusetts had the right to buy the land from the Indians and could sell this right to individuals. If, however, Massachusetts sold the preemption right, the grantee had to have Massachusetts confirm any treaty with the Indians. Furthermore, when the land was purchased from the Indians — recorded in the office of New York's secretary of state — it would become part of New York. The two state legislatures ratified the agreement and submitted it to Congress for approval.

THE PHELPS-GORHAM PURCHASE

On April 1, 1787, Massachusetts sold to Nathaniel Gorham, Oliver Phelps, and their associates preemption right to 6.25 million acres west of the Preemption Line, subject to the Indian title. By treaty with the Indians, signed July 8, 1788, the associates, acting through Oliver Phelps, purchased a tract of land bounded on the north by

---

[2] They kept no record of their negotiations.

[3] A preemption right is the right to purchase something, especially government-owned land, before others; it also refers to a purchase made when such a right is granted. When an individual bought the preemption *right* to land, he or she did not buy the land but rather the right to buy the land.

Lake Ontario, on the south by the Pennsylvania border,[4] and on the east by the Preemption Line. On the west the boundary ran north from the Pennsylvania border to the confluence of Canaseraga Creek and the Genesee River. Thence it followed the river to a point two miles north of Canawagus village (the modern town of Avon), thence due west twelve miles, thence northward so as to be twelve miles distant from the Genesee River to the shore of Lake Ontario. The land was divided into ranges six miles wide running from north to south. Range 1 thus ran along the Preemption Line. Range 7 ran along the Genesee River. The ranges were divided into townships six miles square running from east to west. Township 1 lay on the Pennsylvania border. Township 14 bordered Lake Ontario. Thus the majority of the parcels, except those around the river, were squares six miles on a side. When Phelps bought the land from the Indians, Massachusetts had to confirm the sale, but the land became part of New York. Massachusetts confirmed its title of land east of the Genesee River on November 21, 1788. (The Indians were not willing at that time to sell land west of the Genesee.)

There was a rival claim to the territory by an association of influential New York businessmen — the New York Genesee Land Company, more familiarly known as "the Lessees." Their claim was based on a lease, obtained on November 30, 1787, of all the lands of the Six Nations. Legislatures of both New York and Massachusetts refused to recognize the validity of the lease. Nevertheless, the intrigues of this group persisted. Phelps agreed to convey four townships to them (townships 6, 7, and 8, range 1; and township 9, range 2) in exchange for a release of their claim. Phelps and Gorham reserved for themselves township 10, range 3, at the northern end of Canandaigua Lake, and township 9, range 7, the current town of Geneseo.

OLIVER PHELPS AND NATHANIEL GORHAM

Oliver Phelps was born at Windsor, Connecticut, October 21, 1749, and died at Canandaigua, New York, February 21, 1809. He married

---

[4] The eighty-second milestone on the New York–Pennsylvania border, where present-day Steuben and Chemung counties meet, slightly east of Corning.

Map of the Genessee Lands in Ontario County, from *The Documentary History of the State of New York* by E. B. O'Callaghan (Albany: Weed, Parsons & Company, 1849), vol. 2, p. 114.

Mary Seymour, daughter of Zachariah and Sarah (Steele) Seymour. Mary was born at Hartford on November 16, 1752, and died at Canandaigua September 13, 1826. In 1770 the couple settled in Granville, Massachusetts. They had one son, Oliver Leicester (born September 22, 1775; married Betsey Law Sherman; died at Canandaigua, New York, October 9, 1813; seven children) and a daughter, Mary (born September 5, 1778; married Amasa Jackson; died at New York City September 11, 1859; two children).

Oliver Phelps fought at the battle of Lexington and served in the Commissary Department of the Colonial Army. After the Revolution he moved to Suffield, Connecticut. He was a prominent businessman and was involved in state and national politics. He was a member of the Massachusetts State Assembly, a state senator, and a member of the Governor's Council. He organized the Phelps-Gorham partnership in 1788 and was the active agent in all explorations and negotiations. Phelps relocated to Canandaigua in 1802. He served as the first judge of Ontario County from its erection in

1789 until 1793, and as a New York state representative from 1803 to 1805.

Nathaniel Gorham was born at Charlestown, Massachusetts, May 27, 1738, son of Captain Nathaniel and Mary (Soley) Gorham. He died there of apoplexy on June 1, 1796. In 1763 he married Rebecca Call, daughter of Caleb Call. They had seven (one source says nine) children, including Nathaniel, Rebecca, Mary, Elizabeth Ann, John Benjamin, and Lydia. Gorham became a prominent merchant and was involved for most of his adult life in public affairs. He was a member of the Colonial legislature 1771–75 and a delegate to the Provincial Congress in 1774 and 1775. He was a member of the Board of War from 1778 until 1781, a member of the state Constitutional Convention in 1779, and a delegate to the Continental Congress in 1782–83 and 1785–87, being elected president of that body in June 1786.

Nathaniel Gorham never settled in the Genesee Country. His affairs in New York were handled by his son Nathaniel Gorham Jr., who moved to Canandaigua in 1789.

SALE OF PARCELS TO SPECULATORS AND EMIGRANTS

Original land purchase was often for speculation rather than settlement. The land was often resold quickly, and the original purchaser(s) did not always emigrate. For example, Oliver Phelps sold township 3, range 2, to Prince Bryant of Pennsylvania on September 5, 1789. A month later, on October 2, 1789, Prince Bryant sold the land to Elijah Babcock, who sold various parcels to Roger Clark, Samuel Tooker, David Holmes, and William Babcock.

Also, the original settlers were not always successful. With partial payment they received "articles of sale" instead of deeds; if they could not make the necessary payments, the land reverted to Phelps and was sold again. Table 1 lists original sales to speculators and settlers between April 1788 and November 1790 tabulated according to township and range numbers.

Table 1
PHELPS-GORHAM PURCHASE:
ORIGINAL SALES TO SPECULATORS AND SETTLERS,
APRIL 1788–NOVEMBER 1790

TOWNSHIP, RANGE, TOWN	PURCHASER	NOTES
short range, 2A, Rochester	Ebenezer Hunt, Robert Breck, Quartus Pomeroy, Samuel Henshaw, Samuel Hinckley, Moses Kingsley, Justin Ely	From Springfield and Northampton, Mass.
short range, 2C, Charlotte	Joseph Smith, Horatio Jones	Bounded by Genesee River and Lake Ontario.
T1, R2, Lindley	Col. Eleazur Lindsley, sons Samuel and Eleazur, sons-in-law Ezekiel Mulford and John Seeley, David Cook	By clerk's error "s" dropped in name of town.
T2, R1, Corning	Frederick Calkins, Caleb Gardner, Ephraim Peterson, Justus Wolcott, Peleg Gorton, Silas Wood	Calkins from Vt.; Wood did not emigrate.
T2, R2	Col. Arthur Erwin	Rev. War officer from Bucks Co., Pa.
T3, R2, Campbell	Prince Bryant	From Pa.
13, R5; 14, R6; Canisteo and Hornellsville	Solomon Bennett, Capt. John Jamison, Uriah Stephens, Benjamin Crosby and son Richard	From Wyoming Valley, Pa.
T6, R7	Col. Jeremiah Wadsworth	From Hartford, Conn.; acquainted with Phelps during Rev. War.
T6,7,8, R1; T9, R2	Leasees	—
T7, R2, Jerusalem	Benedict Robinson, Thomas Hathaway	Followers of religious sect founded by Jemima Wilkinson.
T8, R2, Potter	Benedict Arnold Potter	Follower of Jemima Wilkinson.

continued on next page

Table 1 *(cont.)*

TOWNSHIP, RANGE, TOWN	PURCHASER	NOTES
T8, R4, Bristol	Gamaliel Wilder, Joseph Gilbert	—
T9, R1	Benton and Livingston	Two of the lessees' company.
T9, R3,4, 5; Richmond and Bristol	Gideon Pitts, James Goodwin, Asa Simmons, Calvin Jacobs, John Smith	The Dighton Company, from Dighton, Mass. Title to Jacobs and Smith.
T9, R7, Geneseo	reserved for Phelps and Gorham	—
T10, R1	Gen. Israel Chapin, Capt. Dickinson	—
T10, R2, Hopewell	Gen. Israel Chapin, Capt. Nobel	—
T10, R3, Canandaigua	reserved for Phelps and Gorham	—
T10, R4, East Bloomfield	Capt. Wm Bacon, Gen. John Fellows, Elisha Lee, Deacon John Adams, Dr. Joshua Porter	Deacon Adams arrived first; William Bacon of Sheffield, Mass., never emigrated.
T10, R7	William Wadsworth, ___ Wells, ___ Lewis, Isaiah Thompson, Timothy Hosmer	From Conn.; Thompson and Hosmer only purchasers to become residents.
T11, R1	John Decker Robinson, Nathaniel Sanborn	—
T11, R2	Gen. Israel Chapin, Capt. Nobel	—
T11, R3 Farmington	Nathan Comstock, Benjamin Russell,* Abraham Lapham, Edmund Jenks,* Jeremiah Brown,* Ephraim Fish,* Nathan Herendeen, Nathan Aldrich, Stephen Smith,* Benjamin Rickensen,* William Baker,* Dr. Daniel Brown	First sale of purchase. Starred purchasers did not become residents, deed to Comstock and Russell, from Adams (Berkshire Co.), Mass.
T11, R4	Enos Broughton	From Stockbridge, Mass., clerk of William Walker.

TOWNSHIP, RANGE, TOWN	PURCHASER	NOTES
T12, R2 , Palmyra	John Swift, Col. John Jenkins	Agents for a group from Wyoming Valley, Pa. Jenkins was a surveyor.
T12, R4	William Walker	Local agent of Phelps and Gorham.
T12, R5, Pittsford	Simon and Israel Stone	Washington Co.
T13, R4, Penfield	Jonathan Fasset	From Vt.
T13, R5	Gen. Caleb Hyde, Prosper Polly, Enos Stone, Job Gilbert, Joseph Chaplin, John Lusk	From Lenox, Mass.
T14, R1	Talmage and Bartle	—

DISSOLUTION OF THE PARTNERSHIP

The favorable financial outcome envisioned by the original shareholders did not materialize. Fewer emigrants than anticipated reduced the income from land sales. Moreover, a rise in the value of the consolidated securities effectively increased the amount of their debt to four times what they had originally expected. Thus, at the end of the first year they were unable to meet their obligation. Two of the three bonds were canceled, and the third bond was reduced to less than one-third of its original amount. In order to meet even this reduced obligation, the syndicate was obliged to sell the lands it had not disposed of, and Robert Morris purchased about half of the original Phelps-Gorham purchase. The Commonwealth took back the preemption right of the lands west of the Genesee River (which the Indians were not willing to sell) on March 10, 1791. The state then sold the preemption right to this western portion to Robert Morris the next day, March 11, 1791. This land became known as the Holland Purchase because Robert Morris sold it to that group of Dutch bankers with the understanding that he, Morris, would extinguish Indian title (i.e., purchase it from the Indians through treaty), which he finally did in 1797.[5]

---

[5] For additional information on the Holland Purchase, see Chapters 9 and 21.

As part of the agreement with Robert Morris, the survey of the Phelps-Gorham Purchase was repeated and found to be seriously in error. (One source suggests it was deliberate.) The Preemption Line was straightened to include the town of Geneva. An equivalent acreage on the west, the Triangle Tract, was returned to the Indians. In less than a year Morris's London agents sold the tract, at more than double the price, to three Englishmen, Sir William Pulteney, William Hornby, and Patrick Colquhoun.[6] Since at the time noncitizens could not legally hold title to land, Charles Williamson was sent from Scotland and naturalized to hold the land in trust for the owners. Williamson established his own office in Bath, which he named for Sir William's daughter Laura, the countess of Bath. There he continued the work of opening up the Genesee Country to settlement.

SOURCES

Lewis Cass Aldrich, ed., *History of Yates Co., New York* (Syracuse, N.Y.: D. Mason, 1892).

George W. Coles, ed., *Landmarks of Wayne Co.* (Syracuse, N.Y.: D. Mason, 1895).

Lockwood R. Doty, *A History of Livingston County* (Jackson, Mich.: W. J. Van Deusen, 1905).

Howard C. Hosmer, *Monroe County 1821–1971* (Rochester, N.Y.: Rochester Museum and Science Center, 1971).

Blake McKellvey, *Rochester, The Water-Power City, 1812–1854* (Cambridge, Mass.: Harvard University Press, 1945), pp. 18–23.

Charles F. Milliken, *History of the Genesee Country,* Vol. 1, ed. Lockwood R. Doty (Chicago: S. J. Clarke Publishing Company, 1925), Chapters 12–13.

Seymour Morris, "Richard Seymour of Hartford and Norwalk, Conn., and Some of His Descendants," *Genealogies of Connecticut Families: from the New England Historical and Genealogical Register,* 3 volumes (Baltimore: Genealogical Publishing Co., 1983), Vol. 3, p. 328.

---

[6] For additional information on the Pulteney group, see Chapter 19.

Amos Otis, *Genealogical Notes of Barnstable Families,* Vol. 1 (Barnstable, Mass.: F. B. and F. P. Gross, 1888), p. 434.

William F. Peck, *Landmarks of Monroe County* (Boston, Mass.: Boston History Company, 1895).

O. S. Phelps and A. T. Servin, *The Phelps Family of America,* Vol. 2. (Pittsfield, Mass.: Eagle Publishing Company, 1899), pp. 1321–23, 1358–59.

Millard F. Roberts, ed., *Historical Gazetteer of Steuben Co., New York,* Part 1 (Syracuse, N.Y.: the author, 1891).

Richard Sherer, *Steuben County, The First 200 Years: A Pictorial History* (Virginia Beach, Va: Steuben County Bicentennial Commission, 1996).

W. B. Thrall, *Pioneer History and Atlas of Steuben County* (Perry N.Y.: W. B. Thrall, 1942).

Orsamus Turner, *History of the Pioneer Settlement of Phelps and Gorham's Purchase and Morris' Reserve* (Rochester, N.Y.: William Alling, 1851).

Vital Records of Granville, Massachusetts to the Year 1850 (Boston, Mass.: NEHGS, 1914).

CHAPTER 19

Pioneer Settlement
of the Pulteney Estate
and the Morris Reserve

At the close of the Revolutionary War, the new nation was poised for an era of very rapid expansion. In New York State at that time, European settlement ended at the Preemption Line, a roughly north-south line passing through Seneca Lake. A generation later the frontier had passed into Ohio and beyond. The legal machinery for getting the "wild lands" into the hands of individual settlers involved several steps. First, preemption rights were sold to large land speculators; these speculators essentially bought from the state of Massachusetts the right to buy the land from the Indians. After "extinguishing" the Indian rights, the speculators surveyed the land and sold pieces. In some cases the pieces, still large, were sold to other speculators. In other cases individual farms or village lots were sold.

The opening chapter of this migration is told in the preceding chapter in this book, on the Phelps-Gorham Purchase. Oliver Phelps and Nathaniel Gorham purchased the preemption rights to all of western New York in 1787, but were able to buy land from the Indians only as far west as the Genesee River. This portion of the state became known as the "Genesee Country." When Phelps and Gorham defaulted in 1791, they returned the preemption rights west of the Genesee Country to Massachusetts, which sold it to Robert Morris, the financier of the Revolution. Robert Morris also purchased the unsold lands in the Genesee Country, making him by far the largest land owner in the state.

Morris's purchase of preemption rights from Massachusetts involved several deeds, the first of which consisted of a strip approximately

Portrait of Robert Morris, from *The Pennsylvania Magazine of History and Biography*, 28 [1904]:273.

twelve miles wide to the west of the Genesee Country. This piece would become known as the Morris Reserve. Its western boundary, termed the Transit Line, defines the eastern boundary of what was termed the Niagara Country.

The history of the settlement of western New York state is thus conveniently divided into these three regions: the Genesee Country, the Morris Reserve, and the Niagara Country. In this chapter we consider both the remaining history of the Genesee Country under the administration of Charles Williamson, agent for the Pulteney group, and the disposition of land in the Morris Reserve. The Niagara Country was purchased from Robert Morris by the Holland Land Company. Its development is described in Chapter 21.

THE PULTENEY ESTATE

The London Association

Robert Morris held his lands in the Genesee Country for less than a year. In 1791 his London agent, William Temple Franklin, arranged a sale to a group of London businessmen called the London

Association. The association consisted of Sir William Pulteney, nine-twelfths share, John Hornby, two-twelfths share, and Patrick Colquhun, one-twelfth share. Because aliens were not, at that time, permitted to own land in the New York state, the group employed Charles Williamson, a naturalized Scotsman, as their agent in 1792. Thus the Genesee Country was quickly returned to a "retail" footing with regard to land sales, instead of the "wholesale" status of the large land speculators like Robert Morris. The London Association meant to sell land to individuals — to settlers who would clear trees, plant crops, and make the land productive.

When Charles Williamson arrived from Scotland, he was accompanied by Charles Cameron, John Johnstone, James Tower, Henry Tower, Andrew Smith, and Hugh McCartney. Much of the actual work of surveying and building was supervised by these business associates. Charles Williamson was clearly an adventuresome, daring, far-seeing man. He expended prodigious effort, not to mention capital, to attract settlers into his domain. There is hardly an early road in the Genesee Country that he did not build. He built saw mills. He built grist mills. He was made large donations to support the building of churches, schools, and theaters. Elected to the state legislature from Ontario County in 1796, he was also a judge in Ontario County.

Colonization Efforts

One of the early schemes put forward by the London Association was to import colonists who would labor together to build their own village in the wilderness, clear farms, and build roads. The first such experiment involved a German named Guillaume Berezy, who met with Patrick Colquhoun in London, gained his confidence, and was dispatched to Hamburg in 1791 to find suitable settlers. Charles Williamson chose the mouth of Canaseraga Creek at the Genesee River as the site for the new settlement. He plowed 80 acres of land and built several log cabins for the new settlers.

From the first, the enterprise was an exasperating failure. Writing in August 1793, Charles Williamson complained of Berezy: "I suppose'd we were treating with a Man of Honour who would religiously perform his Engagements, for it was supposed they were to be actual Farmers. In place of that, these people were found to consist of every species of idle Vagabonds. . . ."[1] Williamson, as was his custom, provided agricultural and household implements, seed corn, breeding stock of cattle and pigs, milk cows, and more. The settlers wasted these provisions and seemed unwilling and/or unable to perform the labors for which they had contracted. "The Germans engaged to build their own Houses, but Beavers would have built better," he complained in exasperation.[2] "Before I quit this subject it is necessary I should mention that I consider the act of the Germans slaughtering my Cattle, which they seized forcibly as a Robery, as I also do the killing of those delivered for Agricultural Purposes — Those acts I consider as particularly Criminal as there was not the shadow of excuse on accot. of want of Provisions."[3] Berezy claimed to have higher authority than Williamson. He finally instigated a riot, which led to the arrest of several ringleaders. (He himself fled to Philadelphia.) Eventually the London Association cut its losses, made a deal with Gov. Simcoe, and moved the settlers to Toronto.

A second colonization effort had a happier ending. The colonists were from Broadalbin, Perthshire, Scotland. The year was 1798. The location was "Big Springs" in present-day Livingston County, officially renamed Caledonia in 1806. Williamson met with the group in Johnstown, present-day Fulton County, to make his offer. However, they wanted to see the country for themselves. Accordingly, they sent Donald McPherson, Malcolm McLaren, Hugh McDerrmid, James McLaren, and John D. McVean to evaluate the land before accepting.

Donald McPherson wrote: "On our return to Geneva, Col Williamson treated us to peaches and other new fruit of the Genesee Country. He showed us his English stock cattle which we all admired, but much more so the man, Col Williamson. After we

---

[1] Copies of letters to and from Charles Williamson, Charles Cameron, Hector Mackenzie, Robert Morris, John Johnston, William Inman [et. al.] with various other documents relating to the settlement of the Genesee Country, 1791 to 1807, Charles Williamson, no publisher, no date, p. 292.

[2] Ibid., p. 299.

[3] Ibid., p. 302.

arrived in Caledonia again, with our families, we must all acknowledge that we found Col Williamson more noble and generous than he agreed or promised."[4]

Following his usual practice, Williamson erected both a gristmill and a sawmill for his Caledonia settlement and provided much additional assistance to the pioneer settlers. A more detailed, if somewhat florid, account of this enterprise has been written by Arthur Parker.[5]

Capital Expenditures and Land Development

Much of Williamson's expenditure of capital was for construction of roads, gristmills, sawmills, and the like. As the following letter from Robert Morris to Charles Williamson suggests, these expenditures negated any prospect for a quick profit:

> Robert Morris to Charles Williamson,
> Philadelphia, 29 Jul 1793
>
> Your success in the Sale of Settlement of Lands & Towns is very pleasing, and I expect that the information which you transmit upon these subjects to your Friends in London, will make them happy so far as their happiness is connected with this business. I think however that Mr. Colquhoun would be better pleased to receive some remittances from you than to see your drafts upon him continued. This however is only Conjecture for he has not written any thing to me on the subject. — and if he and the other Gentlemen think properly they must see that a little time will put it in your power to gratify them by ample reimbursements.[6]

---

[4] James H. Smith, *History of Livingston County, New York* (Syracuse, N.Y.: D. Mason, 1881), p. 449.

[5] Arthur Parker, *The Scottish Pioneers of Caledonia*, Vol. V (Rochester, N.Y.: Rochester Historical Society, 1926), pp. 275–91.

[6] Williamson et. al. Letters, p. 92.

Bath

Thinking that the influx of settlers into the Genesee Country would come from the south, Williamson began his road building efforts in the southern portion of the Pulteney Estate. In the spring of 1793 he began operations at Bath, named in honor of Sir William Pulteney's daughter, the Countess of Bath. He surveyed the village and built a series of log cabins, including a land office and a tavern. Later he added a sawmill and a gristmill. It would become the site of his permanent home.

In a grand gesture to advertise the transformation of Bath from frontier outpost to cultural center and to attract more settlers, Charles Williamson announced an agricultural fair with horse races to be held at Bath in the fall of 1796. Participants were attracted from New York, Virginia, Maryland, Delaware, New Jersey, Pennsylvania, New England, and Canada. Since roads were still very primitive, Williamson arranged for reliable guides to meet guests at Utica, Albany, New York City, Northumberland, Easton, Harris's Ferry (Harrisburg), Carlisle, Lancaster, Philadelphia, Baltimore, Alexandria, and Richmond. A mile-long circuit had been prepared at Pine Plains, about half a mile from the village of Bath. Guests began to arrive in July; by mid-September about 3,000 people had come. Williamson himself participated in the big race. He entered a mare named Virginia Nell, the favorite. Betting was heavy, but the favorite lost to Silk Stocking, a horse from New Jersey owned by the sheriff of Bath, William Dunn. (Williamson subsequently sold the mare.) Some of those who attended this exposition did return as settlers, but probably not enough to justify the expense.

Although this fair and this horse race have received a good deal of attention from historians, the first fair in Bath had taken place the previous year, 1795.[7] Horse racing was very popular among the sort of people Williamson was trying to attract, and he apparently had organized similar events earlier. In a letter from Robert Morris to

---

[7] The fair has been held every year since then. It has become the Steuben County Fair, the oldest continuous county fair in the country. The horse race has morphed into harness racing, which continues to this day.

Williamson, dated November 24, 1793, Morris wrote, "I see your Races succeeded well and Answered your expectation, indeed it was effecting a good thing, to bring together a Number of People from different places that they might see your fine Country and the improvements & settlements already Effected init."[8] The letter does not specify the location or the exact date. But it confirms, and indeed supports, the motivation of trying to get people to just come and see the country.

Geneva

In the spring of 1794 Williamson began construction of a splendid hotel in Geneva. At this time Geneva was a small, rather rough frontier town, but its location was ideal. He established an old London acquaintance, Thomas Powell, as manager of the hotel and in December 1794 hosted a grand ball to mark the opening of the hotel. Both the ball and the hotel, like the fair and horse racing at Bath, were considered to be good publicity for the Genesee Country. Williamson again was trying to get respectable people to the area, so that they would decide to stay. They did come and many did return to settle — not as many as he hoped, and, like the horse races, perhaps not enough to justify the expense.

Lyons

In the summer of 1794 Williamson created the village of Lyons in present-day Wayne County. Originally called The Forks, he changed the name, saying that the view of the confluence of Ganargua Creek and Canandaigua Outlet reminded him of the confluence of the Roane and Soane rivers in Lyons, France. Through his local agent, Charles Cameron, he had the village surveyed, and built a store house and a distillery. The road from Sodus Point was cut in 1794 and two years later reached Geneva. The town of Lyons was set off from Sodus on March 1, 1811. It is the county seat of Wayne County.

Sodus

In the northern portion of the Pulteney estate, Lake Ontario was seen as a most reasonable way for settlers to reach markets in

---

[8] Williamson et. al. Letters, p. 100.

Montreal and New York City. Sodus Point, in present-day Wayne County, was selected as the site for this commercial enterprise. Williamson drew up plans for a city extending between Salmon Creek and Great Sodus Bay. In the spring of 1794 he began by having roads cut to the site from Palmyra and Phelpstown. He set local agents in place, surveyed the town, built a tavern, and built a gristmill and a sawmill at the falls on Salmon Creek. In another grand gesture to attract the sort of settlers he wanted, he even put a pleasure boat on Sodus Bay. In spite of his expensive efforts, Sodus never developed as a strong commercial site. The town today is a small, popular summer resort.

THE MORRIS RESERVE

At the time of Robert Morris's purchase, the Morris Reserve was part of Ontario County. Early land records will be found there, such as his 1793 sale of the 87,000-acre Triangle Tract to Herman LeRoy, William Bayard, and John McEvers.[9] Robert Morris was a land speculator, not a developer. He was definitely a wholesaler, not a retailer. He sold to other speculators, not to individuals. The Morris Reserve never had a general land agent like Charles Williamson for the Pulteney Estate to the east or Joseph Ellicott for the Holland Land Company to the west. Land in various parts of the reserve became available for purchase by individual settlers at different times.

In 1802 Genesee County was split off from Ontario County. The entire Morris Reserve became part of the new county. Allegany County was taken from Genesee County in 1806, Orleans County in 1824, and Wyoming County in 1841. Table 1 shows the present-day counties and towns that make up the land once known as the Morris Reserve. Also listed are the names of first settlers, where known, and the date of the settlement. To add to the complication of shifting political boundaries, place names also changed. For example, the present town of Granger in Allegany County was known, before 1839, as West Grove.

---

[9] Grantee Deed Index, Ontario County, N.Y., Vol. 1, p. 321.

Table 1
PRESENT-DAY COUNTIES AND TOWNS
ON THE SITE OF THE MORRIS RESERVE

Present County (year formed)	Present Town (year formed)	First Settler(s)	Year of Settlement	Name Changed from (year)
Allegany (1806)	Granger (1839)	Reuben Smith	1816	West Grove (1839)
	Allen (1823)	James Wilson	1806	
	Angelica (1805)	Philip Church	1801	
	Amity (1830)	John T. Hyde	1804	
	Scio (1823)	Joseph Knight	1805	
	Alma (1854)	Myron Hough	1833	
	Grove (1827)	John White	1818	Church Tract (1828)
	Birdsall (1829)	Josiah Whitman	1816	
	West Almond (1833)	Daniel Atherton	1816	
	Ward (1856)	Abraham Walldorf	1817	
	Wellsville (1856)	Nathaniel Dike	1795	
	Willing (1851)	John Ford	1819	
Genesee (1802)	Stafford (1820)	Col. William Rumsey, Gen. Worthy Lovel Churchill	1801	
	Pavilion (1842)	Peter Crosman	1809	Bellona (1813)
	LeRoy	Charles Wilber	1797	
	Bergen (1813)	Samuel Lincoln	ca. 1805	Northwoods
	Byron (1820)	Benham Preston	1807	
Orleans (1824)	Kendall (1837)	Samuel Bates	1812	
	Murry (1808)	Epaphras Mattison	bef. 1809	
	Clarendon (1821)	Eldridge Farwell	1811	Farwell Mills (1821)

continued on next page

Table 1 (cont.)

Present County (year formed)	Present Town (year formed)	First Settler(s)	Year of Settlement	Name Changed from (year)
Wyoming (1841)	Covington (1817)	Jairus Cruttenden, Wm. Miller, Jon & Wm. Sprague	1807	
	Perry (1814)	Josiah Williams	1806	
	Castile (1821)	Robert Whalley	1808	
	Genesee Falls (1846)	John, Samuel & Seth Fields	1804	

Robert Morris intended to hold onto this land, assuming that the price would increase significantly. Like many other speculators of the time, however, he overreached. He had envisioned a wave of immigration from Europe and a strong westward expansion of the growing American population. He gambled and lost. His financial position deteriorated rapidly, and he was forced to sell the entire Morris Reserve to creditors. These tracts bore names like the Hundred Thousand Acre Tract, the Cotringer Tract, the Ogden Tract, the Forty Thousand Acre Tract, and the Church Tract.

In spite of all his efforts, Robert Morris was financially ruined, with debts of nearly $3 million. In 1798 the man who had financed the American Revolution was in debtors' prison. The crowning irony was that, in addition to being unable to earn money to pay his debts, he was required to furnish and to pay rent for his room in the Prune Street Jail. Finally his political allies prevailed and, on April 4, 1800, the Bankruptcy Act was passed, which made it possible for him to be released a year later, on August 26, 1801.

When he was released, Robert Morris had no possessions, no money, and no prospects. His long-time friend Gouverneur Morris had contrived to secure an annuity of $1,500 for Robert Morris's wife, Mary, from the Holland Land Company. This allowed them to live comfortably, if somewhat austerely. Robert Morris died on May 8, 1806.

THE NEXT CHAPTER

The year 1801 also marks significant milestones in the development of the other two regions making up western New York State. To the east, in the Genesee Country, Charles Williamson finally retired from his post as general agent for the Pulteney group, having overstayed his original seven-year contract. He was succeeded by Col. Robert Troup. To the west, the Niagara Country achieved "retail" status. Joseph Ellicott, surveyor and then local agent for the Holland Land Company, opened his land office for business.

SOURCES

Lockwood R. Doty, *History of the Genesee Country* (Chicago: S. J. Clarke, 1925).

Andrea Evangelist, *Remembering Wayne* (Lyons, N.Y.: Wayne County Historical Society, 1999).

Robert French, *History of Allegany County, New York* (Corning, N.Y.: Southern Tier Library System, 1954).

History of Wyoming County, N.Y. (New York: F. W. Beers, 1880).

John Horton, Edward Williams, and Harry Douglas, Chapter 1, "Wyoming County," in *History of Northwestern New York: Erie, Niagara, Wyoming, Genesee and Orleans Counties*, Vol. I (New York: Lewis Historical Publishing Company, 1947).

John Kennedy, *The Genesee Country* (Batavia, N.Y.: Calkins & Lent, 1895).

John Minard, *Allegany County and Its People: A Centennial Memorial History of Allegany County, New York* (Alfred, N.Y.: W. A. Fergusson, 1896).

Arthur Parker, *Charles Williamson: Builder of the Genesee Country, Publication Fund Series*, Vol. VI (Rochester, N.Y.: Rochester Historical Society, 1927), pp. 1–34.

Isaac Signor, ed., *Landmarks of Orleans County, New York* (Syracuse, N.Y.: D. Mason, 1894).

James H. Smith, *History of Livingston County, New York* (Syracuse, N.Y.: D. Mason, 1881).

Thomas Stackpole, ed., *The Heritage of Bath, NY, 1793–1993* (Bath, N.Y.: Historical Foundation of Bath, 1998).

Arad Thomas, *Pioneer History of Orleans County, New York* (Albion, N.Y.: H. A. Bruner, 1871).

Orsamus Turner, *History of the Pioneer Settlement of Phelps and Gorham's Purchase, and Morris' Reserve* (Rochester, N.Y.: W. Alling, 1852).

Frederick Wagner, *Robert Morris, Audacious Patriot* (New York: Dodd, Mead, 1976).

Eleanor Young, *Forgotten Patriot, Robert Morris* (New York: Macmillan, 1950).

CHAPTER 20

The Development of Prattsburg, New York

C hapter 17 discussed the Phelps-Gorham Purchase, which began settlement of the Genesee Country in western New York State. Here we concentrate on the settlement of one small part of this tract, the town of Prattsburg.

Briefly, Oliver Phelps of Windsor, Connecticut and Nathaniel Gorham of Charlestown, Massachusetts, obtained title to land east of the Genesee River on November 21, 1788. Because of financial difficulties, they transferred the lands they had not disposed of to Robert Morris on November 18, 1790. In less than a year after Morris took possession of the tract, his London agents sold it, at more than double the price, to three Englishmen, Sir William Pulteney, William Hornby, and Patrick Colquhoun.

The Phelps-Gorham tract had been divided into ranges, each a strip six miles wide running from north to south. Range 1 ran along the eastern border, the so-called Preemption Line. Range 7 ran along the western border, the Genesee River. The ranges were divided into townships, each a strip six miles wide running from east to west. Township 1 lay on the Pennsylvania border, while township 14 bordered Lake Ontario. The standard parcel was thus 36 square miles. On 16 June 1802, Capt. Joel Pratt, of Spencertown, Columbia County, New York, and William Root of Albany County, New York, contracted with the Pulteney group for township 6, range 3, on the northern border of Steuben County.[1] Advertisements at the time

An earlier version of this chapter was posted at *www.NewEnglandAncestors.org* February 12, 2002.

[1] Joel Pratt would later buy out William Root's share. For more information about the Pulteney group, see Chapter 19.

assured the public that "the soil was fertile; the forests abounded with game, the lakes with fish; the climate was delightful and healthy." Other promotional materials highlighted the possibilities for "easy communications with different markets" and encouraged "those who wish their estates in a few years to increase in extent and value" to consider settling on the "Steuben Frontier."[2]

Captain Joel Pratt, born in Colchester, Connecticut, journeyed to the present site of Prattsburg as early as 1799 and built a log cabin. He returned in February 1800 with his son Harvey, four teams of oxen, and six men (including subsequent settler Uriah Chapin). That season they claimed to have cleared 110 acres of heavy forest and sowed it to wheat in the fall. They then returned to Columbia County. Jared Pratt, nephew of Captain Joel Pratt, and his wife arrived with the others next season. They built a barn to store the harvest, and they threshed the wheat throughout the winter. They then sent it the short distance to Bath on oxcarts and ground some of it to flour. In the spring of 1802, the wheat was floated to Baltimore on arks and sold for $8,000.[3]

This easy communication with "civilization" accelerated the process of transforming frontier land into an established community. In contrast to the first settlers on the east coast of North America, whose supply line stretched across the Atlantic Ocean, settlers in the "Steuben Frontier" faced a half-day journey to Bath and, as Joel Pratt's wheat crop demonstrated, a river journey of a few days to reach large commercial centers such as Harrisburg, Columbia, Baltimore, and other Atlantic coast ports. Irvin W. Near writes in his *History of Steuben County*:

> During the high water season in the early years of the settlement of this valley this river was navigable for arks from Liberty in the town of Cohocton, this county [Steuben], where they were built, and in which the products of the vicinity were shipped to markets in Pennsylvania and Maryland. At Bath and other places on this river storehouses

---

[2] Julie Roy Jeffrey, *Converting the West* (Norman: University of Oklahoma Press, 1991), Chapter 1, pp 3–4.

[3] With the given price of $2.50/bushel, one may calculate that the 110 acres yielded 3,200 bushels or 29 bushels/acre.

were built and yards established for the accumulation and keeping of property awaiting shipment by these river crafts.[4]

Prattsburg's most famous citizen is Narcissa Prentiss, who migrated west to Oregon with her husband, Marcus Whitman, to establish a mission for Native Americans in 1836. Prentiss was born in Prattsburg in 1808, daughter of Stephen Prentiss, one of the earliest settlers. During her lifetime, Prattsburg was transformed from a forest to a thriving community of several thousand people. Stephen Prentiss was born at Grafton, Massachusetts, in 1777.[5] He married Clarissa Ward in Onondaga County, New York, January 3, 1803.

CHILDREN OF STEPHEN AND CLARISSA PRENTISS

Stephen Turner Prentiss	b.1804; m. Jane Holbrook; an organ builder.
Harvey Pratt Prentiss	b.1805.
Narcissa Prentiss	b.1808; m. Marcus Whitman; moved to Oregon.
Jonas Galusha Prentiss	b.1810; owned dry goods store in Angelica, N.Y.
Jane Abigail Prentiss	b.1811; unmarried; kept house for brother Edward.
Mary Ann Prentiss	b.1813; m. _____ Judson, a minister.
Clarissa Prentiss	b.1815.
Harriet Prentiss	b.1818; m. John Jackson; moved to Oberlin, Ohio.
Edward Warren Prentiss	b.1820; minister.

EARLY HISTORY OF PRATTSBURG

Most settlers came to the Steuben Frontier from the eastern counties of New York and from the state of Connecticut. Captain Joel Pratt, a devout Congregationalist, was a significant force in the religious life of the new community. He required new settlers purchasing land from

---

[4] Irvin W. Near, *History of Steuben County* (Chicago: Lewis Publishing, 1911), p. 3.

[5] Stephen Prentiss's paternal lineage: Stephen (1777–1862), son of Stephen (1744–1831), son of Stephen (1719–), son of Solomon (1673–1758), son of Solomon (1646–1719), son of Henry, who emigrated from England and settled in Cambridge, Mass., before 1640. Source: Clifford Merrill Drury, *Marcus and Narcissa Whitman and the Opening of Old Oregon*, Vol. I (Glendale, Calif.: The Arthur H. Clark Co. 1973), pp. 97–114.

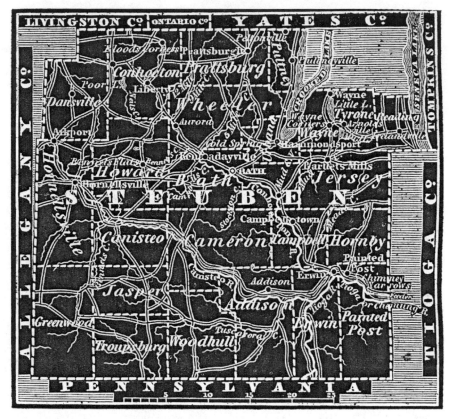

Map of Steuben County, from *Gazetteer of the State of New York* by Thomas Gordon (Philadelphia: the author, 1836).

him to pay an annual fee of $15 per 100 acres to the trustees of the Religious Society, which handled the spiritual affairs of the community. Pratt induced Rev. John Niles to come by offering him 80 acres of land. Niles arrived in the autumn of 1803 and held the settlement's first religious services at the home of Jared Pratt. William P. Curtis, Samuel Tuthill, Pomeroy Hull, and Salisbury Burton arrived in 1804. Settlers present by 1806 were Enoch Niles, Rufus Blodgett, Jesse Waldo, Judge Hopkins, John Hopkins, Dea. Ebenezer Rice, Robert Potter, Dea. Gamaliel Loomis, Samuel Hays, Dea. Abiel Lindsley, Moses Lyon, Uriel Chapin, Asher Bull, Rohan Hills, and Stephen Prentiss.

In 1806, Ira Pratt and Joel Pratt Jr. opened a general store in the village of Prattsburg. The first post office opened in 1807 with Joel

Pratt Jr. as postmaster. Post riders traveling weekly between Geneva and Bath now stopped there. The first public schoolhouse was built near the church in 1812. Table 1 lists some early businessmen and tradesmen of Prattsburg.

Table 1
EARLY BUSINESSMEN AND
TRADESMEN OF PRATTSBURG, NEW YORK[6]

Henry Allis	blacksmith, manufactured iron farm implements
Aaron Bull	opened the first tavern/hotel, 1806
____ Bidwell	blacksmith
William P. Curtiss	erected a distillery with Stephen Prentiss
John Hopkins	shoe maker
Samuel A. Johnson	cabinet maker
Moses Lyon	built first tannery
Noah Niles	physician, farmer
Stephen Prentiss	sawmills and gristmills, carpenter
Henry Pomeroy	cloth dresser
Robert Porter	built first gristmill, 1807
Israel Skinner	tanner, harness and saddle shop
Timothy Skinner	shoe maker
Cyril Ward	farmer, sawmill
Jesse Waldo	wagon maker

Over 300 families and more than 2700 people resided in the township by 1820. Framed houses, orchards, and gardens flourished where forests once were, and many types of mills were in full operation. The 1825 state census indicated that only 18 percent of Prattsburg families owned unimproved land. Stephen Prentiss owned more improved land than 80 percent of the town's citizens, with 67 acres of such land and two mills to his name.

---

[6] Near, *History of Steuben County.*

In 1822, plans were put forward to build the Franklin Academy for Advanced Studies, ("advanced studies" meaning beyond elementary school). Named for Benjamin Franklin, the academy was funded by local subscription. The $2,000 pledged for construction and $4,000 for maintenance, all from town residents, was a sure indicator that Prattsburg could no longer be considered a frontier outpost. The first academy building, a two-story structure adorned by an ornamental cupola, was erected on land purchased from Judge Porter. The first students were admitted in 1824 and the school became so successful that in 1827 a "female department" was added. Narcissa Prentiss, then 19, was one of the first female students to attend.

EPILOGUE

In June 1834, Stephen Prentiss moved his family about 40 miles southwest of Prattsburg to a new community in neighboring Allegany County called Amity (since changed to Belmont). Presumably this new community had ready work for a carpenter and joiner. Shortly afterward, they moved again to nearby Angelica, where his son Jonas operated a dry goods store. Narcissa Prentiss married Dr. Marcus Whitman on February 18, 1836. They both fulfilled long-held dreams to become missionaries and were sent to Oregon to work with the Cayuse tribe. Marcus eventually went back to the East Coast but soon returned, leading the first large migration to the West via the Oregon Trail. Unfortunately, the mass migration triggered a deadly measles outbreak that decimated the population of the Cayuse tribe. Surviving members of the tribe, enraged by the loss of nearly all their children, took revenge and killed the Whitmans along with twelve other pioneers on November 29, 1847.[7]

The Prentiss family story is illustrative of the history of many of the early settlers of Prattsburg and Steuben County. They came from New England bringing with them their Congregationalist faith, their belief in the value of education, and their strong sense of community.

---

[7] An article on the Prentiss family was published by Rev. Levi Fay Waldo in *Whitman College Quarterly* 1 (1897):3. Whitman College, named after Marcus Whitman, is in Walla Walla, Washington.

They built a new home on the frontier, and then, in a generation or two, moved on. Some families, however, stayed and put down roots. Their history is imprinted on the very names of the streets in the village of Prattsburg. Pratt Street crosses Main Street, appropriately enough, by the acre of land that Joel Pratt donated in 1806 as a cemetery. Waldo Road recalls wagon maker Jesse Waldo,[8] and Porter Street commemorates Judge Robert Porter.[9]

On February 28, 1923, the Franklin Academy was destroyed by fire. It was rebuilt as Prattsburgh Central School. The house in which Narcissa Prentiss was born is now preserved as a museum and leases space to the Prattsburg Community Historical Society, which shows the house to visitors during the summer.

---

[8] Jesse Waldo was born at Mansfield, Conn., in 1761, and died in 1826. He married Martha Hovey, who was born at Mansfield in 1770. They had three sons Otis (b. 1794), Lucius (b. 1802), and Charles (b. 1805).

[9] Robert Porter was born at Farmington, Conn., 6 Oct. 1773, son of Noah and Mary (Lewis) Porter. He married Roxana Root, of Litchfield, Conn., 28 Nov. 1799.

CHAPTER 21

The Holland Purchase: Pioneer Settlements in Western New York State

A t the close of the Revolutionary War, a major focus of the new country was westward expansion. Land speculation became a fever. Pioneers into western New York purchased their land not from the state, but by a contract with the Holland Land Company. This consortium of Dutch bankers purchased 3.3 million acres comprising present-day Allegany, Cattaraugus, Chautauqua, Erie, western Genesee, Niagara, Orleans, and Wyoming counties. (View a map of this area at *www.hlc.wny.org/wnymap.jpg.*) The first contracts were written in 1801. In 1810 the population exceeded 23,000, and by 1820, when approximately half of the land had been sold, it exceeded 100,000. In this chapter we look at the Holland Land Company, the Holland Purchase, and the men who administered it. Chapter 8 discusses the genealogical information available in the archives of the Holland Land Company and how to access those records.

THE FORMATION OF THE HOLLAND LAND COMPANY

At the close of the Revolutionary War, John Adams helped to negotiate sufficient financial backing from Dutch investors to stabilize the fledgling government of the United States. By 1796 the Dutch held the entire foreign debt of the new country — about $12 million. In 1789, a joint venture was proposed by four Amsterdam banking houses with experience in American investing: Pieter Stadnitski and Son, Ten Cate & Vollenhoven, Nicholass and Jacob Van Staphorst,

An earlier version of this chapter was posted at *www.NewEnglandAncestors.org* February 21, 2003.

and P. & C. van Eeghen. Later, in 1795, two other firms — W. & J. Willink and Rutger Jan Schimmelpenninck — were added, to form the Hollandische Land Compagnie.

THE HOLLAND PURCHASE

On November 30, 1789, the company hired Theophilus Cazenove as their general agent. He was to manage all of their U.S. investments, one of which was to be a 3.3 million-acre tract west of the Genesee River. This transaction became known as the Holland Purchase. Unlike Pennsylvania, where the company also made large purchases, New York State law forbade aliens from owning land.[1] Thus, for the New York purchases Cazenove created a board of trustees to hold the land for the company. In a series of five deeds in 1792 and 1793, Robert Morris sold this land to Herman LeRoy, John Linklaen, Gerrit Boon, William Bayard, and Matthew Clarkson.[2] Although the sale included an agreement by Robert Morris to assist in the extinction of Indian rights to the land, this was not accomplished until the Treaty of Big Tree on September 15, 1797. Several tracts, ranging in size from one to seventy square miles, were not part of this treaty: the reservations of Cannawagus, Little Beard's and Big Tree, Squakie Hill, Gardeau, Caneadea, Oil Spring, Allegany, Cattaraugus, Buffalo, Tonawanda, and Tuscarora. The larger reservations may still be located on a current state map.

THE SURVEY

Before the land could be sold, this vast territory had to be mapped and surveyed. Cazenove had engaged Joseph Ellicott as principal surveyor in 1794. This was a logical choice considering that Joseph Ellicott's older brother Andrew, who became Surveyor General

---

[1] Later the state would pass a series of acts making the use of trustees unnecessary. The first, passed April 11, 1796, was titled "An act for the relief of Wilhem Willink, Nicholaas Van Staphorst, Christiaan Van Eeghen, Hendrick Vollenhoven, Rutger Jan Schimmelpenninck, and Pieter Stadnitski, being aliens."

[2] Robert Morris's wife, Mary, received an annuity from the Holland Land Company of $1,500 for release of dower on lands sold. Although a seeming pittance at the time these deeds were executed, the sum became crucial some five years later when Morris's financial position collapsed and he found himself facing debtors' prison.

of the United States, trained Joseph and made him his assistant in surveying the city of Washington. Joseph Ellicott served the Holland Land Company at other locations, principally in western Pennsylvania, until the Treaty of Big Tree was signed. He then began the task of surveying the boundaries of the New York land and subdividing it into townships and ranges. He and his crew of about 150 men began in March 1798 and finished in October 1800, at a total cost to the company of close to $71,000. He employed the transit method to avoid the types of errors that plagued the eastern boundary of the Phelps-Gorham purchase. This method required line-of-sight measurements, which in turn required the crews to cut clear swaths along each line. The survey was slow, labor intensive, and accurate.

The company needed the survey in order to describe the land involved in each sale. When the state later created towns and counties, the political boundaries often, but not always, followed the

Joseph Ellicott, surveyor and agent of the Holland Purchase, from *Pioneer History of the Holland Purchase of Western New York* by O. Turner (Buffalo, N.Y.: Jewett, Thomas & Co./Geo. H. Derby & Co., 1850; reprinted Geneseo, N.Y.: James Brunner, 1974), frontispiece.

existing township and range boundaries. Thus the present-day boundary between Cattaraugus and Erie counties divides ranges 5, 6, 7, and 8 of township 6 between the two counties.

LAND SALES BEGIN

In 1799 Theophilus Cazenove resigned as general agent of the Holland Land Company. His successor was Paul Busti.[3] Busti had worked for the company since 1796, and continued to do so until he died in office on July 23, 1824. His chief clerk, John J. Vanderkemp, succeeded him. It was Busti who suggested the name of Batavia for the community in which the first local land office was located, taking it from the republic in which Amsterdam was located. On November 1, 1800, the company named Joseph Ellicott as their local agent, in charge of the sale of the land he had surveyed. Settlement was initially slow but picked up from about 1807 until the outbreak of the War of 1812. Some settlers in present-day Niagara and Erie counties were devastated by that war. O. Turner, in his *Pioneer History of the Holland Purchase,* speaks of "the smoking ruins of the once pleasant, delightful and flourishing village of Buffalo" and describes refugees streaming into Canandaigua.[4]

THE MIDDLE YEARS

Recovery from the war seems to have been speedy. Even so, lack of access to markets and the resulting shortage of cash meant that the majority of settlers became delinquent in their payments. Economic depression in 1819 further slowed sales and payments. Joseph Ellicott became involved in local politics, leading to difficulties for the company. In 1821, Paul Busti demanded, and received, Ellicott's resignation.

---

[3] Paul Busti was born October 17, 1749 in Milan, Italy, and was employed in his uncle's counting house in Amsterdam. He was a brother-in-law of Ten Cate, one of the bankers in the Holland Land Company. The town of Busti in Chautauqua County bears his name.

[4] O. Turner, *Pioneer History of the Holland Purchase* (Buffalo, N.Y.: Jewett, Thomas & Co./Geo. H. Derby & Co., 1850; reprinted Geneseo, N.Y.: James Brunner, 1974), p. 605.

Artist's representation of an early Holland Purchase pioneer, from *Pioneer History of the Holland Purchase of Western New York* by O. Turner (1849), p. 562.

Ellicott's successor was Jacob S. Otto, who served until his death in 1826.[5] During his tenure the company began to accept payment in kind from farmers who had little cash, an idea originally proposed by Joseph Ellicott and resisted by the company. Cattle and grain were delivered to depots that the company established. Each year agents advertised the time, place, and price for accepting cattle.

Upon Otto's death, his assistant (and Ellicott's nephew) David E. Evans became the last local agent in Batavia, and he remained in office until 1837, when company business ceased. In September 1827, the company decided to refinance contracts, rather than begin foreclosure proceedings. The following year they sold 60,000 acres of land in Chautauqua County to the Cherry Valley Company.[6] (See Table 1.)

---

[5] Otto attended the celebration of the completion of the Grand Canal in Lockport on October 26, 1825. He caught cold and died May 2, 1826. The town of Otto in Cattaraugus County bears his name.

[6] James O. Morse, Levi Beardsley, and Alvan Stewart.

Table 1
LANDS SOLD TO CHERRY VALLEY COMPANY IN 1828

LOCATION	TOWN	LOCATION	TOWN
T1R10	Carroll	T1R11	Kiantone & Busti
T2P10	Poland	T2R11	Ellicott
T3R10	Ellington	T4R11	Charlotte
T4R10	Cherry Creek	T5R11	Arkwright
T5R10	Villenova	T6R11	Sheridan
T6R10	Hanover	T1R12	Busti & Harmony

END GAME

In spite of all efforts to avoid foreclosures, relations between the company and settlers went from bad to worse, although the completion of the Erie Canal contributed to growing prosperity. In 1833 the legislature passed a law taxing the company for debts still owing to it upon land sales. Efforts to collect arrears were largely ignored. Newspaper articles were published painting the company as composed of evil, grasping foreigners. The settlers tried, unsuccessfully, to challenge the company's title to the land, and soon the company carefully began to divest itself of its holdings in New York.

In 1834, some mortgages newly subject to taxation were sold to the New York Life Insurance & Trust Company. Evans recommended selling a few of the more troublesome townships in order to demonstrate that the new landlord would not be an improvement. In the summer of 1835 three townships were sold: Orangeville in Genesee County (T9R2), Charlotte in Chautauqua County (T4R11), and Boston in Erie County (T7R8). In the same year, men interested in a projected Erie Railroad[7] bought reverted and unsold land in Allegany and Cattaraugus counties, and the towns of Java and China in Genesee County. The Farmers Loan & Trust Company of New York bought out the interests in Erie, Orleans, Niagara, and Genesee counties.

---

[7] E. Lord, S. B. Ruggles, and Nicholas Devereaux of Utica.

Paul Evans describes the settlers' change of heart.

> When it became known early in 1835 that the Company
> was making preparations to sell out its interest to native
> landlords, the news was greeted by the settlers with some-
> thing like consternation. Though they had been quick to
> criticize the faults of the Company, most of them realized
> perfectly well that it had been extraordinarily lenient in its
> treatment of backward debtors. Petitions poured into the
> Batavia office from the settlers praying the Company not to
> 'sell them out.' . . . Had it not been so serious it would have
> been comic. Those who had protested most loudly in the
> past years were now rushing to get deeds before the
> Holland company should turn them over to the tender
> mercies of the native landlords.[8]

Remaining lands and securities in Chautauqua County were sold to
Trumbull Cary and George Lay of Batavia. Company agents Evans
and Vanderkemp could scarcely believe the favorable terms they
were offered and readily agreed. These new proprietors made the
same demands — that back interest and deferred payments be paid.
They also offered, like the Holland Land Company, to renew
expired, unpaid contracts. However, the new contract would be
based on then-current land prices, not the price at the time of the
original contract. They threatened to evict the current occupant and
sell the land to a new tenant if payments were not made.

The settlers refused and on February 6, 1836, they destroyed the
land office in Mayville, Chautauqua County. This led to the fortifi-
cation of the land office in Batavia, which staved off a similar mob
attack. Some leniency on the part of the new proprietors, a new local
agent in Mayville, and the passage of time eventually restored calm.
The estimated profit to the Holland Land Company shareholders
was 5 to 6 percent per year.

---

[8] Paul D. Evans, *The Holland Land Company* (Buffalo, N.Y.: Buffalo Historical
Society, 1924), p. 394.

SOURCES

William Chazanof, *Joseph Ellicott and the Holland Land Company* (Syracuse, N.Y.: Syracuse University Press, 1970).

David M. Ellis, James A. Frost, Harold C. Syrett, and Harry J. Carman, *A History of New York State* (Ithaca, N.Y.: Cornell University Press, 1967).

Paul D. Evans, *The Holland Land Company* (Buffalo, N.Y.: Buffalo Historical Society, 1924).

O. Turner, *Pioneer History of the Holland Purchase* (Buffalo, N.Y.: Jewett, Thomas & Co./Geo. H. Derby & Co., 1850; reprinted Geneseo, N.Y.: James Brunner, 1974).

Andrew W. Young, *History of Chautauqua County* (Buffalo: Matthews and Warren, 1875).

CHAPTER 22

The Erie Canal:
"Mother of Cities"

A t the time of its completion in 1825, the Erie Canal, begun in 1817, was the longest canal in the world. It connected Albany, on the Hudson River, with Buffalo on Lake Erie, and thus opened up the state to travel, immigration, and commerce. Some cities, such as Rochester and Lockport, were created because of the canal, giving rise to its most flattering alias "Mother of Cities." Other established communities, such as Geneva and Canandaigua, were eclipsed because the canal bypassed them. Canal construction required a great deal of manpower. Initial reliance on part-time labor by local farm workers proved to be inefficient. The shift to construction crews offered job opportunities that were snatched up by unskilled European immigrants, most notably the Irish. As each section of the canal was put into operation, travel and trade expanded, attracting more settlers into the region. Your ancestors may have been among these new arrivals. Or, if your ancestors were already living in New York State, they may have moved in response to the "Big Ditch." In this article we examine the effect of the canal on communities on and off its route.

BUILDING THE CANAL

The original Erie Canal was forty feet wide at the top, twenty-eight feet wide at the bottom, and four feet deep. The original locks were fifteen feet wide and ninety feet long. This was just big enough to accommodate two-way traffic using the canal boats of the time. The

An earlier version of this chapter was posted at *www.NewEnglandAncestors.org* July 2, 2004.

canal was dug by hand using shovels, men, wheelbarrows, and mules. No power tools. If your ancestor helped dig the canal, it is a good assumption that he was young, strong, a hard worker, and probably unmarried.

A berm was constructed on one side of the canal and a ten-foot-wide towpath on the other side. Numerous bridges were constructed over the canal to enable local farmers to reach their fields. They were less than eight feet above the water level causing boat passengers to hunker down to avoid an unwanted dip.

Construction began on July 4, 1817, in Rome. This site was chosen in part because the canal route west of Rome contained long flat stretches and required relatively few locks. The original route went through a swamp to the south of Rome, rather than through the town center, which greatly displeased the citizenry.[1] The eastern route near Albany was more rocky and harder to dig. The western route near Lockport included a seventy-foot drop in elevation, requiring a complex series of locks. Each section was put into operation as soon as it was completed, the tolls being used to help fund the project. Table 1 shows when each section was completed.

TABLE 1

YEAR	CANAL SECTION OPENED FOR USE
1819	Utica to Rome
1820	Syracuse to Utica
1821	Rome to Little Falls
1822	Little Falls to Schenectady and Rochester to Syracuse
1823	Schenectady to Albany and Brockport to Rochester
1824	Lockport to Brockport
1825	Buffalo to Lockport

---

[1] When the canal was relocated in mid-century the route was moved closer to the center of Rome and ten feet lower than the level of the original route. This drained the Great Rome Swamp, creating rich farmland.

Rome's rival, Utica, was a tiny settlement before it became a major port on the Erie Canal. The population of this upstart quickly outstripped that of Rome. From 1820 to 1830 the population of Utica rose from 2,947 to 12,782, an increase of 334 percent. In comparison, the population of Rome in the same time period rose from 3,569 to 4,360, an increase of 22 percent.

If your ancestors lived in Schenectady at this time, they may have found the canal to be a mixed blessing. Schenectady had been the eastern terminus of the navigable portion of the Mohawk River. The new canal threatened the prosperous warehousing and boat building businesses as well as the inns and taverns that had developed around this transfer point. In fact, from 1820 to 1830 the population of Schenectady actually decreased slightly from 12,876 to 12,347, or 4 percent.

Other western boomtowns such as Syracuse, Buffalo, Rochester, and Lockport were essentially created by the arrival of the canal. The population growth in these towns was accomplished in part by settlers new to the state, and in part by a shift from established communities not on the new canal route. Take, for example, the case of Lyman Spalding. In 1820 Lyman Spalding opened a grocery store in Canandaigua, the county seat of Ontario County. Located on the northern tip of Canandaigua Lake, Canandaigua had been chosen by Phelps and Gorham as the site of their land office. It had been connected to eastern markets by a toll road in 1804 and enjoyed a deserved reputation as a promising site for business. The grocery store prospered. Canandaigua was the most important community in the region before the construction of the canal. However, the route of the Erie Canal passed thirteen miles to the north and state officials denied the town's request to build a feeder canal. Business declined and in 1822 Spalding followed his customers to Rochester. While the population of Rochester grew from 1,502 in 1820 to 9,207 in 1830, or 513 percent, the population of Canandaigua grew from 4,680 to 5,162, or only 10 percent.

The canal route also bypassed the salt-producing community of Salina. However, a mile-long side cut from the canal south to Onondaga Creek was put in to connect the salt works with the canal. The new town of Syracuse, which had a population of 250 in

1820, grew up at the junction of the canal and the side cut. It eventually expanded to absorb Salina and its salt works.[2]

The town of Lockport is justly named. At this point the water level changes seventy feet through a series of five pairs of locks, accommodating two-way traffic. The town simply did not exist in 1820. In the summer of 1821 there were three families living in this frontier. By 1830 the population had mushroomed to 2,022.

When the canal reached Buffalo in 1825, the time required to transport goods to and from New York City dropped from six weeks to ten days and the cost of transport dropped to one-fifth of the former amount. If your ancestor was a businessman in the area, he faced numerous interesting opportunities. Some enterprising merchants stocked canal boats and brought groceries, dry goods, and household goods to what had been empty frontier only a few years before. Show boats brought legitimate theater into the local halls of communities that never before had contact with such culture.

OPENING CELEBRATIONS

The opening of each section of the canal was celebrated with various dignitaries making speeches in canal boats along the new route. If your ancestor lived anywhere along the route, it is likely that the whole family would have taken part in at least one of these events. In October 1819 the first fifteen-mile stretch from Rome to Utica was opened. The canal boat *Chief Engineer of Rome* traveled from Rome to Utica and returned the next day. On July 4, 1820, in a more elaborate show, seventy-three new canal boats traveled from Syracuse to Rome to celebrate the completion of the middle section of the canal.

The final celebration was particularly impressive. The stops made along that journey from Buffalo to Albany followed the full original canal route. A flotilla of canal boats assembled in Buffalo, to be joined by others as they proceeded eastward. The first boat, *The*

---

[2] In its third configuration Syracuse would no longer be on the canal. Today the canal route between Rome and Syracuse is marked by the Old Erie Canal State Park. The Erie Canal Museum, 318 Erie Boulevard, Syracuse, records canal history.

Seneca Chief, carried Governor DeWitt Clinton and other dignitaries (including the Marquis de Lafayette), a barrel of water from
Lake Erie (to be poured into the harbor at New York City), and a
second barrel containing water from the Amazon, Columbia,
Gambia, Ganges, Indus, LaPlata, Mississippi, Nile, Orinoco, Rhine,
Seine, and Thames rivers. The second boat, *Noah's Ark,* carried "a
rare assortment of birds, fish, and insects, including a pair of eagles,
a pair of fawns, a fox, two young bears, and two Seneca Indian
boys."[3]

The entire 425-mile route from Buffalo to New York City was lined
with war cannons, thirty-two pounders, used by Commodore Perry's
fleet against the British on Lake Erie during the War of 1812. The cannon were spaced so that each gunner was within earshot of the next.
George Condon describes what occurred at ten o'clock on the morning of Wednesday, October 26, 1825, as the boats prepared to set off.

> [The] first gunner lighted the fuse . . . fearsome enough to
> be heard by the next, unseen, gunner down the line because
> it seemed as if the echoing boom from the northeast came
> so quickly as to step on the lingering reverberations of the
> first roar. . . . It rolled through the country of the Mohawks,
> the Senecas, the Onondagas, the Cayugas, the Oneidas, and
> the Tuscaroras . . . moved east, through the Niagara Country,
> the Genesee Country, the Montezuma swampland, through
> the Mohawk Valley, past the Catskills, and down the Hud-
> son. . . . It took the cannon telegraph relay only one hour
> and twenty minutes to reach the island of Manhattan and
> deposit its historic word before turning about for the
> return relay to Buffalo.[4]

At the first stop, Lockport, more boats were to join the procession.
The local welcoming delegation, however, convened at the foot of
the great array of five locks and ascended to the top of the Niagara

---

[3] George E. Condon, *Stars in the Water, the Story of the Erie Canal* (Garden City,
N.Y.: Doubleday, 1974), p. 6.

[4] Ibid., p. 8.

Aqueduct of the Erie Canal, from *Pictorial Geography of the World* by S. G. Goodrich (Boston: C. D. Strong, 1841), p. 238

escarpment, thus officially opening the locks themselves. They then sailed west to meet the oncoming flotilla, returned with them, descended through the locks, and took everyone off to the Washington House for an elegant banquet. The next day, Thursday, they arrived in Rochester, where the grandly named canal boat, *The Young Lion of the West,* joined the fleet. In Weedsport the celebration was dimmed by tragedy when the explosion of a cannon killed two gunners. Saturday afternoon, October 29, they reached Syracuse for a banquet at Williston's Mansion House.

In Rome a group of citizens who resented the decision to position the canal route a mere half-mile to the south formed a solemn procession and protested by pouring a barrel of tar into the canal. Having made their point, they then joined the celebration at Starr's Hotel that evening. The canal boats stopped in Utica on Sunday morning for church and reached Little Falls Sunday night. They arrived after dark, the canal being illuminated by burning barrels of tar, which had been placed along the edge of the cliffs above the locks. In Fort Plain the next evening, Monday, October 31, their arrival was also illuminated; this time the burning barrels had been placed on top of high poles on Prospect Hill and appeared to hang in the air. The reception Tuesday afternoon in Schenectady was subdued due to an increased awareness among the town's businessmen of the negative aspects of the canal on their town. Dinner was polite, but restrained.

In the thirty miles between Schenectady and Albany the land dropped 218 feet, requiring twenty-six locks. The city of Albany provided dinner outdoors for 600 on the Columbia Street Bridge. On November 4, the tenth day of travel, the boats arrived at Sandy Hook in New York Harbor. The party that followed was stunning. Ceremonies in the harbor lasted all day, followed by more festivities on land the next day including a grand parade with floats, exhibits (remember the animals?), and finally, a grand ball. After the events concluded in Manhattan, the boats returned to Buffalo and closed the circle by pouring a barrel of water from the Atlantic Ocean into Lake Erie.

The canal was more successful than anyone had predicted — and the predictions were very high. The total cost of building the canal was $7,700,000. Income in 1826, the first year after it was completed, exceeded $1 million. This income was raised with the operation of 160 freight boats and a few packet (passenger) boats. Tolls were reduced in 1833, but traffic grew so fast that profits still increased. By 1836 the remaining debt, $3,500,000, was paid off and there were 3,000 boats on the canal. If the boats had been spaced evenly, this would be equivalent to about one boat every seventy feet. Not surprisingly, in 1835 and again in 1862, the canal was widened and the route altered — all accomplished while the canal was in use. A system of secondary feeder canals grew up. But, by the time of the Civil War, railroads were offering serious competition and the "Big Ditch" faded from the public consciousness.

Since this essay was written, much has been accomplished to revitalize the Erie Canal as a recreational outlet. The New York State Canal Corporation, a subsidiary of the Thruway Authority, maintains a website at *www.nyscanals.gov* for current information. Another site, *www.eriecanal.org,* is devoted to the history of the canal.

SOURCES

Betty Bantle, *Perinton, Fairport, and the Erie Canal* (Perinton, N.Y.: Perinton Historical Society, 2001).

George E. Condon, *Stars in the Water, the Story of the Erie Canal* (Garden City, N.Y.: Doubleday, 1974).

Emerson Klees, *The Erie Canal in the Finger Lakes Region: The Heart of New York State* (Rochester, N.Y.: Friends of the Fingerlakes Publishing, 1996).

Carol Sheriff, *The Artificial River, The Erie Canal and the Paradox of Progress, 1817–1862* (New York: Hill and Wang, 1996).

Barbara Shupe, Janet Steins, and Jyoti Pandit, *New York State Population, 1790–1980: A Compilation of Federal Census Data* (New York: Neal-Schuman Publishers, 1987).

CHAPTER 23

The Brown Tract

I n 1798, John Brown of Providence, Rhode Island, acquired 210,000 acres of land in upstate New York, which became known as the "Brown Tract." The majority of this tract (167,000 acres) is located in present-day Herkimer County. The rest is in Lewis County (40,000 acres) and Hamilton County (3,000 acres). At a time when settlers poured into the state, fueling an enormous population boom, three generations of the Brown family failed utterly in their attempts to develop their "wild lands." In this chapter we look at the history of John Brown's tract to discover why your New York ancestors probably chose some other region of the state in which to settle.

THE BROWN FAMILY

John Brown was born in 1736, son of James and Hope (Power) Brown, and great-grandson of Chad Brown, one of the earliest settlers of Providence.[1] John Brown married Sarah Smith and the couple had four children. Their son James Brown never married. Their eldest daughter Abigail (Abby) married John Francis (1763–96), son of Tench and Anne (Willing) Francis, on January 1, 1788. They had a son, John Brown Francis. Their middle daughter Sarah (Sally) married Charles Frederick Herreshoff (1763–1819), son of Charles and Agnes (Muehler) Herreshoff, on July 1, 1801. They had a son, John

---

An earlier version of this chapter was posted at *www.NewEnglandAncestors.org* November 19, 2004.

[1] This John Brown should not be confused with the famous abolitionist of the same name.

srown Herreshoff. John and Sarah Brown's youngest daughter Alice married James Mason (ca. 1774–1845) on July 16, 1800.

ACQUISITION OF THE BROWN TRACT

At the close of the Revolutionary War, the state took over all Crown lands as well as lands held by loyalists. In 1792 Alexander Macomb bought an astonishing 4 million acres from the state at eight cents an acre. Cash flow was a problem for early land speculators and Macomb was bankrupt within six months. He sold 1.9 million acres to William Constable for £50,000. Six months later Constable sold 1.3 million acres to Samuel Ward for £100,000 and became one of the very few land speculators in the region to make a profit. Ward sold the 210,000 acres that later became the Brown Tract to James Greenleaf for $24,000. Greenleaf was a business partner with Robert Morris, financier of the Revolution.

One reason businessmen of the time experienced cash-flow problems was that there was simply not enough money in circulation. Businessmen used letters of credit as a substitute. To raise money, James Greenleaf mortgaged his 210,000 acres to John Livingston for $38,000. In 1794 John Francis, a son-in-law and business partner of son James Brown, accepted a second mortgage on the land as payment for a shipload of tea. Considering the prestige of the Greenleaf–Morris partnership at the time, it was a reasonable business transaction.[2] However, the panic of 1796 put both Greenleaf and Morris in debtors' prison. When it finally became clear that James Greenleaf's financial state was not going to recover sufficiently to honor his note, John Brown sent his son James to visit the area in August 1798. James did not go to the Brown Tract itself but instead traveled to Utica and Rome (the two largest settlements in the area), and to Boonville. He wrote that "these regions although settled only about ten or twelve years are thickly inhabited and

---

[2] This latest information contradicts the established version found in such sources as Alfred L. Donaldson's *A History of the Adirondacks* (Harrison, N.Y.: Harbor Hill Books, 1977), Vol. I. See Henry A. L. Brown and Richard J. Walton, *John Brown's Tract: Lost Adirondack Empire* (Canaan, N.H.: Published for the Rhode Island Historical Society by Phoenix Pub., 1988) p. 121.

many of the inhabitants are again emigrating."[3] John Brown did not have first-hand information about the land in question. At this point he made the business decision not to accept the loss, but to buy the land by paying off John Livingston's first mortgage. According to Brown and Walton, "If Brown had not bid on it, the land's selling price, if anybody wanted to buy it, would have been much lower, not even enough to cover the Livingston Mortgage."[4] John Brown got the deed to the tract on December 5, 1798.

FIRST-GENERATION DEVELOPMENT ATTEMPTS (1798–1803)

John Brown had his tract surveyed into eight townships, which he named Industry, Enterprise, Perseverance, Unanimity, Frugality, Sobriety, Economy, and Regularity. We find the following instructions to his surveyor, John Hammon, in a letter dated March 31, 1799:

> You'l be very particular in Your Field book & Note Every thing of Importance, so as to Give Me the Value of Every Town as near as posable by its Number. You'l be sure to Note Every Mill place, Every Good place for a Compact Town, the ore, the Salt Springs if aney, the kind of Timber, the Lay of the Ground Weither good or bad or Indifferent, Weither Broken, or Even or Weither Large or Small Hills and Every other Observation You think worthey of My Knowing.[5]

Brown laid plans for a village at the confluence of north and middle branches of the Moose River, with a gristmill and sawmill, and he hoped to build about 500 miles of roads. His expectation was that settlers would come, plant crops, have good harvests, and thus attract more settlers. It was, after all, what was happening in the Black River Valley a few miles west. He hired James Sheldon as his agent to oversee the clearing of the land. Early surveyor reports of

---

[3] Brown and Walton, *John Brown's Tract* 1988, p. 112.

[4] Quoted in ibid., p. 121.

[5] Ibid., p. 125.

the tract having rocky ground instead of rich farmland did not dissuade John Brown. In a letter to Sheldon, he blithely praised the virtues of stone walls:

> There is nothing in My Mind that can Impeade the Rappid Settlement of my Lands unless there is too Maney Stones which from the account of those who had Reconorterd to Westward I confess give accts of more stones than I wish to have had, tho a large proportion of Stones Would in time be an Advantage Rather than Disadvantage to the Land, as no Fence in the World is Equilly Valuable to a Good Stone wall.[6]

The work of building roads, bridges, and mills went slowly. Sheldon was not able to clear land for crops, so all supplies had to be hauled in. Few settlers came and fewer stayed. In January 1800 John Brown wrote to Sheldon, "I must close by beging you to make use of all the Oconnemy in Your power and Reduce the Expenses already Exceeded my Expectation. More than Double Considering there is no produce Yet Raised & but Little Land prepared."[7]

Brown's efforts to turn a profit on this venture ended with his death on September 20, 1803. The townships of Industry, Enterprise, and Perseverance went to his wife, Sarah; Unanimity went to his daughter, Abby Francis; he left Frugality to his daughter Sarah Herreshoff; Sobriety was given to his daughter Alice Mason; Economy to his grandson John Brown Francis; and Regularity to his son James Brown.

John Brown had built a dam, a sawmill, a gristmill, a store, a few houses, and a road from Boonville crossing the Moose River into Old Forge. His will describes the improvements made in the townships of Industry ("2 Log Houses, a good Barn & considerable improvements of cleared land") and Economy ("a Grist Mill & Saw Mill, House, Store etc. on this Town is the best of Pine Timber which may be floated to the Mill & saw'd in to the best Pine Boards, very

---

[6] Ibid., p. 139.

[7] Ibid., p. 157.

cheap"). For all his effort and expense, there were probably fewer than a dozen people living on the tract when he died.[8]

SECOND-GENERATION DEVELOPMENT ATTEMPTS (1806–19)

The first of the second generation to try to settle the "wild lands" of the Brown Tract was James Mason, husband of John Brown's youngest daughter, Alice. In April 1806 he hired Joseph Shaw to go to what is now Old Forge and attempt to attract settlers. James and Alice Mason made the first sale at the end of 1807, when Oliver Ingalls of Windham, Connecticut, purchased 1,000 acres for $2,000. In May of 1808 they sold parcels to three settlers, a total of 940 acres for $1,850.

In 1811, Charles Frederick Herreshoff, husband of John Brown's middle daughter Sarah, arrived at the Brown Tract with his nephew, John Brown Francis. They found all of John Brown's earlier work on the roads, bridges, and mills of the tract in disrepair. Herreshoff began again, but all his ventures seemed doomed to failure. In 1815 he decided to try sheep ranching. The sheep died. The next year he wanted to establish a nail factory on the tract. The necessary loan was refused. This was also the "Year without a Summer," because of the eruption of the Tambora volcano in present-day Indonesia in 1815. This resulted in heavy snowfall in the second week of June, ruining most crops. In 1817 he built a forge (thus giving a name to present-day Old Forge). He wrote to his daughter Anna: "There is no more doubt but what we have two sources of the most valuable ore, and both inexhaustible."[9] Even though Herreshoff stayed on site through the winter of 1817–18 to work on the mine, the ore quality was actually rather poor. He died on site on December 19, 1819, apparently by his own hand. James Mason had died the same year.

THIRD-GENERATION DEVELOPMENT ATTEMPTS (1819–50)

In 1819, Sarah, widow of John Brown, turned over the three townships she owned to her daughter Abby Francis, her grandson, John

---

[8] Ibid., p. 96.
[9] Ibid., p. 239.

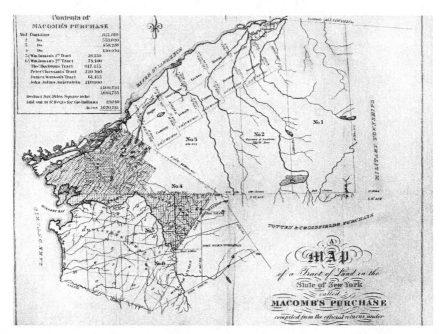

Map of Macomb's Purchase by Charles C. Brodhead, from *The Documentary History of the State of New York* by E. B. O'Callaghan (Albany: Weed, Parsons & Company, 1850) vol. 3, p. 1070.

Brown Francis, and her daughter Sarah Herreshoff. Abby Francis died intestate on March 5, 1821, at age 54. Sarah Herreshoff died on August 2, 1846, nearly 73. What remained of the Brown Tract was then in the hands of John Brown's two grandsons and namesakes — John Brown Francis and John Brown Herreshoff.

There followed years of tentative offers, none of which reached fruition. Land reverted to the state for payment of back taxes and was sometimes later redeemed within the allowable two-year period. The township of Sobriety, inherited by Alice Mason, was not redeemed. Even though the taxes were quite low (approximately $700 per year), the estate was producing no income. It was a steady drain on the family finances.

Finally, on March 20, 1850, John Brown Francis sold his interest in the Brown Tract — approximately 93,000 acres spread over six townships — to Lyman Rasselas Lyon. A few weeks later, on April 4, 1850, John Brown Herreshoff sold his remaining interest — approximately 69,000 acres in three townships — to the same Lyman Lyon.

Lyman Lyon, who would now try to make a going commercial concern out of this land, was the son of Caleb Lyon, an early settler in the region. A biography in Hough's *History of Lewis County* begins: "Lyman Rasselas Lyon, than whom no citizen of Lewis County, past or present, is more entitled to the touch of the biographer's pen, was born in what is now Walworth, Wayne County, N.Y., in 1806, and came a lad of twelve years with his father to Lewis County."[10] The biography goes on to describe Lyman Lyon's political and business activities, including the Moose River and Otter Lake tanneries. Father and son were also involved in railroads. The Sackett's Harbor & Saratoga Railroad Company was incorporated on April 10, 1848, but not actually organized until January 10, 1852. Caleb Lyon performed the groundbreaking ceremony on April 8, 1852, near Dayanville. Lyman Lyon was one of the directors, having contracted the Brown Tract to the company. By the fall of 1854, construction had ceased. The name was changed to Lake Ontario & Hudson River Railroad Company on April 6, 1857, and fresh capital was sought in England. In 1860 the name was changed to the Adirondack Estate and Railroad Company. The project was stopped by the Civil War. The company went bankrupt and came through receivership to Thomas C. Durant, who was connected with the Union Pacific Railroad.[11] Lyman Lyon died on April 7, 1869, the largest single landowner in Lewis County.[12]

THE JOHN BROWN TRACT TODAY

With the completion of the Erie Canal, settlers poured into upstate New York. By 1842 the population in the region from Utica to Buffalo had increased to over a million people. At this same time the 328-square-mile Brown Tract was home to about fifty to sixty people — about six square miles per person. Even today only one substantial

---

[10] Franklin Benjamin Hough. *A History of Lewis County in the State of New York, from the Beginning of Its Settlement to the Present Time* (Albany, N.Y.: Munsell & Rowland, 1860), p. 441.

[11] Ted Aber and Stella King. *The History of Hamilton County* (Lake Pleasant, N.Y.: Great Wilderness Books, 1965).

[12] Joseph F. Grady, *The Adirondacks; Fulton Chain-Big Moose Region; the Story of a Wilderness* (Little Falls, N.Y.: Press of the Journal & Courier Co., 1933).

road (Route 28) crosses the southern edge. The failure of the Brown family to develop the area discouraged others from trying. Today the entire tract is within the "forever wild" Adirondack Forest Preserve, created by the New York State Legislature in 1885.[13]

So what went wrong? We might try to second-guess some of the business decisions, such as the iron mine and forge, but ultimately one must come back to the land itself. To a geologist, it is clear that there are sharp changes over the course of just a few miles. The land in the Brown Tract was not (and is not) suitable for farming. It is rocky. The growing season is short, less than 100 days. The winters are harsh. Settlers simply could not raise enough food during the summer to support themselves. And there was good land farther to the west, which was available on equal or better terms. Thus, even though it was close to Albany, one of the oldest settled areas in the state, the Brown Tract remained a wilderness long after the West was "won." Genealogically speaking, it is a desert.

[13] *www.adirondack-park.net/mainframe.html.*

CHAPTER 24

Early Palatine Families
of New York

After the death of Charles II of Spain in 1700, Philip V, grandson of King Louis XIV of France, was named to succeed him. Louis refused to keep his grandson from the line of succession to the French throne, which prompted fears of expansion. These actions led to the War of the Spanish Succession, which moved into America in 1702, where it was known as Queen Anne's War. The conflict, which lasted from 1702 to 1713, pitted France and Spain against England, Austria, the Netherlands, and Portugal. The armies of Louis XIV invaded the Palatinate region of Germany, forcing residents to flee first to Holland, then by boat from Rotterdam to London. As they were victims of Britain's enemy, these German-speaking Protestants were at first welcomed in London, and in 1709 the government issued sixteen hundred tents for Palatine encampments in Blackheath and elsewhere. The flood of immigrants that followed, estimated to be 10,000 to 30,000 (or 2 to 5 percent of the city's population in 1710), became unsupportable. (Boston today has roughly the same population as the London of 1710. Imagine the same number of immigrants sailing into Boston Harbor and setting up a tent city on the Common.)

This situation led Her Majesty's government to formulate a plan by which refugees needing aid could be transformed into colonists producing profit. The government proceeded to send several thousand of these German families to New York to produce naval supplies needed for the war by the Royal Navy. In return for passage to New York

An earlier version of this chapter was posted at *NewEnglandAncestors.org* July 25, 2003.

and maintenance, the Germans were to produce tar, turpentine, and ship's masts. When the debt was repaid, each family would receive forty acres of land free from taxes or quit rents for seven years. Some three thousand people set sail for New York in 1710. They labored for about three years, but the project was an economic disaster and much ill will was generated. Finally, in 1713, the project was terminated, leaving the Palatines still in debt to the crown. Without permission, many left for the land that they claimed Queen Anne had promised them, in the Schoharie Valley where the Schoharie Creek flows into the Mohawk River. Their claim was not recognized in Albany, and in 1723, after a decade of violent dispute, the settlement disbanded and many of the settlers moved south into Pennsylvania.

ARRIVAL OF PALATINES INTO NEW YORK, 1709–10

These Palatines were not the first group of German-speaking settlers to arrive in New York. An earlier group of forty-one persons (ten men, ten women, and twenty-one children), led by Evangelical minister Joshua Kockerthal, was sent to New York by royal order of Queen Anne on May 10, 1708. This group was not part of the Naval Stores project described in the preceding paragraph. Filby lists the arrival in 1709 of Joshua Kockerthal, age 39, his wife Sibylla Charlotta, 39, and children Benigna Sibylla, 10, Christian Joshua, 7, and Susanna Sibylla, 3.[1] Rupp lists the names, ages, and occupations of "Those Who Accompanied Rev. Joshua Kocherthal, who settled on lands on Quassick Creek, then Dutchess County, NY in the Spring of 1709."[2] They were given five hundred acres of land to form the town of Quassic, now Newburg (near the junction of Interstates 84 and 87) and remained there.

The main group of about three thousand distressed Germans sailed for New York in ten ships, arriving June 13, 1710 with Robert Hunter, the newly appointed royal governor. The passengers experienced much sickness during the voyage, and nearly five hundred

---

[1] P. William Filby, ed., *Passenger and Immigration Lists Index* (Detroit: Gale Research Co., 1981), Vol. II, p. 1123.

[2] D. Rupp, *A Collection of Thirty Thousand Names of German, Swiss, Dutch, French, and Other Immigrants in Pennsylvania, 1727–1776* (Philadelphia: Leary, Stuart Co., 1927), Appendix IV.

were lost at sea. Upon arrival, they were quarantined for several months on Nutten (now Governor's) Island due to typhus on board. Thus they could not begin work until the spring of 1711. Genealogical information on over eight hundred of these families is available in Henry Z Jones's two-volume work *The Palatine Families of New York: A Study of the German Immigrants Who Arrived in Colonial New York in 1710*.[3] His primary sources (original sources, not published transcriptions) include Rotterdam Sailing Lists of 1709, the London Census of Palatines of 1709, Hunter Subsistence Lists 1710–12, the West Camp Census 1710–11, and the Simmendinger Register.

NAVAL STORES PROJECT, 1709–12

As early as 1699, the Earl of Bellomont, appointed governor of New York, Massachusetts Bay, and New Hampshire, had proposed that the colony of New York be used for the production of naval supplies. He also suggested using garrisoned soldiers as the labor force in this initiative. Colonel Robert Hunter, who himself would later become governor of New York, coupled this suggestion with the exploding refugee problem and substituted the Palatines as the labor force. As described in this excerpt from a report by the Board of Trade dated December 5, 1709, the settlement was to be located along the Mohawk River:

> [W]e have considered the proposals made to us by Colonel
> Hunter for settling 3000 Palatines at New York, and
> Employing them in the Production of Naval stores, and
> thereupon humbly Represent to your Majesty . . . the most
> proper Places for the seating them in that Province, so as
> they may be of benefit to this Kingdom by the Production
> of Naval Stores, are on the Mohaques River, and on the
> Hudsons River. . . . A Tract of land lying on the Mohaques
> River containing about 50 miles in length and four miles
> in breadth, and a Tract of land lying upon a creek
> [Schoharie Creek] which runs into the said River,

---

[3] Universal City, Calif.: the author, 1985. See also Henry Z Jones, Jr., *More Palatine Families* (Universal City, Calif.: the author, 1991).

containing between 24 and 30 Miles in length. This land mentioned, land of which your majesty has the possession, is claimed by the Mohaques, but that claim may be satisfied on very easy terms. . . . We therefore humbly offer that the governor or commander in chief be Directed upon their Arrival . . . to grant under the Seal of that Province, without fee or Reward, 40 acres per head to each family, after they shall have repaid by the produce of their Labour, the charges the publick shall be at in setting and subsisting them there. . . . As these people are very necessitous, they will not be able to maintain themselves there, till they can reap the benefit of their labour which will not be till after one year at the soonest. . . . Lastly, we humbly offer that the said Palatines upon their arrival there, be naturalized . . . that they may enjoy all such privileges and advantages as are Enjoyed by the present Inhabitants of that province.[4]

For whatever reason, Governor Hunter decided against a settlement on Crown land. The Germans were then settled not on the banks of the Mohawk River, but on land along the Hudson River sold to the province by Robert Livingston, commissioner of Indian affairs. Four villages made up East Camp, located on the east side of the river at the present site of Germantown, in Columbia County. Three villages comprised West Camp, on the west side of the river at the present site of Saugerties. Governor Hunter also awarded to Livingston the contract for providing food and supplies to the Germans. At least two sources claim that Livingston cheated them. The reason is not clear. It may have been simple politics. Hunter was a Tory, Livingston a Whig. The Whigs, who had taken over the government while Hunter was en route to New York, ceased funding the project. For some reason Hunter continued to pay for the Germans' supplies until he had emptied his purse. In any case, the Germans knew they were being cheated and blamed the governor.

---

[4] Lester E. Hendrix and Anne Whitbeck Hendrix, comp. and ed., *The Sloughters' History of Schoharie County* (Schoharie, N.Y.: Schoharie Historical Society, 1995), p. 30.

In the spring of 1711 they began work. Nearly one hundred thousand trees were felled and prepared. Roads were constructed to bring tar to the banks of the river. Coopers made barrels and cauldrons were made ready. The work did not prosper, however, perhaps because neither the supervisors nor the workers knew how to extract tar or produce turpentine, or perhaps because the species of pine available to them did not contain useful amounts of pitch. (The best pine for tar and turpentine is the longleaf pine, Pinus palustris, found only in the south. The best source colonists in New York had would have been the pitch pine, Pinus rigida, found from southern Maine to northern Georgia.[5]) Wallace explains the failure thus: "Sackett was a local farmer who had persuaded the Governor (who understood nothing about the tar business) that he (Sackett) understood everything; and who, having been put in charge of production, had proceeded with great energy and confidence to have his hundred thousand trees barked in the wrong way."[6]

By the autumn of 1712, Hunter could no longer afford the expense and the Germans were left to fend for themselves, still in debt to the crown. Disgusted, many left for the land along the Schoharie Creek, which they claimed had been promised to them by Queen Anne.

SCHOHARIE INTERLUDE, 1712–23

In the winter of 1712–13, about fifty families walked to the Schoharie Valley. More joined them in the spring, making a total of between five hundred and seven hundred people. They founded seven "dorfs," or farming villages, along the Schoharie Creek.[7] The southernmost, Weiser's Dorf, named for Conrad Weiser, was at the site of present-day Middleburgh and contained about forty dwellings. Hartman's Dorf, named after Hartman Winteker and located between Middleburgh and Schoharie, contained sixty-five dwellings. Brunnen Dorf, at the site of present-day Schoharie

---

[5] Elbert L. Little. *The Audubon Society Field Guide to North American Trees, Eastern Region* (New York: Knopf, 1980).

[6] Paul A. W. Wallace. *Conrad Weiser 1696–1760, Friend of Colonist and Mohawk* (Philadelphia: University of Pennsylvania Press, 1945), p. 12.

[7] Jeptha R. Simms. *History of Schoharie County and Border Wars of New York* (Albany: Munsell & Tanne, 1845), p. 48.

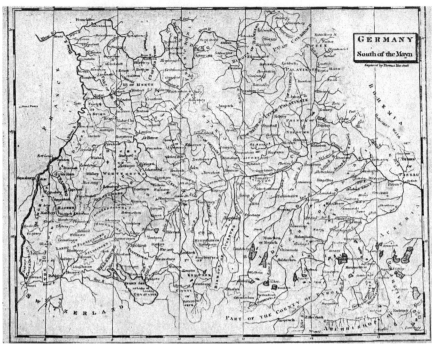

Map of the Palatine, detail from "Germany South of the Mayne," from *A New and Elegant General Atlas* by Aaron Arrowsmith (Boston: Thomas & Andrews, 1805), p. 22.

Village, translates to "Fountain Town"; it was named for a large spring located near the current courthouse. Smith's Dorf, named after Johannes George Smidt, was located about one mile north of Brunnen Dorf. Next to Smith's Dorf were Fox's Dorf and Fox's Creek, both named for William Fox. Garlock's Dorf, named for Elias Garlock, was between Schoharie and Central Bridge. Kneiskern's Dorf, named for John Peter Kneiskern, was the most northerly settlement, on the east side of the Schoharie River opposite the mouth of Cobel's Kill.

Because the settlers were viewed in Albany as squatters, conflict was inevitable. On November 3, 1714, Governor Hunter sold the Huntersfield Patent to a group of businessmen (Myndert Schuyler, Peter Van Brugh, Robert Livingston, Jr., John Schuyler, Henry Wileman, Lewis Morris, Jr., and Andrus Coeman) known as the "Seven Partners of Schoharie."[8] Earlier, on August 26, Adam Vrooman had

---

[8] Ibid., p. 62.

obtained a patent to four hundred acres in the area. Vrooman, then aged 75, apparently bought the land for his son Peter, who occupied it the same year with his own eldest son Bartholomew. Peter Vrooman was not well received by the Palatines, as his subsequent complaint makes clear:

> I have mannured a great part of the Land and Sowed Considerable grain thereon they still drove their horses on in by night, I then hired my sones to go with me and build me a house . . . but on the 4th day of this Instant In ye night following they had a Contryvance to tie bells about the horses necks and drive them too and fro In which time they pulled my house Stones and all to the Ground the next day I spok with some of them and they used such Rebelious Expressions that was never heard off. . . . John Conradus Wiser has been the Ring Leader of all factions for he has had his son some time to Live among the Indians and now he is turn'd their Interpreter. . . . I am no wayes secure of my Life their for after I came away they went and pulld my son off of the wagon and beat him and said they would kill him or his father or anybody Else that came their John Conradus Wiser & 2 or 3 more has made their Escape by way of Boston and have said they will go for England but has left his son which is their Interpreter to the Indians and every day tells the Indians many Lyes. . . . I am well Informed who are their Chiefes: for those that are good Subjects among them and will not Joyn with them are afraid the others will Burn their houses down by their threatening words. . . .[9]

When the sheriff was sent to intervene, he was mobbed by a group of determined Palatine women:

> When the sheriff began to meddle with the first man, a mob of women rose, of which Magdalene Zee was captain. He [Sheriff Adams] was knocked down, and dragged

---

[9] Hendrix and Hendrix, *Sloughters' History,* p. 37.

through every mud-pool in the street; then hung on a rail and carried four miles, thrown down on a bridge, where the captain took a stake out of the fence, and struck him in the side, that she broke two of his ribs and lost one eye; then she pissed in his face, let him lie and went off.

Knowing that discretion is the better part of valor, the wounded Adams made off for Albany. For a good time to come, the men of Schoharie stayed away from that city, sending women instead, but not forever. After things cooled, the partners had a sheriff's posse waiting and a group of visiting Palatines, including Weiser junior, was seized and jailed.[10]

At this time (1718) an enumeration was made of the German families in New York A total of 394 families was tallied, including 170 in the "Seven Townships" in Schoharie and 7 in "Wessels pretended land." (See Table 1.) One of the signers of the account was Joshua Kocherthal, presumably the same Rev. Joshua Kocherthal who led the first group of Palatines.

Although there were signs of division amongst the families, the majority agreed to send a committee to London to plead their cause before King George I. (Queen Anne had died August 1, 1714). In 1718 the elder Conrad Weiser, William Scheff, and Gerhardt Walrath set forth on an ill-fated journey to London. Waylaid and robbed by pirates, they were jailed for debt when they finally reached their destination. Both Scheff and Walrath died in London. In 1723 Conrad Weiser returned empty-handed to find that the group had fragmented. Some had stayed in the area, and others had moved west or south.

DISPERSAL FROM SCHOHARIE

In 1719 Governor Hunter became the governor of Jamaica and a new governor, William Burnet, was installed in Albany. In 1721 Conrad Weiser, Jr., petitioned the new governor for redress of their grievances. As a result, those who wished to stay in the area were able to purchase

---

[10] Ibid., pp. 37–38.

Table 1
AN ACCOUNT OF THE FAMILIES
OF GERMANS SETTLED ON HUDSON'S
RIVER IN THE PROVINCE OF NEW YORK, 1718

ON THE EAST SIDE OF HUDSON'S RIVER	LOCATION	FAMILIES	PERSONS
	Hunterstown	25	109
	Kingsberry	33	104
	Annberry	17	71
	Haysberry	16	75
	Rheinbeck	35	140
In Schoharie	Seven Townships	170	680
On the West Side	New Town	14	56
	George Town	13	52
	Eliz. Town	9	36
	Kingstown	15	60
	Wessels pretended land	7	28
	Kingstown Sopes	10	40
	At New York & places adjacent	30	150
		394	1601

The widows & orphans are not included in this list.

This to the best of our knowledge is the Accot of those people settled, amounting to 394 families, containing abut 1601 persons.

[signed] Joshua Kocherthal and John Fred. Hager

[endorsed] "New York, List of the Palatines settled in New York Province Recd wth Brig. Hunters Lr of 7 Aug 1718" [11]

---

[11] E. B. O'Callaghan, *The Documentary History of the State of New York*, Vol. I (Albany: Weed, Parsons & Co., 1849), pp. 692–93.

land from the "Seven Partners" at reasonable terms at Stone Arabia in the Mohawk Valley. Information about these families may be found in the records of the Reformed Dutch Church of Stone Arabia.[12] The earliest surnames are Lauks, Sutz, Dilleback, and Allstein.

Other Palatine families obtained land in the Burnetsfield Patent in 1722. They founded the town of Herkimer near Utica. Table 2 lists those settlers who formed the Herkimer Church (north side) and the Fort Herkimer Church (south side).[13] Each person, not each family, received one hundred acres, and at least three acres was to be cultivated in three years.

Table 2
SETTLERS WHO FOUNDED THE HERKIMER
AND FORT HERKIMER CHURCHES, HERKIMER, NEW YORK

PATENTEES ON NORTH SIDE	PATENTEES ON SOUTH SIDE
Eva Staring (wife of John Adam [Staring])	Jacob Bowman
John Jost Temouth	Christopher Fox
Mary Beerman	Johannes Reslaer
Augustines Hess	Nicolas Kaslaer
Johannes Poenradt	Anna Dacksteder (wife of Jurgh Dacksteder)
Gertruy Poenradt (wife of Johannes [Poenradt])	Johannes Miller
Henry Heger	Nicholas Staring
Elisabeth Hellmer (wife of Lendert Hellmer)	Joseph Staring
Hendrick Spoon, Jr.	Conradt Orendorf

[12] *Records of the Reformed Dutch Church of Stone Arabia in the town of Palatine, Montgomery County, New York* (Schenectady, N.Y.: Schenectady Genealogical Society, 1941).

[13] W.N.P. Dailey, *History of the Old Fort Herkimer Church, German Flats Reformed Church, 1723* (St. Johnsville, N.Y.: St. Johnsville Enterprise and News, no date), p. 3.

PATENTEES ON NORTH SIDE	PATENTEES ON SOUTH SIDE
Johan Adam Staring	Hendrick Orendorf
Lodwick Pares	Peter Spels
Johannis Beerman	Lawrence Herter
Philip Helmer	Ffrederick Pellinger
Frederick Pell	Conrady Ryckert
Anna Mary Pell	John Mitchall Edigh
Mary Catherine Koens (widow)	Hendrick Spoon
Melgert Ffols	Johannes Hess
Johan Veldelant	Nicholas Weileven
Adam Michael Smith	Ludolph Korsing
Johan Jurgh Kast, Jr.	Anna Mayor
John Adam Helmer	Catharine Pears
Nicholas Ffeller	Margaret Pellenger (wife of Johannes Pellenger)
Jacob Wever	Jacob Edich
Johan Jurgh Smith	Michael Editch
Johan Jost Petre	Hans Conradt Ffelmore
Hendrick Mayer	Christina Ffelmore
Thos. Shoemaker	Ludolph Shomaker
Anna Catherena Lant (widow)	Mary Ffeller (wife of Nicholas Ffeller)
Johan Adam Bowman	Jacob Wever, Junr.
Godfree Reele	Mark Petrie
Nicholas Wever	Odelia Koring (wife of Ludolph Koring)
Tedrigh Temouth	Anna Margaret Helmer (wife of Johan Adam Helmer)
Jurgh Dacksteder	Andries Wever
Ledwick Rickert	Godfrey Reele, Junr.
Johannes Pellinger	Ephraim Smith
Lendert Helmer	Elisabeth Spels (wife of Peter Spels)
Johan Jurgh Kast	Appolone Herter

continued on next page

Table 2 *(cont.)*

PATENTEES ON NORTH SIDE	PATENTEES ON SOUTH SIDE
Peter Pellinger	Mark Rykert
Frederick Staring	Marte Smith
Gertruyt Petrie (wife of Johan Jost Petrie)	Jacob Ffols
Johannes Velden Staring	Ludwick Kones
Ellizabeth Edigh	John Velde Staring, Junr.
Margaret Pellenger (wife of Peter Pellenger)	
Catharrine Rickert	
Anna Veldelant	
Frederick Helmer	

The younger Conrad Weiser persuaded approximately sixty families to move south with him to Tulpehocken, Berks County, Pennsylvania. An account of that settlement may be found in any of the several published biographies of Conrad Weiser, Jr.,[14] or from the Tulpehocken Settlement Historical Society in Womelsdorf, Pennsylvania. According to Peter Kalm, as quoted in Rupp, these German settlers related their side of their experiences in New York to their friends and relatives.[15] They advised against settling in New York and directed the newcomers to Pennsylvania. Thus in the eighteenth century, areas such as Bucks County and Lancaster County experienced a large influx of German farmers who might otherwise have settled in the Mohawk Valley.

---

[14] For example, Wallace, *Conrad Weiser 1696–1760.*

[15] Rupp, *Thirty Thousand Names*, Appendix X, p. 452.

CHAPTER 25

Early Nineteenth-Century Welsh Immigrants in Upper New York State

M any groups participated in early nineteenth-century immigration into upper New York State. In this chapter we take a look at a quiet, unassuming group — the Welsh. Welsh immigration began earlier than the nineteenth century, of course. Fourteen generals of the Revolutionary army were Welshmen, as were eighteen signers of the Declaration of Independence.[1] Both Thomas Jefferson and John Adams claimed some Welsh ancestry.[2] The years between 1800 and 1850 saw several waves of Welsh immigration to America. At the time there was some degree of social unrest in Wales because of low farm prices, high rents, and a shift to industrialization. Farmers' children had to leave the land to work in the mines. In America they saw the promise of cheap land, religious freedom, and a chance for advancement. Although the Welsh came to America in groups and settled together, they did not cling to their ethnic background as the Palatines or the Irish did; within two or three generations they were assimilated. As a result, "Welshness" can be hard to spot. You may have Welsh ancestors and not even know it. In this article we look at ways of identifying these elusive Welshmen, using the Welsh community in Cattaraugus County as an example.

An earlier version of this chapter was posted at *www.NewEnglandAncestors.org* November 19, 2004.

[1] Jan Morris, *The Matter of Wales* (New York: Oxford University Press, 1984), p. 334.

[2] Ibid., p. 335.

[3] Gertrude Barber, "Cattaraugus County, N.Y. Cemeteries" (typescript, 1930).

Gertrude Barber's work on cemetery inscriptions in the county includes records from a "Welch" cemetery in the town of Freedom.[3] An early history of Cattaraugus County describes a Welsh community in the town of Freedom thus:[4]

> In 1841, Robert Williams, John Higgins, Thomas Rees, Daniel Morgans, H. O. Roberts, John Lewis, and others came in from Oneida Co., N.Y., and formed the nucleus of a welsh settlement, which has prospered and increased in numbers until there are found in this and the adjoining towns of Farmersville and Centreville a population of at least 500 of these thrifty, law-abiding, enterprising people.

In addition to listing the names of these six immigrants, the same article mentions Ebenezer Baptist Church (Welsh), organized May 2, 1843, with forty-two members, and Salem Church (Welsh Calvinistic Methodist, first meeting in 1851). A more recent county history continues the history of these churches: "Freedom Ebenezer Church, which is Welsh Baptist, observed its centennial in 1943. The old records were written in Welsh but Rev. R. J. Williams of Scranton, Pa. translated them and so furnished an excellent history to be read at that meeting."[5] The author goes on to say that by 1895, the town had established Bethel Baptist Church to accommodate Welsh children who wanted services in English. In 1919 the two churches were combined, forming Freedom Baptist Church. The Calvinistic Methodist Church changed to Presbyterian in 1892. From this we have a picture of a group of families moving west, forming a supportive frontier community. Within fifty years use of the Welsh language was greatly diminished and before a hundred years had disappeared altogether.

A search for the "others" that accompanied or followed the six named pioneers is conveniently begun using the 1850 federal census, which records place of birth. A survey for heads of household born

---

[4] Franklin Ellis, *History of Cattaraugus County, New York* (Philadelphia: L. H. Everts, 1879), p. 392.

[5] O. M. Howlett, *150 Years of Freedom 1811–1961*, 2nd ed. (Freedom, N.Y.: Freedom Sesquicentennial Committee, 1962), p. 5.

in Wales for the town of Freedom, Cattaraugus County, yields the names in Table 1. The names are presented alphabetically by page number. Although the entire census for Freedom occupies pages 430 to 450, half of the names in the table are clustered on pages 430 to 434, and nearly three-quarters are on pages 430 to 438. This supports the idea of close proximity. The six names listed in the early county history — Williams, John Higgins, Thomas Rees, Daniel Morgans, H. O. Roberts, John Lewis — are all there.[6] Undoubtedly a similar survey of the 1850 census records of adjoining towns, not forgetting neighboring Allegany and Wyoming counties, would yield similar results.

Table 1
HEADS OF HOUSEHOLD
BORN IN WALES: 1850 FEDERAL CENSUS,
FREEDOM, CATTARAUGUS COUNTY, NEW YORK

FIRST NAME	SURNAME	PAGE	FIRST NAME	SURNAME	PAGE
David	Francis	430	Thomas	Jones	435
Lewis	Griffith	430	David O.	Davis	436
David	Phillips	430	Griffith	Griffith	436
Hugh	Richards	430	John	Higgins	436
Stephen	James	431	John T.	Owens	436
William	Philips	431	Hugh	Roberts	436
Daniel	Reese	431	Hugh O.	Roberts	436
Thomas	Reese	431	William E.	Williams	436
Hugh H.	Roberts	431	William	Jones	437
Thomas	Wiggin	431	Thomas	Morgan	437
Thomas	Evans	432	John	Lewis	438
Thomas W.	Morgan	432	Daniel	Morgan	438

continued on next page

---

[6] The coincidence of finding the same six names is suggestive but not definitive. Further research would have to be done to determine whether those listed in the 1850 census are the same as those listed in the county history.

Table 1 (cont.)

FIRST NAME	SURNAME	PAGE	FIRST NAME	SURNAME	PAGE
Benjamin	James	433	John R.	Rogers	438
John	Jones	433	William J.	Williams	438
Robert P.	Roberts	433	Thomas	James	440
Robert	**Williams**	433	Hugh M.	Jones	442
Daniel	Edwards	434	John R.	Jones	443
Benjamin	Pairs	434	Stephen W.	Owens	444
John J.	Jones	435			

But what can we learn about these families' lives from the years before their migration to Cattaraugus County? Because these Welsh settlers were said to have entered Cattaraugus County in 1841 from Oneida County, we might look for their names in the 1840 federal census of that county. In fact, such a search yields one or more matches for every one of them. Some of the names are quite common. For example, I found eighteen entries for "John Jones," three for "John R. Jones," but only one "John J. Jones." All the name matches in the 1840 census come from ten contiguous towns in the northeastern section of Oneida County — Lee, Western, Steuben, Remsen, Boonville, Floyd, Trenton, Whitestown, Marcy, and Deerfield. All these towns are east of the city of Rome and north of the Mohawk River.[7]

By comparing ages and family makeup, we can in some cases be reasonably certain of a match between a family in Cattaraugus County in 1850 and a family in Oneida County in 1840. I chose two households as a test case — Hugh O. Roberts and William E. Williams, entered next to each other on page 436 in the 1850 census for Freedom.

---

[7] Settlement in this location is typical for the early nineteenth century. Settlement spread first up the Hudson River, then west along the Mohawk.

Table 2
1850 FEDERAL CENSUS, FREEDOM,
CATTARAUGUS COUNTY, NEW YORK, P. 436

NAME	AGE	SEX	BORN
Hugh O. Roberts	50	M	Wales
Elizabeth Roberts	53	F	Wales
Robert Roberts	23	M	N.Y.
Benjamin Roberts	18	M	N.Y.
Jane Ann Roberts	15	F	N.Y.
Elizabeth Roberts	13	F	N.Y.
Owen Roberts	12	M	N.Y.
William E. Williams	61	M	Wales
Margaret Williams	55	F	Wales
Samuel W. Williams	22	M	Wales
William Williams	15	M	N.Y.
John Williams	12	M	N.Y.
Elen Williams	6	F	N.Y.

Assuming that each household represents a married couple and their children, we can already say something about when the families left Wales. Samuel W. Williams, age 22, was born in Wales, but his younger brother, William Williams, age 15, was born in New York. On this evidence, we can deduce that the family of William E. Williams left Wales after 1828 and settled in New York before 1835. By similar reasoning, the birthplace of Robert Roberts, age 23, in New York, limits the emigration of Hugh O. Roberts to before 1827.

The 1840 federal census for Oneida County contains entries for Hugh O. Roberts, town of Western, and William E. Williams, town of Trenton, which seem to match, allowing for older children to have left home.

Table 3
COMPARISON OF 1840
FEDERAL CENSUS RECORDS FOR ONEIDA COUNTY WITH
1850 FEDERAL CENSUS RECORDS FOR CATTARAUGUS COUNTY

HUGH O. ROBERTS		WILLIAM E. WILLIAMS	
1840 Western	1850, Freedom	1840 Trenton	1850 Freedom
1M <5	Owen, 12	1M <5	John, 12
1M 5–10	Benjamin, 18	1M 5–10	William, 15
2M 10–15	Robert, 13	1M 10–15	Samuel W., 22
	[son, 20-25]	1M50–60	William E., 61
1M 30–40	Hugh, 50		Elen, 6
2F 5–10	Jane Ann, 15	2F 15–20	[2 dau. 25–30]
	Elizabeth, 13	1F 50-60	Margaret, 55
1F 15–20	[dau. 25–30]		
1F 40–50	Elizabeth, 53		

To the writers of early county histories, these events were quite recent. Pomroy Jones, writing in 1851 about the town of Remsen in Oneida County, states, "David Mound, John James, Griffith I. Jones, John Owens, Hugh Hughes came about 1808 to Remsen from Wales."[8] These Welsh became successful dairy farmers and wrote back to Wales encouraging others to come. It seems likely that only part of the Welsh community in Oneida County moved to Cattaraugus County, for Jones further states, "At least three-fourths of its population is Welsh. It is said that Remsen, Steuben, Trenton, and portions of Deerfield, Marcy, and Boonville are almost as well known in Wales as in Oneida County."[9] All the churches in Remsen were Welsh, as were six of the seven churches in the town of Steuben.

---

[8] Pomroy Jones, *Annals and Recollections of Oneida County* (Rome, N.Y.: the author, 1851), p. 306.

[9] Ibid.

By the end of the nineteenth century, the Welsh had assimilated enough that it's hard to find clues of Welsh origins in records from later years. In an 1896 county history, Daniel Wager described the twilight of the Welsh as a separate community in Oneida County. After speaking of the arrival of Welsh settlers in Marcy, Remsen, and Steuben, he gives these particulars of Thomas Thomas:

> About the year 1800 the family of Thomas Thomas, another Welshman, settled in this town [Steuben]. He had been a sailor and was a victim of the British press gangs. He afterwards lost his right leg in an engagement with a French ship; this occurred in 1796, and he was taken to Halifax, thence to Greenwich Hospital, and finally married and returned to America. He died at the age of eighty-seven years, and was the last survivor of the Welsh pioneers of this town.[10]

Even though a Welsh community melted into the mainstream quickly on a genealogist's time scale, it maintained its identity long enough to leave local traces. In addition to the sources cited earlier, place names — for example, "Welsh Creek" or "Wales Hollow" — can be a clue. Table 4 contains a list of some place names in New York State[11] containing "Welsh/Welch" or "Wales." Consider the entry for "Welsh Hill," a summit in the town of Plainfield in Otsego County. Was there once a Welsh community in Plainfield? I searched on the word "Welsh" on the Otsego County section of *RootsWeb.com*[12] and found reference[13] to the Welsh Congregational Church of Plainfield, organized in 1861, first pastor Hugh R. Williams. Further research should readily determine how this congregation came to Plainfield.

---

[10] Daniel E. Wager, ed., *Our County and Its People, a Descriptive Work on Oneida County New York,* (Boston: Boston History Co., 1896), p. 550.

[11] Obtained from *http://geonames.usgs.gov/*.

[12] See *www.rootsweb.com/~nyotsego/churches/plainfield.htm.*

[13] D. Hamilton Hurd, *The History of Otsego County, New York, 1740–1878* (Philadelphia: Everts & Fariss, 1878).

Table 4
PLACE NAMES IN NEW YORK
STATE CONTAINING "WELSH" OR "WALES"

PLACE NAME	COUNTY	TYPE	LATITUDE	LONGITUDE
Welsh Corners	Herkimer	locale	430934N	0745914W
Welsh Hill	Lewis	pop. place	433810N	0752739W
Welsh Cemetery	Madison	cemetery	424730N	0751558W
Welsh Hill	Otsego	summit	424809N	0750942W
Welsh Camp	Rockland	locale	411354N	0740405W
Welsh Corners	Schoharie	locale	422726N	0743401W
Welsh Hill	Schoharie	summit	422842N	0742953W
Welsh Brook	St. Lawrence	stream	443146N	0744430W
Welsh Church	St. Lawrence	church	442434N	0752359W
Welsh Creek	St. Lawrence	stream	441430N	0750702W
Welsh Vly	Warren	swamp	432842N	0735628W
Welsh Hollow Cemetery	Washington	cemetery	432903N	0732956W
Welsh Cemetery	Oneida	cemetery	432122N	0752726W
Wales Center	Erie		424606N	0783149W
Wales Hollow	Erie		424433N	0782919W
Walesville	Oneida	pop. place	420655N	0752157W
Wales, Town of	Erie	civil	424346N	0783112W
Wales Hollow	Erie	school	424548N	0783108W
Wales Center	Erie	pop. place	424606N	0783149W

From U. S. Board on Geographic Names, U. S. Geologic Survey,
http://geonames.usgs.gov/.

Table 4 contains three entries in St. Lawrence County. A search of the RootsWeb site[14] of an associated Welsh community yielded a sample of text in the Welsh language — a newspaper obituary for Rev. David Jones.

> Died. Jones. In Gouverneur, June 3, 1886, of kidney disease, Rev. David Jones, pastor of the Welsh Congregational church, Richville, aged 64 years, 10 months and 24 days. *BU FARW. Mehefin 3, 1886, yn Richville, N.Y. y Parch David Jones, Gweinldog yr Eglwys Gunulleidfaol Gymreig, yn 65 mlwydd oed: weedi bodyn pregethu yr efengyl amtua deugain mlynedd. Yr oedd el gymheriad yn ddilychwin. Yn ci amser goreu yr oedd yn un o'r pregethuyr mwyafcraffus a sylweddol. Cafodd gladdedlgaeth barchus Saboth y oed Cyf. Gweinyddwyd ar yr achlusur gan y Parch Mr. Morris, Crary's Mills, yn hypon effaithiol. Bydded nodded "Barnwr y gweddwon a Thad yr Ymmddifaid" dros y teulu.*[15]

From this necessarily brief look at Welsh immigration into upper New York State, we glimpse a prosperous community with a strong religious foundation. They were people looking for opportunities and open to change. If your family tree contains an Owens, or a Morgan, or a Reese, they may have arrived from Wales in the nineteenth century

[14] See *www.rootsweb.com/~nystlawr/html/searching_st_lawrence_county_.html*.

[15] "Births, Deaths, Marriages from Gouverneur, NY Herald, St. Lawrence County, NY (approx. 1864-1904)," database online at *www.rootsweb.com/~nystlaw/herald/hrldtxt10.htm*.

CHAPTER 26

From France to New York:
The Story of Three Sisters
Named Marie

W hen lands in central New York State became available for purchase after the Revolutionary War, a flood of settlers poured into the region. Against the background of this mass migration, a tiny drama played out in the south central part of the state involving French aristocrats driven from their homeland during the French Revolution. In the style of traditional immigration stories, but with a twist, I relate this tale of three Maries who sailed to Philadelphia to start a new life. These were the three wealthy d'Ohet sisters, Marie Jeane (d'Ohet) d'Autremont, Marie Genevieve (d'Ohet) LeFevre, and Marie Claudine d'Ohet. My tale also includes brief mention of a few characters, namely Victor du Pont de Nemours and Captain Joseph Juliand. My information comes from several sources[1] and is, by turns, ambiguous, contradictory, or wrong. In the process of attempting to corroborate these "family myths" with readily available primary records, it becomes apparent that the events were not as tidy as related in these county histories.

An earlier version of this chapter was posted at *www.NewEnglandAncestors.org* April 20, 2002.

[1] John S. Minard, *Allegany County and Its People* (Alfred, N.Y.: W. A. Fergusson & Co., 1896); Arch Merrill, *Pioneer Profiles* (New York; American Book-Stratford Press, 1957); Alexander C. Flick, ed., *History of the State of New York in Ten Volumes* (New York: Columbia University Press, 1934), Vol. 5: *Conquering the Wilderness;* T. Wood Clarke, *Emigrés in the Wilderness* (New York: Macmillan, 1941); J. W. Ingham, *A Short History of Asylum, Pennsylvania, Founded in 1793 by the French Exiles in America* (Towanda, Pa.: Towanda Printing Company, 1916); James H. Smith, *History of Chenango & Madison Counties* (Syracuse, N.Y.: D. Mason, 1880).

THE THREE MARIES

Unless a specific source is given, the information comes from one or more of the six references noted in footnote one. Most of the substantiating data are available on various county web pages in the USGenWeb collection for New York (*www.rootsweb.com/~nygenweb/*) and Pennsylvania (*www.pagenweb.org/*).

Marie Jeane d'Ohet (born 1745; died August 29, 1809, or January 29, 1810) married Hubert d'Autremont 3 or 5 February 1770, and bore him three sons, Alexander Hubert, Louis Paul, and Augustus François Cecile. Hubert d'Autremont was guillotined early in the French Revolution.

Marie Genevieve d'Ohet (born 1752; died August 23, 1834) married Antoine Bartholemy Louie LeFevre (unknown birthdate; died February 1, 1830). They had two sons (Alexander and one who died young) and two daughters (Cecilia and Augustine).

Of the three Maries, the least is known about Marie Claudine d'Ohet (born 1758; died January 10, 1810). She was a nun in France whose convent had been destroyed during the revolution. She moved to Nantes, then sailed to New York in 1806 and came to her sister's home in Angelica. She died there at age 52.

THE VOYAGE

On June 19, 1792, Marie Jeane d'Autremont, her three sons, and her brother-in-law LeFevre were among a group of refugees who sailed with Charles Felix de Boulogne from Le Havre to Philadelphia. According to tradition, LeFevre's passport allowed only himself, one daughter, and one son to leave the country. The son died shortly before sailing, so the other daughter was smuggled aboard in his stead. Marie Genevieve LeFevre and their remaining son, Alexander,[2] followed two years later.

I searched for Boulogne, d'Autremont, and LeFevre in Filby's Passenger and Immigration Lists Index, but found no record of a

---

[2] Alexander LeFevre reportedly enlisted in the army in the War of 1812 and died of sickness at Carlisle, Pa.

1792 voyage from France to Philadelphia. There is, however, an arrival in 1796 of Louis Paul d'Autremont.[3]

THE BUTTERNUT SETTLEMENT

In the sources cited, Charles Felix de Boulogne[4] is variously termed an agent of the land speculators or the leader of the colony. Through his efforts, the group acquired a tract of nearly twenty-five square miles, purchased in 1792 from patentees Malachi Treat and the ubiquitous Robert Morris. The best estimate of the location of this land is the juncture of Butternut Creek and the Unadilla River in Chenango County. This junction is today in the town of Greene, about two miles north of exit 9 on U.S. Interstate 88. Smith[5] lists Lefevre and Boulogne (but not d'Autremont) as new arrivals in 1793, as well as Shamont, Bravo, DuVernet, and Obre. Other sources say the group, headed by Boulogne, arrived in October 1792.

This first "Butternut" settlement was not successful. Several sources speak of aristocrats unable to cope with building shelter, planting crops, and spending a pitiful winter in a drafty one-room log cabin. Their hardships were compounded by a questionable title to the land, their inability to make payments, and the death of Boulogne. All these circumstances led them to leave in 1794 or 1795 to join a more successful French settlement farther south in Bradford County, Pennsylvania, called Asylum.

THE ASYLUM SETTLEMENT AND THE RETURN TO FRANCE

In the online Bradford County Archives (*www.rootsweb.com/~srgp/jmtindex.htm*), I found a listing for taxables in 1796 containing both Widow d'Autremont and Anthony B. Lafevre, as well as Oliver Dodge. In 1797, middle son Alexander Hubert d'Autremont (born

---

[3] P. William Filby, *Passenger and Immigration Lists Index* (Detroit: Gale Research Co., 1981), 1:427.

[4] Boulogne is said to have drowned while attempting to ford Loyal Sock Creek at Hillsgrove, Pa., on 20 July 1796. The water was very high at the time. His body was recovered and buried at Hillsgrove.

[5] Smith, *History of Chenango & Madison Counties.*

12 March 1776; died 4 April or August 1857), married Abigail, daughter of Major Oliver Dodge of Tarrytown, four miles below Asylum on the Susquehanna River.

Meanwhile in France, Napoleon staged a successful coup d'état in November 1799. In 1800, he granted amnesty to the aristocrats who fled during the Revolution and promised the restoration of their estates. Many of the émigrés returned to France. Louis Paul d'Autremont (born November 7, 1770; died 1860), eldest son of Marie, returned to Paris and took a wife. He died in 1840, leaving one daughter who married a man named Bridet. Her two sons took their mother's maiden name, d'Autremont, by decree of the emperor in 1852.

MARIE JEANE D'AUTREMONT

Marie Jeane d'Autremont reportedly returned to the Butternut location in Chenango County with her two younger sons. However I have found no evidence of her presence. The 1800 federal census for Chenango County does contain a record for Alexander Dutrimone in the town of Greene (see Table 1). Marie Jeane d'Autremont would have been 55 at the time of the census, her son Alexander would have been 24, and her son Augustus François Cecile would have been 17. The census information shows that while this household could consist of Alexander, his wife Abigail, his daughter, his brother Augustus, and one other unknown male, the age of his mother does not match up. I also found no d'Autremont, searching several spelling variants, in the 1800 census for Pennsylvania.

In 1806, Marie Jeane apparently bought land from Philip Church on the western frontier on the Genesee River in Allegany County, town of Angelica, where she died.[6]

---

[6] This is the so-called Church Tract, a six- by twenty-six-mile tract on the Genesee River named for Philip Church, who acquired the land in 1800. As an aside, it is possible that the d'Autremont and Church families were well acquainted. Both were intimately acquainted with both Lafayette and Talleyrand. Philip Church was the grandson of General Philip Schuyler and the nephew of Alexander Hamilton's wife. Two points here also hint at a close relationship: first, Alexander d'Autremont named his youngest daughter Sophia Church; second, Philip Church married Anna Matilda, eldest daughter of Gen. Walter Stewart of Philadelphia and Augustus d'Autremont married a Sarah Ann Stewart.

THE D'AUTREMONT/DAUTREMENT SONS IN ANGELICA

Records for the two younger d'Autremont sons in Allegany County are relatively plentiful. The 1808 list of freeholders for the town of Angelica lists both Alexander and Augustus "Dautrement" and here they seemed to settle. The naturalization of Augustus (1783–1860) is recorded in court proceedings of June 1809. The Allegany County website at *www.rootsweb.com/~nyallega/* contains a list of jurors that served between 1807 and 1810. Alexander served October 26, 1808; June 9, 1809; October 24, 1809; January 16, 1810; and 26, June 1810. Augustus served October 26, 1808, and October 23, 1810. The 1810 census (Table 1) lists Alexander Deutremont and Augustus Dautimonte in Angelica. Alexander would have been about 44 years of age, his younger brother about 37.

Table 1
EXTRACTS FROM 1800 AND 1810
FEDERAL CENSUS RECORDS, NEW YORK STATE
FREE WHITE PERSONS, INCLUDING HEADS OF FAMILIES

YEAR	1800	1810	1810
NAME	Alexander Dutrimone	Alexander Deutremont	Augustus Dautrmonte
TOWN	Greene	Angelica	Angelica
COUNTY	Chenango	Allegany	Allegany
M <10	—	2	—
M 10–16	—	1	—
M 16–26	2	—	1
M 26–45	1	1	—
M >45	—	—	—
F <10	1	2	—
F 10–16	—	—	—
F 16–26	1	—	—
F 26–45	—	1	—
F >45	—	—	—

Minard lists children of Alexander Dautremont and Abigail Dodge (see Table 2). From this list we can account for all persons in the 1810 census record for Alexander except one male between the ages of 10 and 16. I also found the 1820 record, which contains two unknown males between the ages of 16 and 26. Since Alexander is listed in the 1850 census as a 75-year-old farmer,[7] it is likely that these "extra" young men were farm workers. The eldest daughter Adeline is missing in 1820. She would have been 20 and could have been married to Ithemer Smith by then. There is a listing for Ithemer Smith in the town of Covington, Genesee County.

Table 2
CHILDREN OF ALEXANDER DAUTREMONT
AND ABIGAIL DODGE

NAME	BIRTHDATE	SPOUSE
Adeline	12 July 1800	Ithemer Smith
Amelia du Pont	28 April 1803	Hugh Magee
Louis Paul	28 Jan. 1805	Hannah Magee
Victor du Pont	16 Aug. 1807	Isabella Common
Caroline	8 Dec. 1809	Charles Brundage
Janet	30 Nov. 1814	Ephriam Smith
Charles	26 June 1818	Sarah Collins
Alexander	2 April 1821	Diana Howard
Virginia	30 July 1824	unmarried
Sophia Church	3 Aug. 1829	Lucian P. Wetherby

John S. Minard, *Allegany County and Its People* (Alfred, N.Y.: W. A. Fergusson & Co., 1896).

Auguste François Cecile d'Autremont married Sarah Ann Stewart in 1816. One source says she was of New Castle, Delaware, and that Augustus d'Autremont moved to Delaware to work for the du Pont brothers (see below). She died in 1840 and he in 1860. They had ten children, which included two sets of twins. See Table 3.

---

[7] Also listed in his household is Abigail Dautremont, age 79, born in Conn., presumably his wife Abigail Dodge.

Table 3
CHILDREN OF AUGUSTUS DAUTREMONT
AND SARAH ANN STEWART

NAME	BIRTHDATE	SPOUSE
Matilda	1 June 1817	
Josephine	17 Jan. 1820	Harden P. Mather
Augustus, Jr. Mary Hubbard	29 Feb. 1822	Adaline Mather,
Mary Amanda	27 July 1824	
Francis Paul	27 July 1824	
Caroline Elisabeth	27 April 1827	Ralph Taylor
Victorine	17 June 1830	
Eveline Ellen	17 April 1833	
Glodine	16 Dec. 1835	
Sarah Andrina	16 Dec. 1835	Samuel A. Farman

The 1820 census record for an "Agustus" Dautrimont is consistent with husband, wife, and two youngest daughters plus five other males and one female. In the 1850 census, Agustus was an innkeeper,[8] so these "extras" in 1820 may have been guests at the inn or staff.

Also readily found in the 1870 census are the following married children of Alexander Dautremont:

> Victor, 42, a painter; Isabella, 39, born in England; and three children
> Charles, 32, merchant; Sarah, 28
> Adelline, 34; Ithemar Smith, 47, farmer born in Connecticut; six children
> Amelia, 47; Hugh Magee, 50, innkeeper in Hornells, Steuben County
> Sophia, 21; Lucian P. Wetherly, 29, lawyer

---

[8] Apparently his eldest son, Augustus, Jr., followed in his father's profession. His occupation is also that of innkeeper. Glodine, who would have been age 14, is more likely dead than married.

MARIE GENEVIEVE (D'OHET) LEFEVRE

Anthony LeFevre did not return to France, but moved his family across the river from the now-abandoned Asylum settlement to Lime Hill, where he kept an inn. In support of this, I find in the list of taxables for 1812–13 the names Anthony Lafevre and Alexander Lafevre. The elder daughter Cecilia married John Prevost in 1815 and died in Wyoming County, Pennsylvania, in 1876. Augustine, the younger daughter, married John Huff; they had no children. Anthony Lefevre died February 1, 1830, and his wife, Marie Genevieve, died August 23, 1834.

THE DU PONT CONNECTION

Victor du Pont de Nemours, son of Pierre Samuel du Pont de Nemours, bought five hundred acres in the Church tract in 1806, the first deed recorded in the county. He became active in local politics and opened a store. Some connection with the d'Autremont family is found in the names of the children. Alexander d'Autremont named a daughter Amelia du Pont (born 1803), and a son Victor du Pont (born 1807). Augustus d'Autremont named a daughter Victorine (born 1830). Victor du Pont is listed as one of the freeholders in Angelica in 1808. The store reportedly did not prosper and Victor quarreled with the local squire, Philip Church. Victor is said to have left Angelica in 1809 to join his brother Irénée in Delaware. This tale, however, became tangled when I looked deeper.

The DuPont Company's website (*www.dupont.com*) gives a few facts regarding the founding of the firm. On July 19, 1802, Eleuthère Irénée du Pont de Nemours purchased property on the Brandywine River and began construction of Eleutherian Mills. On 1 May 1804, the company began to manufacture and sell gunpowder. By 1811 it was the largest manufacturer of gunpowder in America.

In 1810, however, both brothers were involved as plaintiffs in court cases in Angelica (see Table 4). The 1820 federal census for Delaware lists an E. J. DuPont in New Castle County, but no Victor.[9] It seems more likely that the two brothers jointly launched two separate

---

[9] Series M33, roll 4, page 121, spelled "Dupont."

business ventures, one in New York State and one in Delaware. Were it not for the vagaries of business acumen, the DuPont name might have flourished in New York instead of Delaware.

Table 4
1810 COURT CASES INVOLVING
MEMBERS OF THE DU PONT FAMILY,
TOWN OF ANGELICA, ALLEGANY COUNTY, NEW YORK

PLAINTIFF	DEFENDANT	DATE	VERDICT
E. J. DuPont	Cornelius Borgardus	June 1810	Defendant confessed damages to $51.67
Eleuthère I. DuPont	Luke Goodspeed	Oct. 1810	Clerk assessed $9.11 in cause
Victor DuPont	Silas Knight & Asahel Franklin	June 1810	Defendant confessed damages to $48.58

CAPT. JOSEPH JULIAND: THE MAN
WHO BOUGHT BUTTERNUT

Clarke tells of a Captain Joseph "Juliard," a native of Lyons, who studied medicine, gave it up, and became commander of a merchant ship. On a visit to America he spent some time in New Haven and married "a girl" from that town. While living near Greenfield, Massachusetts, he heard of a French colony in southern New York. Heading there, he arrived as the "Butternut" colony in Chenango County was breaking up. He then bought up the entire site of the village of Greene.[10] In support, Smith lists a "Capt. Joseph Juliand, born Lycos, France, joined French Village in 1796."[11]

Although there is no Joseph Juliard recorded in the 1790 census records of Massachusetts or Connecticut, I have found a Joseph *Juliand* in the 1800 census of Chenango County, town of Greene. The household contains one male under 10, two age 10–16, 1 age 16–26, and one over 45. There is one female under 10 and one age 16–26 as well.[12]

---

[10] T. Wood Clarke. *Emigrés in the Wilderness.*

[11] Smith. *History of Chenango & Madison Counties*, p. 195.

[12] 1800 U.S. Census, Town of Greene, Chenango County, New York (NARA Series M32, Reel 28), p. 742.

The 1850 census record (see Table 5) for Greene, Chenango County, contains the name of Hannah Juliand, 87, born in Connecticut, living in the household of Joseph Juliand, 53, merchant, born in New York. It is tempting to identify Hannah as the "girl" Juliand married in New Haven, and to name the other Juliands — Joseph, age 53; Lewis, age 46; George, age 45; and Frederick, age 42 — as his sons. If so, however, Hannah's age does not agree with the 1800 census record. But there is a female, age 60–70, listed with Frederick Juliand in the 1840 census.[13] This woman would have been between 20 and 30 in 1800, which is consistent with the 1800 record. This suggests that her husband, Joseph Juliand, may have died before 1840.

There is a final Connecticut connection. Living in the household of Lewis Juliand is one Joseph Bulton, 75, a merchant born in Connecticut. This may be the Joseph Bulton listed in the 1800 federal census in the town of Sangerfield, Chenango County (3 males under 10; 1 male 16–25; 2 females under 10; 1 female 16–25). Perhaps this Joseph Bulton is living in 1850 in the house of his married daughter and his son-in-law, Lewis Juliand. Perhaps Lewis Juliand's son, "Jos. B," is Joseph Bulton Juliand, named after his grandfather.

As this chapter illustrates, French ethnicity does not loom large in New York state. Certainly it does not have the importance it has in, say, Maine or Louisiana. Instead it is a thin thread running through a largely British and Dutch heritage. Some French immigrants, like the Marie d'Ohet sisters, came fleeing the murder and mayhem of the Reign of Terror. Others, like the du Ponts and Capt. Juliand exemplify the energy of the entrepreneur looking for new challenges. The brief look at each of these three families also illustrates a widespread, irritating fact of genealogy. Sources don't always agree. County histories, particularly those written toward the close of the nineteenth century, are richly spiced with hearsay and oversimplification. A healthy skepticism comes in handy.

---

[13] All four Juliand households are listed in the 1840 census in Chenango County. None besides Frederick contains any other person over the age of 50.

Table 5
1850 FEDERAL CENSUS RECORDS,
TOWN OF GREENE, CHENANGO COUNTY, NEW YORK

NAME	AGE	SEX	OCCUPATION	BIRTHPLACE
Joseph Juliand	53	M	merchant	NY
A.M. Juliand	45	F		NY
Hannah Juliand	87	F		Conn.
Anna M. Juliand	14	F		NY
J. E. Juliand	6	M		NY
Lewis Juliand*	46	M	farmer	NY
C. E. Juliand	40	F		NY
Wm. L Juliand	12	M		NY
Jos. B. Juliand	8	M		NY
E. C. Juliand	2	F		NY
Joseph Bulton	76	M	merchant	NY
Frederick Juliand**	42	M	merchant	NY
Catharine Juliand	39	F		NY
Jno. R. Juliand	14	M		NY
Sarah J. Juliand	4	F		NY
F. H. Juliand	6/12	M		NY
George Juliand	45	M	farmer	NY
Charlotte Juliand	31	F		NY
Charles Juliand	13	M		NY
Henry Juliand	6	M		NY

* In birth records on the website of Chenango County (*www.rootsweb.com/~nychenan/*), I find the birth of Emma C. Juliand, b. 12 April 1847 to Lewis and Cornellia Juliand.

**In birth records on the website of Chenango County, I find the birth of Frederick H. Juliand, b. 30 March 1850 to Frederick and Catharine Juliand.

CHAPTER 27

Jemima Wilkinson,
the Public Universal Friend

J emima Wilkinson is one of those colorful but little-known historical figures whose discovery delights genealogists. She was the first in a succession of religious leaders associated with upper New York State, which included Mormon Church founder Joseph Smith, pioneers of Spiritualism Margaretta and Kate Fox, and other movements of lesser note such as the New Light Baptists. Wilkinson is also recognized as the first American-born woman to organize a religious group.

A modern biography of Jemima Wilkinson was written by Herbert Wisbey,[1] who cautions his readers about an earlier effort[2] by saying, "The only book devoted exclusively to Jemima Wilkinson was a small biography first published in 1821, and reprinted in 1844, which unfortunately contains some completely fictitious episodes and is largely inaccurate as to fact and misleading in interpretation." Lockwood Doty wrote in *History of the Genesee Country*[3] that Stafford Cleveland's *History of Yates County*[4] "contains the most

---

An earlier version of this chapter was posted at *www.NewEnglandAncestors.org* December 20, 2001.

[1] Herbert A. Wisbey, *Pioneer Prophetess Jemima Wilkinson, the Publick Universal Friend* (Ithaca, N.Y.: Cornell University Press, 1964).

[2] David Hudson. *History of Jemima Wilkinson, a Preacheress of the Eighteenth Century; Containing an Authentic Narrative of Her Life and Character, and of the Rise, Progress and Conclusion of Her Ministry* (Geneva, N.Y.: S. P. Hull, 1821).

[3] Lockwood R. Doty, *History of the Genesee Country*, Volume I (Chicago: S. J. Clark, 1925), p. 452.

[4] Stafford C. Cleveland, *History and Directory of Yates County* (Penn Yan, N.Y.: the author, 1873).

reliable and fair-minded account of Jemima Wilkinson, gathered at the scene of her ministry in the Genesee Country, and much of it derived from those yet living who had been associated with her."

Jemima Wilkinson was born in 1758 in Cumberland, Providence County, Rhode Island. She was the eighth of twelve children born to Jeremiah and Amy (Whipple) Wilkinson. Her father was a farmer of modest means, and her mother was a Quaker who died when Jemima was eight. About 1774, she encountered religious zealots called Separatists who "rejected church organization and insisted upon constant and direct guidance from Heaven."[5] She began regularly attending their meetings and experienced a sudden change of personality as she became more involved with the group's beliefs. Wilkinson changed from a normal, happy teenager into a sullen, introspective loner who took to locking herself in her room. In 1776, at the age of 18, she underwent a religious conversion described in Lewis Aldrich's *History of Yates County, N.Y.* as follows:

> In the summer of 1776, then being eighteen years old, she fell sick . . . she wasted in bodily strength. . . . Jemima constantly told them [her family] of her strange visions. . . . [I]n October she appeared to fall into a trance state and appeared almost lifeless for a space of about thirty-six hours. . . . To the great surprise of her family she suddenly aroused herself, called for her garments, dressed, and walked among the assembled members of the household. . . . [S]he disclaimed being Jemima Wilkinson, but asserted that the former individuality had passed away and that she was another being, a minister of the Almighty sent to preach his gospel and to minister to the spiritual necessities of mankind. She took to herself the name of the Public Universal Friend.[6]

Known hereafter as the "Universal Friend" or "the Friend," Wilkinson began to preach in her native Rhode Island but soon spread her

[5] Ibid., p. 89.

[6] Lewis Cass Aldrich, ed. *History of Yates County, N.Y.* (Syracuse, N.Y.: D. Mason, 1892), p. 78.

message across Massachusetts, Connecticut, and Pennsylvania. She developed a following known as the Society of Universal Friends that established a settlement in 1788 on the west shore of Seneca Lake in the current town of Torrey. Wilkinson and her followers constituted the first actual settlers in the Genesee Country of central New York State at the end of the eighteenth century. This chapter first presents an overview of the society's history and its settlements, followed by a detailed look at some of pioneer families.

THE PIONEER SETTLEMENT AT KASHONG

As the number of the Friend's various followers grew, they became determined to consolidate their scattered congregations and establish a community of their own. In 1786, Ezekiel Shearman was sent into the Genesee Country[7] to find a suitable location for a permanent settlement. Owing to unsettled relations with the local Indian tribes, his report was unfavorable. By the next year, Indian relations in the area had stabilized somewhat and Thomas Hathaway, Richard Smith, and Abraham Dayton formed a committee to search for a suitable site. They first explored areas of Pennsylvania, particularly in the Wyoming Valley, but soon set their sights on New York. After visiting Kanadesaga (now Geneva) at the northwest corner of Seneca Lake, they came down the west side of the lake to Kashong (now Torrey, Yates County), where waterfalls provided several sites for gristmills and sawmills. This time their report was favorable, and the earliest settlers moved there in 1788, before they even had title to the land. James Parker, William Potter, and Thomas Hathaway attended a land sale in Albany and obtained a certificate of title dated October 10. 1792, for 14,040 acres to be used by the men and their associates as tenants in common. The first settlement of the society included pioneers Abel Botsford, Peleg Briggs, John Briggs, Isaac Nichols, George Sisson, Ezekiel Shearman, and Stephen Card. By the spring of 1790, the original settlement of 25 members grew to 260 (taken from census), and the Friend, accompanied by her closest companion, Sarah Richards, moved into her permanent home. Elijah Malin built the dwelling, and Anna Wagener primarily funded the project.

---

[7] For more information about the Genesee Country, see Chapter 17.

The Universal Friend's Log Meeting House, from Stafford C. Cleveland's *History and Directory of Yates County* (Penn Yan, N.Y.: the author, 1873), p. 62.

PREEMPTION LINE MOVED

The land purchased at Kashong was originally thought to be to the east of the neighboring Phelps-Gorham tract (see Chapter 17). However, when Robert Morris acquired the land about 1792–93, a new survey of its eastern boundary (the so-called preemption line) moved the line more than a mile eastward, causing it to pass through the society's settlement. Those twenty-three members who had farms west of the new preemption line thus found that their state grant was void. The members affected, many of them of the original families, were Benajah Botsford, Eleazer Ingraham, Solomon Ingraham, Richard Smith, Abel Botsford, Enoch Malin, William Davis, John Briggs, Elnathan Botsford, Daniel Ingraham, Richard Mathews, Elnathan Botsford, Jr., Asahel Stone, Samuel Doolittle, John Davis, Benedict Robinson, Philo Ingraham, Samuel Parsons, Jonathan Davis, Elijah Malin, Thomas Hathaway, Mercy Aldrich (sister of the Friend, and wife of William Aldrich), and Elisha Ingraham.[8]

DISSENSION AND THE MOVE TO JERUSALEM

Sometime after 1792, for reasons that are unclear, both James Parker and William Potter became dissatisfied with the workings of the society and withdrew from its membership, which marked the decline of the Friend and her followers. Both Parker and Potter were directly involved in the internal hostilities that had begun to rage against the Friend and her society, which led to the Friend's change of residence from the Seneca Lake region to Jerusalem (now in Yates County). On 2 September 1790, Thomas Hathaway and Benedict Robinson purchased a 36-square-mile parcel at Jerusalem, and many of the society's members relocated to this remote area. Much of the land was subsequently conveyed to Sarah Richards, in trust to the Friend (who did not own property in her own name). In the spring of 1794, after a residence of four years in the original settlement, the Friend removed to her new abode.

DECLINE OF THE SOCIETY

In the autumn of 1799, on the complaint of William Potter, magistrate and former society member James Parker issued a warrant against the Friend for blasphemy. She successfully eluded three attempts at arrest, but the following June, she was brought before a grand jury at the circuit court in Canandaigua. The grand jury listened to all the evidence and unanimously agreed that there was nothing on which to base an indictment. Communal ownership of the land also became a source of instability for the society and led to litigation. William Potter sued George Sisson over a portion of the original tract and "claimed the sole title, by a deed from Parker and Hathaway to himself, their common title resting on a deed from the State."[9] Determination in June 1800 was in favor of the plaintiff. Interestingly, the court offered the opinion that the Friend's cause might find relief in equity. However, following the court's suggestion

---

[8] Robert Morris sold the land to a group of London businessmen whose agent was Charles Williamson, "a man of remarkable fairness and liberality in his dealings with all the settlers" (Cleveland, *History and Directory of Yates County*, p. 56). These twenty-three members wrote a letter to Williamson dated "13th of the 1st month, 1794," and he confirmed their titles.

[9] Cleveland, *History and Directory of Yates County*, p. 58.

proved disastrous to the society. Society Trustees Richard Smith, John Briggs, and George Sisson advanced a note of $1,500 as a retaining fee to lawyer William Stewart, which he then sold without providing services. Full payment of the note was demanded, and since the note was given to the lawyer without the society's permission, the three men were held solely accountable. Sisson and Briggs, both poor, were forced to sell all of their property and personal possessions, and Sisson was jailed in Canandaigua for debt.

Sarah Richards, head of the Friend's household, died in 1793. Her heir was Rachel Malin. Enoch (Rachel's brother) and Eliza (Richards) Malin claimed that Eliza, as Sarah's daughter, was entitled to at least some of her mother's land, and they proceeded to sell off portions of it. In 1811, Rachel Malin brought suit against them, but by the time the case was finally decided in 1828, Enoch, Eliza, and the Friend were dead.

The Friend died in 1819. The society, fearing that physicians were conspiring to take her body and dissect it, deposited it in a vault in the basement of the house she had occupied since 1814 in Jerusalem. The body was later removed to a private graveyard for her followers. The entire graveyard was later disinterred and all remains were removed for burial at Penn Yan. The Friend's will names Rachel and Margaret Malin as both heirs and executors.

Only one portrait of Jemima Wilkinson is known to exist. It is in the possession of the Yates County Genealogical and Historical Society. According to the terms of her will, the portrait is never to be reproduced.

Margaret Malin died in 1844, willing her interest in the estate to James Brown, Jr., with the wish that he replace her in the society and in the late Friend's household. Rachel Malin died in 1848, leaving her property to the descendants of her brothers and sisters. From this time the society may be considered extinct.

SOCIETY OF UNIVERSAL FRIENDS
BIOGRAPHICAL INFORMATION

James Parker

James Parker[10] was one of the Friend's earliest converts and perhaps the most influential, owing to his wealth, strong character, and position as a magistrate in Rhode Island. He was born in South

Kingston, Rhode Island, about 1743, the seventh child of George and Catharine (Cole) Parker of London. Although a Quaker, he served as a captain in the Rhode Island militia during the Revolutionary War. Parker was also the first justice of the peace in what is now Yates County.

His first wife was Elizabeth Shearman. They had seven children:

Henry	d. young
Mary	m. Griffin B. Hazard
Alice	m. Thomas Prentiss
Oliver	m. his cousin, Hannah Shearman
Elizabeth	m. Otis Barden
Nancy	m. Levi Benton, Jr.
Catherine	m. James Whitney of Hopewell

Parker's first wife died before he came to New York in 1789 with their seven children. His second wife was Esther Whitney, daughter of Jonas Whitney. His third wife was Miriam, widow of Jonathan Hazard and sister of Reuben Gage. Parker died in 1829 at nearly 86 years of age and was interred in the family burial ground of his son-in-law Otis Barden in the present town of Benton.

William Potter

William Potter[12] was born at South Kingston, Rhode Island, January 21, 1722, son of Col. John and Mercy (Robinson) Potter. In 1750, at the age of 28, William Potter married Penelope Hazard, b. February 11, 1730/31, daughter of Thomas and Alice (Hull) Hazard.

---

[10] Augustus G. Parker, *Parker in America 1630–1910* (Buffalo, N.Y.: Niagara Frontier Publishing Company, 1911), pp. 46–47.

[12] For more on the Potter and Hazard families, see Caroline E. Robinson, *The Hazard Family of Rhode Island 1635–1894* (Boston: the author, 1895).

Children of William and Penelope:

Mercy	b. 26 Nov. 1751, d. 1794; m. Joshua Perry in 1769 in Rhode Island, where he died leaving three children: *Jonathan, Susanna,* and *Anna.*
Thomas Hazard	b. 8 Dec. 1753, d. Sept. 11, 1807; m. Patience Wilkinson (d. 1819), sister of the Friend. Children: *Susan, Eliza,* and *John.*
Alice	b. 20 April 1756; d. 1818; m. Capt. Arnold Hazard.
Susanna	b. 25 April 1758; d. in Rhode Island, unmarried.
William Robinson	b. 13 July 1760; d. young.
Benedict Arnold	b. 12 Sept. 1761; d. 1810; m. Sarah Brown. He dropped the name Benedict after the Revolutionary War. He died on a trip to Harrisburg, Pa., and was buried there. Children: *William, Arnold,* and *Penelope.*
Penelope	b. 7 March 1764; d. 1813; m. 1784 Benjamin Brown, Jr.
William Pitt	b. 10 April 1766; d. 6 Nov. 1800; m. 1793 Mary Hazard.
Edward	b. 15 Feb. 1768; d. 12 Aug. 1849; m. Eliza Johnson, who d. at age 75. Children: *William, Susan, William Pitt, Samuel J., Penelope,* and *Francis M.*
Simeon	b. 25 April 1770; d. 1 Feb. 1817; m. Catharine Klice. Children: *Lucinda, Penelope, Mary,* and *Sarah Ann.*
Sarah	b. 13 Dec. 1771; d. 1830; m. 1805 George Brown.

| John | b. 24 May 1774; d. 1815; m. Catherine Garrison. |
| Pelham | b. 7 Dec. 1776. |

William Potter was a senator in the colonial legislature, treasurer of the State of Rhode Island, and was elected chief justice of the Court of Common Pleas in Washington County in 1775. He resigned the latter office in 1780 and joined the Friend's society. Judge Potter was by far the wealthiest adherent of the Friend, and the society's tract of 14,040 acres on Seneca Lake reverted largely to him upon the division of the original compact. After leaving the society, Potter returned to Rhode Island, sold his estate there in 1807, and resided with his son [Benedict] Arnold, whom he survived. He died suddenly at the age of 92 while returning from Jerusalem after a visit with his son-in-law George Brown.

Ezekiel Shearman

Also from Rhode Island, Ezekiel Shearman was the brother of James Parker's first wife Elizabeth. Born about 1764,[13] he married in 1790 Mary (Supplee) Bartleson, sister of John Supplee of Pennsylvania, and widow of John Bartleson.[14] Mary died in 1843 at the age of 83. Ezekiel and Mary (Supplee) (Bartleson) Shearman had three children:

Isaac	b. 1792; m. Susan Prentiss.
John	d. young.
Bartleson	b. 1797; m. Hannah Potter.

David, Susanna, and Anna Wagener

David Wagener of Worcester, Montgomery County, Pennsylvania, joined the society with his sisters Susanna and Anna in 1782 after the Friend came there to preach. Susanna married first Peter Supplee, and second ____ Clanford.

---

[13] In his *History and Directory of Yates County*, Cleveland states that Ezekiel Shearman died in 1824 at the age of 60, but that he was 26 in 1786, when he made his survey of the Genesee Country.

[14] John Bartleson and their two children are buried in Pennsylvania.

Thomas Hathaway

Thomas Hathaway was a native of New Bedford, Massachusetts. His wife died shortly after the Revolutionary War, and he joined the society in 1784. Hathaway began to build a sawmill in 1796, but he died of a fever in 1798 before it could be completed. Thomas Hathaway and his wife had four children: Thomas, Mary, Elizabeth, and Gilbert.

In 1793, Thomas Hathaway, Jr., married Mary Botsford, daughter of Elnathan Botsford. He died in 1850, aged 84 years. His wife died in 1866 at the age of 96. They had seven children:

Lucy	m. Oliver Hartwell.
George	m. Louisa McMath.
Susan	m. Henry A. Wisner.
Thomas (twin)	m. Mary Headly.
Gilbert (twin)	m. Mary Hurd.
Mary	m. her cousin Capt. William Hathaway, Jr., of New Bedford.
Caroline	m. John Tims Raplee.

Gilbert, son of Thomas Hathaway, Sr., married Mary, daughter of Richard Hurd, of Rock Stream, New York. Their children were Gilbert, Jr., Deborah, Bradford G. H., Richard H., Maria, and Charles. Gilbert lived to be 87 years old.

Richard Smith

Richard Smith was a native of Groton, Connecticut. He married Elizabeth Allen and had five children:

Russell	d. in Connecticut.
David (twin)	b. 1778; d. 1805 of yellow fever.
Jonathan (twin)	b. 1778
Avery	b. ca. 1780; m. Lament, daughter of David Wagener.
Sarah	

Richard Smith left his family to immigrate to the new settlement and there built a gristmill in July 1790. His family joined him about ten years later. Richard Smith died in 1836 at 90 years of age. His wife Elizabeth died two years later at the age of 84.

Abraham Dayton

Abraham Dayton is listed in the 1790 census as living in Jerusalem, Ontario (now Yates) County, New York. Around this time, the Friend began to consider a more remote site for the society. Dayton was sent to Canada to negotiate with Governor John Graves Simcoe and succeeded in securing a grant of land in the township of Beauford, Canada West [Ontario], Canada. The governor annulled the charter on the grounds that it was made under the mistaken impression that the members of the society were Quakers, for whom he had great respect. The grant, however, was renewed to Dayton in his own name. He moved his family and property to the township and lived there during the remainder of his life. Abraham Dayton and his wife Abigail had two daughters, Dinah and Anice. It has been suggested that he may be the Abraham, son of Henry and Abigail (Norton) Daton of Brookhaven, New York, who was said to have left Long Island for Connecticut in 1770.[15]

Abel Botsford

Abel Botsford came from New Milford, Connecticut, with his wife Mary and his brothers Elnathan (and wife Lucy) and Jonathan (and wife Elizabeth). Abel died in 1817. His daughter Mary married Robert Buckley.

Elnathan and Lucy Botsford had five children:

Mary	m. Thomas Hathaway, Jr.
Benajah	m. Deborah Wilkinson, youngest sister of the Friend.[16]

---

[15] Donald Lines Jacobus and Arthur Bliss Dayton. *The Early Daytons and Descendants of Henry, Jr.* (New Haven, Conn.: New Haven Colony Historical Society, 1959), p. 35.

[16] Benajah Botsford died in 1801 by falling from a load of hay; his widow then married Elijah Malin.

Sarah	b. 1766; d. 1845; m., after 1776, Achilles Comstock (b. in Conn. 1757, d. 1832).
Lucy	m. Stephen Wilkinson, brother of the Friend.
Ruth	m. (1) Daniel Comstock, brother of Achilles; (2) Rufus Gale.

Jonathan and Elizabeth Botsford had six children:

Elizabeth	m. Abel Hunt.
Abigail	m. Jacob Nichols.
Achsa	m. John Supplee.
Peace	m. John Fitzwater.
Jonathan	d. young.
Elijah	m. Margaret Scott.

Peleg Briggs and John Briggs

Peleg Briggs (b. 1729; d. 1807) came from North Kingston, Rhode Island. He married Margaret Vaughn (d. 1800). They had five children:

Joanna	b. 1756; d. 1826; m. George Bates of North Kingston, R.I. (b. 1754, d. 1827). Children: *Mercy, George, Peleg, David, Mary, Lucy,* and *Anna*
Sarah	
Francis	b. 1763; d. 1850; m. (1) Isabel Albro (10 children), (2) Olive Bell (2 children).
Peleg Jr.	b. at North Kingston, R.I., 1765; d. 1837; m. Elizabeth Chambers in R.I. (b. 1765, d. 1834). Children: *James C., Peleg, Ester, Robert V., Stephen R.,* and *Hamilton J.*
Mary	

John Briggs, cousin of Peleg Briggs, married Elizabeth Bailey of Rhode Island. They had four children:

John	m. Ardery Place in Rhode Island; d. age 70, about 1825
David	b. at East Greenwich, R.I., 1776; d. 1857; m. Anna Chambers (b. 1779, d. 1869).
Ruth	m. Peleg Gifford of Cape Cod.
Ann	
Esther	

Isaac Nichols

Isaac Nichols was born near Newport, Rhode Island, in 1748, and died in 1829. He married Anna Boon, also of Rhode Island (b. 1754, d. 1838). They had four children:

George	m. Hannah Green.
Alexander	m. Polly Chambers.
Benjamin	unm.; d. at about 80 years.
Jacob	m. Abigail, daughter of Jonathan Botsford.

George Sisson

George Sisson married Bethany Luther. Their son Jonathan married Catharine Vosbinder and they had children: William, George, Joshua, David, Harrison, and Bethany. Both Jonathan and Catharine died in 1857; he was 73, and she was 70.

Stephen Card

Stephen Card was born at North Kingston, Rhode Island, in 1761 and died in 1836. He and his brother-in-law John Reynolds arrived in 1788 to clear land and soon became the first residents to sow wheat in western New York. They returned to their eastern homes during that winter. Card married Hannah Reynolds (b. 1758, d. 1851), a devoted adherent of the Friend, and they had two children, John (m. Jane Brown) and Sarah (m. George W. Hazard).

Jonathan Davis

Jonathan Davis was born about 1777 and died 1870. He was originally a Quaker. In 1801, he married Rachel Updegraff (b. 1777, d. 1858) in Philadelphia. Their children were Mary, Isaiah, Leah, Lydia. Anna, a sister of Jonathan, was the wife of Jared Cohoon.

John, Tamar, and William Davis

John Davis married Leah ____. His sister Tamar married ____ Stone. William Davis married Anna ____. It is not known what relation, if any, relation William had to John and Tamar.

Elisha, Eleazer, and Nathaniel Ingraham

Elisha Ingraham and Eleazer Ingraham (wife Lydia) were brothers who came to the settlement with their cousin Nathaniel (wife Experience). Elisha's children were Jerusha, Asa, and Lament.

The children of Eleazer and Lydia Ingraham were Daniel, Philo, Eleazer, Jr., John (wife Anna), Abigail, Lydia, Rachel (d. unmarried in 1873, "one of the two last survivors of the Friend's colony"[17]), Lament, Patience (m. Asa Brown), and Menty (m. Samuel Davis).

Nathaniel and Experience Ingraham had a daughter Mary (unmarried) and a son Solomon. They were associated with the Friend in Philadelphia. Solomon turned against the society in 1814 and "was about to join Daniel Bracket, an eccentric religious zealot, when he was accidentally buried in a well he was digging and lost his life."[18]

Elijah Malin

Elijah Malin was a carpenter from Philadelphia who built the Friend's house in the first settlement. He married Deborah, widow of Benajah Botsford and youngest sister of the Friend. Enoch Malin, who married Eliza, the only daughter of Sarah Richards,[19] was also a carpenter. He died in Canada. Sisters Rachel (d. 1848) and

---

[17] Miles A. Davis. *History of Jerusalem* (Penn Yan, N.Y.: the author, 1912), p.22.

[18] Cleveland, *History and Directory of Yates County*, p. 85.

[19] Eliza Richards's care was entrusted to the Friend on the death of her mother, Sarah Richards, the head of the Friend's household. Apparently Eliza did not share the Friend's regard for celibacy; she eloped one night to marry Enoch Malin.

Margaret Malin (d. 1844) lived in the Friend's household and were named as her heirs and executors

Benedict Robinson

Benedict Robinson, born at Jamestown, Rhode Island, 10 February 1758, was the only child of Robert and Phebe (Carr) Robinson. Robinson was a surveyor who married his housekeeper, Susannah Brown (b. at Stonington, Connecticut, 3 September 1760; d. 10 June 1837) on 1 September 1792. Benedict Robinson died 18 February 1832. They had four children:

Phebe	b. 1793; d. unmarried 1864.
Daniel Arnold	b. 1795; d. 1871.
James Carr	b. 1797; d. 1856; m. 1819 Susan Stewart.
Abigail	b. 1802; m. 1824 Dr. John Hatmaker.

CHAPTER 28

The Oneida Community: A Utopian Experiment in Central New York State

The first half of the nineteenth century witnessed a revival of religious fervor in this country and a related proliferation of utopian communities. In a previous chapter we looked at the small, obscure community headed by Jemima Wilkinson, which melted away leaving scarcely a trace. Here we consider the Oneida Community, founded by John Humphrey Noyes, which, like the phoenix, rose from its own ashes to become Oneida Ltd., manufacturer of quality tableware. From 1848 to 1879 members of the Oneida Community, or Oneidans, succeeded in living together and sharing the fruits of their labor. Within the community they were economically communist; in their dealings with the outside world they were highly successful capitalists. Unlike many other utopian communities, Oneidans bore and raised children. Their religion, "Christian Perfectionism," was based on the idea that some Christians can lead morally perfect lives. They practiced mutual criticism, male continence, complex marriage (otherwise known as "free love"), and stirpiculture (selective breeding of children). Their writings designate these Noysian concepts, just like "Christian Perfectionism," with capital letters.

JOHN HUMPHREY NOYES

John Humphrey Noyes was born September 3, 1811, at Brattleboro, Vermont,[1] and died April 13, 1886, at Niagara Falls, Ontario, Canada.[2] He was one of nine children. His father, John Noyes, was

---

[1] Vital Records of Brattleboro, Vermont to 1814, database online at *www.NewEnglandAncestors.org*.

[2] Ontario deaths 1886, Reg. # 041386.

a graduate of Dartmouth College, the village schoolteacher, minister, clerk in a Brattleboro store, and a U.S. congressman. He married Polly Hayes, eldest daughter of Rutherford and Chloe (Smith) Hayes.[3] Rutherford Hayes was born in New Haven, Connecticut, but had settled in Brattleboro, Vermont.[4] John and Polly (Hayes) Noyes had nine children:

1. Mary, married Larkin G. Mead, an attorney of Brattleboro.
2. Joanna, married Samuel Hayes of New Haven, removed to Trinidad, died of a tropical fever.
3. Elizabeth, married Dr. F. A. Ransom, and settled in Michigan, where she died.
4. **John Humphrey, founder of the Oneida Community.**
5. Horatio, became a successful business man and banker.
6. Harriet, joined the Oneida Community.
7. Charlotte, joined the Oneida Community.
8. George, died at 10 years of age.
9. George, joined the Oneida Community.

While a student at Yale Divinity School, John Humphrey Noyes developed the concept of Christian Perfectionism: the idea that some men and women could obtain salvation from sin in this world. Because of his public preaching of this unorthodox doctrine, he was denied ordination by Yale. Nevertheless he persisted, publishing his views in small newspapers and periodicals. In 1838 he married Harriet Holton, an orphan, who had grown up in Westminster, Vermont, with her grandfather, Mark Richards, a lawyer. Gradually Noyes gained a small following, which included his younger sisters Harriet and Charlotte, his younger brother George, his invalid father, and finally his mother. He arranged marriages between his sisters and two of his close followers. Harriet married John L. Skinner, a teacher, the son of Quaker parents; Charlotte married

---

[3] George Wallingford Noyes. *Religious Experience of John Humphrey Noyes, Founder of the Oneida Community* (New York: Macmillan, 1923).

[4] President Rutherford B. Hayes was his grandson and Polly's nephew.

John Humphrey Noyes, ca. 1851. (From the Collection of the Oneida Community Mansion House, Oneida, N.Y.)

John R. Miller, a storekeeper. Early in 1841 Noyes's father died, dividing his considerable estate among his eight surviving children. The four Perfectionist children now had two farms and other property in Putney, Vermont, and this property formed the nucleus of a community of their followers. In 1844 the group, now numbering thirty-seven, pooled all their individual resources and formed a communist association. A $9,000 legacy from his wife's grandfather further stabilized their financial position in 1846.

At this time Noyes introduced his ideas of mutual criticism, complex marriage, and male continence to community leaders. Mutual criticism arose from Noyes's experience of the force of peer pressure during his years in seminary at Andover.[5] In the practice of mutual criticism, a committee of six to twelve community members openly describes an individual's faults and virtues. Noyes declared himself exempt, saying that it would be bad for community morale to dwell on any failings of their leader. In complex marriage, all women were

[5] Maren Lockwood Carden, *Oneida: Utopian Community to Modern Corporation* (Baltimore: Johns Hopkins Press, 1969), p. 71.

considered to be married to all men. Sexual intercourse was permitted between any consenting couple, the assignation being brokered by a third party to insure mutual consent. Exclusive attachments were not permitted. Male continence was Noyes's term for *coitus reservatus* (intercourse without ejaculation) and would prove to be an effective method of birth control.[6]

An attempt in 1848 to include Harriet Hall, a woman Noyes claimed to have cured by faith, and her husband Daniel in the inner circle led to trouble. Apparently Daniel Hall had an unfavorable view of Noyes's rules, for he went to the state attorney general, who indicted Noyes for adultery. Consequently, it became necessary for the group to leave Putney, and he fled to Connecticut.

FOUNDING OF THE ONEIDA COMMUNITY

A Perfectionist convert, Jonathan Burt, had bought land and a sawmill on the former Oneida Indian Reserve. A small group led by William Gould, an Oneida-area physician had joined him. Burt welcomed the Putney group, but was ousted by Noyes, who took over the leadership role. The group had sufficient capital to buy two adjoining farms that were for sale. By the end of 1848 the group numbered eighty-seven. In the 1850 federal census for the town of Lenox in Madison County, the Oneida Association is listed as family #1182. Most of the people list New England states as their birthplace, although there is a sizable representation from New York and New Jersey as well, and a few people list Michigan, Ohio, and England as birthplaces. The most common occupation is farmer (25), followed by printer (7), carpenter (7), shoemaker (4), blacksmith (3) machinist (2), miller (2), gardener (2), carriage maker (2), cabinet maker (2), and editor (1).

Their numbers increased slowly because the group was very selective in whom they admitted. In his story of the Community, Spencer Klaw points out:

---

[6] "In a community of well over two hundred adults, accidental pregnancies occurred at a rate of fewer than one a year." Spencer Klaw, *Without Sin: The Life and Death of the Oneida Community* (New York: Penguin Press, 1993), p. 132.

At the outset Noyes saw the community he had established at Oneida as having two distinct though related purposes. One purpose was to enable Perfectionists to foil the devil by leading, under Noyes's inspired guidance, a truly holy life. At the same time Oneida would serve as a bridgehead in Christ's campaign to conquer the world. Here the faithful would gather and, through the medium of a free daily newspaper, summon people everywhere to cast aside sin and thereby prepare themselves for the fast-approaching time when heaven and earth would be united and death would die.[7]

Family units did not live together. The adults lived in a three-story Mansion House, which they built.[8] Each man and woman had his or her own small room; thus the mansion was enlarged several times and at the end contained more than 200 rooms. Sexual intercourse took place in a few apartments set aside for that purpose. In the evenings, Oneidans gathered in common rooms, where they would hear a sermon by John Noyes and discuss community business. Other activities included dancing, pantomimes, play-acting, concerts, chess, checkers, and cards.[9] After 1850 the Oneida Community was open to the public for tours. During the year 1866, they entertained about 4,000 visitors.[10] In 1869 the Midland Railroad established a branch line with a stop near the Mansion House and day trips became even more popular. Guests were given escorted tours and invited to dine with the Community.

Children lived apart. After weaning, they were turned over to the Community nursery at an adjoining farm, where they lived until the age of about 12. They were then admitted as junior members of the community and were no longer required to attend school, although

---

[7] Ibid., p. 191.

[8] The Mansion House still stands. A National Historic Landmark, it has dining and banquet facilities, guest rooms, tours, gardens, and apartment rentals. See the website, *www.oneidacommunity.org*.

[9] Pierrepont B. Noyes, *My Father's House: An Oneida Boyhood* (New York: Holt, Rinehart and Winston, 1965).

[10] Carden, *Oneida*, p. 81.

most did continue with their education. Classes were offered to teenagers as well as adults in mathematics, science, English, and Latin. Some of the young men were sent away to college. In 1864 Theodore Noyes and George Cragin were sent to Yale Medical School to supply the community's need for physicians. Until that time the Oneidans called on the services of area doctors, but only for setting broken bones and stitching cuts.

The Oneidans tried numerous cottage industries as experiments. Community member Sewall Newhouse had invented an improved animal trap. William Inslee, a machinist, devised a method of mass production. John Hutchins helped design traps of various sizes. They invented the lazy Susan, a mechanical mop wringer, mechanical potato peeler, washing machine, more comfortable ladies' shoes, and the garter belt. They started a cannery to preserve fruit from their own fruit trees, and a silk mill, which produced silk sewing thread. They published a newspaper.

The 1860 federal census for the town of Lenox in Madison County lists the Oneida Association as family #732. New occupations give a sense of the various attempts the community made to prosper. The community now included a beekeeper, several trap makers, a dairy superintendent, dressmakers, tailors and tailoresses, and a teamster, weaver, soap maker, sadler, millwright, joiner, and silk merchant. William Hinds, who would cause so much trouble for the community in the future, gives his occupation as "phonographical reporter."[11] The Lenox [Madison Co.] Business Directory of 1868 describes the Community thus:

> The "Oneida Community" is an association, located on
> Oneida Creek, four miles south of Oneida. It is organized
> on a peculiar social and religious basis, and was established
> in 1847, by John H. Noyes, from whom most of their reli-
> gious and social tenets were received. They form a general
> community, holding common interest in all things. They

---

[11] According to *Webster's New Twentieth Century Dictionary* (New York: Simon & Schuster, 1972), phonography is "any system of shorthand based on a phonetic transcription of speech; especially, the system invented by Isaac Pitman (1813–97)."

call their peculiar social system *"complex marriage."* They number about two hundred; are located on a farm of over 500 acres, and engaged in horticulture and manufacturing. Their farm and dwellings are in Lenox, but some of their shops are in Oneida County. Their principal manufactures are steel-traps, sewing machine twist, and preserved fruits. They make eight sizes and descriptions of traps, suitable for catching everything, from a house rat to a grizzly bear. Their sales of traps last year amounted to over $100,000. Their sales of machine twist and sewing silk amount to about $75,000 per year, and of preserved fruits of various kinds to about $25,000. They have a saw-mill, a foundry, a carpenter shop and packing box manufactory, and a machine shop, where they make their own silk machinery. In some departments they employ hired help, superintended by their own people. "The Circular," published weekly, is "free to all," but "those who choose to pay, may send one dollar a year."[12]

The same directory lists John H. Barron as superintendent of the fruit-preserving department; Charles A. Cragin, superintendent of the silk department; Myron Kinsley and S. Newhouse, superintendents of the trap department; and Theodore R. Noyes, editor of "Community Circular." In 1877 when the trap business began to falter, Oneidans began manufacturing tin-plated spoons.

In 1846 Noyes wrote that the perfection of the human race would happen in their generation. By 1856, however, his ideas of the kingdom of heaven had receded, and Noyes decided that the Perfectionists should have children. In 1869 the Community began a formal program of stirpiculture.[13] Stirpiculture required that the best breeding stock be selected — by Noyes. Fifty-three women and thirty-eight men signed an agreement to be parents. From 1869 to

---

[12] *1868–69 Lenox Business Directory, Lenox, Madison Co., N.Y.,* accessed at *www .RootsWeb.com/~nymadiso/68lenox.htm.*

[13] Stirpiculture, from Latin *stirps,* a stock, and *cultura,* culture, means selective breeding for desirable characteristics. Applied to humans, stirpiculture — as practiced by the Oneidans — became a form of eugenics.

South view of main dwelling, 1870 (From the Collection of the Oneida Community Mansion House, Oneida, N.Y.)

1879 forty-four women bore a total of fifty-eight live children. By the late 1870s there was internal turmoil, and fights occurred between Noyes and his son Theodore. Younger men and women did not feel that Noyes should be making decisions on who could be parents. This, coupled with a general decline and fall of Perfectionism caused the community to abandon stirpiculture and complex marriage in 1879.

TRANSFORMATION FROM ONEIDA COMMUNITY TO ONEIDA COMMUNITY LTD.

In common with most utopian communities, the Oneida Community foundered over the question of a successor to their leader. John Humphrey Noyes himself wished the leadership to pass to his son Theodore. Theodore Noyes was a graduate of Yale Medical School and had good business sense. He did not however, have his father's charisma. Put in charge in 1877, he was not accepted by the Community, and the following year John Humphrey Noyes quickly resumed control. For the first time the

Community as a whole began to question Noyes's judgment. Factions developed.

An internal revolt was led by James William Towner, a former Universalist minister and lawyer who handled the Community's legal business. His ally was William Hinds, who had been with the community since its origin. Towner and Hinds believed young girls' sex lives should be overseen by their parents, not by Noyes and his inner circle. Further, adults should be able to sleep with whomever they liked. When the dust had settled, Noyes had moved to a Perfectionist community in Canada, where he remained for the rest of his life. The Community built him a house and provided six acres of land, fruit trees, a garden, horse and carriage, and $1.50 per month for expenses. Complex marriage had been abandoned. All property was turned over to Oneida Community, Ltd., shares of which were to be held by all community members. Members would be given preference for jobs in their various businesses, and they could live in Mansion House at low rent. Elderly members could receive lifetime support in place of stock if they wished. Children received no stock, but they got free education up to age 16, then $200. People who had contributed money would get half the value back in shares.

The rest of the stock was distributed to members based on the number of years they had lived in the Community. Stock was divided among 226 people, 15 minors and 211 adults. Table 1 gives some idea of the distribution.

Table 1
DISTRIBUTION OF STOCK, ONEIDA COMMUNITY LTD.

STOCK VALUE	NUMBER OF PEOPLE	STOCK VALUE	NUMBER OF PEOPLE
<$675	1	$2,000-3,499	84
$675–999	11	$3,500–4,999	60
$1,000–1,999	49	>$5,000	5

Sewell Newhouse opposed the settlement. He had invented the animal trap, which was so profitable for the community, and thought he should have received more. His share was held in trust until he accepted it at age 79.

All this went into effect 1 January 1881. There were three Townerites (including Towner) on the first nine-member board, four board members loyal to Noyes, and two "neutralists" — Theodore R. Noyes and Francis Wayland-Smith — who were sympathetic to Noyes. Towner's victory was short-lived. The loyalists had lived longest at Oneida, and Noyes himself became controlling stockholder. Towner was not reelected the following year. His faction was being snubbed in the Mansion House. Towner and thirty-five of his followers left Oneida and moved to California.

After a rocky start, Pierrepont Noyes, a son of John Humphrey Noyes and Harriet Worden, was made general manager in 1899 and served in that office until he resigned in 1917. He focused the company on the silverware business. The chain business was sold in 1912, the silk industry ceased in 1913, and the canning industry ceased in 1915. Today Oneida Ltd. (*www.oneida.com*) manufactures stainless steel, silverplate, and sterling flatware, china dinnerware, and crystal and glassware items. Net sales figures in fiscal year ending January 2004 were $453 million.

FURTHER READING

Books published by members of the Oneida Community

Corinna Ackley Noyes, *The Days of My Youth* (Kenwood, N.Y.: Mansion House, 1960).

George Wallingford Noyes, *Religious Experience of John Humphrey Noyes, Founder of the Oneida Community* (New York: Macmillan, 1923).

Pierrepont B. Noyes, *My Father's House: An Oneida Boyhood* (New York: Holt, Rinehart and Winston, 1965).

Constance Noyes Robertson, ed., *Oneida Community: An Autobiography, 1851–1876* (Syracuse, N.Y.: Syracuse University Press, 1970).

Books published about the Oneida Community

Dolores Hayden, *Seven American Utopias: The Architecture of Communitarian Socialism, 1790–1975* (Cambridge, Mass.: MIT Press, 1976).

Spencer Klaw, *Without Sin: The Life and Death of the Oneida Community* (New York: Penguin Press, 1993).

Robert Allerton Parker, *A Yankee Saint: John Humphrey Noyes and the Oneida Community* (New York: G. P. Putnam's Sons, 1935).

Walter D. Edmonds, *The First Hundred Years, 1848–1948* (New York: Oneida Ltd., 1948).

CHAPTER 29

New York's Failed
Annexation of Vermont

T hose with eighteenth-century ancestors in Vermont may not realize that those ancestors were once New Yorkers (well, almost). And some New Yorkers who obtained patents for land now in Vermont never actually possessed their land. In the years preceding the Revolutionary War, the governors of both New Hampshire and New York were each dispensing grants for the same land. The vigilante group known as the Green Mountain Boys, led by Ethan Allen, rather rudely dispatched New York surveyors sent in to establish boundaries in existing settlements. Consequently, the Green Mountain Boys were declared outlaws and ended up with a price on their heads. Vermont finally acted on its own and seceded — from New York, from New Hampshire, and from the Confederation of the United States. Read on.

The Treaty of Paris in 1763 ended the conflict known in Europe as the Seven Years War and in North America as the French and Indian War. As a result of this treaty, the territory that would eventually become Vermont passed out of French control. New Hampshire considered territory west of the Connecticut River and south of Canada to be a part of that colony and the region became known as the "New Hampshire grants." The first royal governor of New Hampshire, Benning Wentworth, was appointed in 1741.[1] In 1749

An earlier version of this chapter was posted at *www.NewEnglandAncestors.org* August 30, 2002.

[1] Benning Wentworth was the son of John Wentworth, lieutenant governor of Massachusetts from 1717 to 1730. He was named for his paternal grandmother, Mary Benning.

he granted the town of Bennington, six miles square on the western border of New Hampshire, and by 1754 he had granted fifteen townships. As of 1761, sixty townships, each six miles square, had been granted on the west side of the Connecticut River.

Wentworth collected a sizable £20 fee from each grantee, of which there were sixty per town. He also reserved 500 acres in each township for himself. When he resigned the office in 1766 to his nephew John, Benning Wentworth had become a very wealthy man.

Not to be outdone in the land speculation game, the governor of New York, Robert Monckton, had also been granting the same land as part of the county of Albany. His claim to the territory was the grants by Charles II to the Duke of York in 1664 and 1674. On December 28, 1763, Cadwallader Colden, acting governor of New York, issued a proclamation claiming all the land west of the Connecticut River for New York, annulling the grants Wentworth had made. Wentworth replied with a proclamation on March 13, 1764, declaring the grant to the Duke of York obsolete.

New York submitted a petition to the Privy Council in London purported to be signed by settlers on the New Hampshire grants wanting the western bank of Connecticut River established as the eastern boundary of New York. (Subsequent action makes one wonder who did sign this petition.) Surprisingly, on July 20, 1764, the Crown so ordered. The matter might have ended there if the New Hampshire grants had simply been transferred to the jurisdiction of New York, and if the original settlers had been confirmed in their claims. New York, however, insisted that the decree was retroactive — and thus all the settlers' claims were invalid. If the settlers wanted to keep farms they had labored to carve out of the wilderness, they were required to buy them again from New York. New Hampshire did not press its claim, but the settlers resisted the "Yorkers" firmly. In 1766 they appointed Samuel Robinson of Bennington as their agent to represent them in the Court of Great Britain.

As a display of authority, New York created Cumberland County to include land in the New Hampshire grants on July 2, 1766. The Crown annulled this act on June 26, 1767, and a month later ordered that the governor of New York could make no more grants.

New York ignored this annulment and again passed legislation to form the county.

In October 1767, the settlers' representative, Samuel Robinson, died of smallpox in London. Nevertheless, the settlers continued their local resistance. Ethan Allen and his brother Ira defended those taken to court for eviction. They lost in court but continued to resist

Chorographical map of the disputed area, from E. B. O'Callaghan, *The Documentary History of the State of New-York*, Volume IV (Albany: Charles Van Benthuysen, 1851), p. 330.

and formed associations, some of them military. Ethan Allen was appointed "colonel commandant" and Seth Warner, Robert Cochran, Gideon Warner, and Allen's cousin Remember Baker were appointed captains. Surveyors from New York were met with a "reception committee" of Green Mountain Boys armed with guns, clubs, and stones. Zadock Thompson describes the scene when the sheriff of Albany County attempted to serve writ on James Breckenridge, a farmer in Bennington:[2]

> Whenever the sheriff appeared upon the grants for the purpose of arresting rioters, or ejecting the settlers, he was sure to be met by a party larger than his own, fully determined to frustrate his object. Being required to serve a writ of ejectment on James Breckenridge, the sheriff, by order of the governor, called to his assistance a posse of 750 armed militia. [John Pell claims a more realistic posse of 150.[3]] The settlers having timely knowledge of his approach, assembled to the number of about 300, and arranged their plans to resist him. An officer with 18 men was placed in the house, 120 men behind trees near the road by which the sheriff must advance, and the remainder were concealed behind a ridge of land within gun shot of the house; and the forcing the door by the sheriff was to be made known to those concealed without by raising a red flag at the top of the chimney.
>
> When the sheriff approached all were silent, and he and his men were completely within the ambuscade before they discovered their situation. Mr. Ten Eyck, the sheriff, went to the door, demanded entrance as sheriff of the county of Albany, and threatened, on refusal, to force it. The answer from within was, "attempt it, and you are a dead man."

---

[2] Zadock Thompson, *History of Vermont* (Burlington, Vt.: privately published, 1853), pp. 21–22.

[3] John Pell, "The Secession of Vermont," Chapter 1 in Alexander C. Flick, ed., *History of the State of New York, Volume 5: Conquering the Wilderness* (New York: Columbia University Press, 1934).

Woodcut of Ethan Allen, champion of the Vermonters during the controversy, from Henry W. De Puy, *Ethan Allen and the Green-Mountain Heroes of '76* (Buffalo: Phinney & Co., 1859), frontispiece.

> On repeating this demand, with a threat of using force, . . . the two divisions exhibited their hats on the points of their guns, which made them appear much more numerous than they really were. The sheriff and his posse seeing their dangerous situation, and not (says Ira Allen) being interested in the dispute, made a hasty retreat, without a shot being fired on either side.

Remember Baker was once arrested from his home, and he, his wife, and small son were wounded. Thompson, flaunting his bias against New York, describes the event thus:[4]

> Having assembled ten or twelve of his friends and dependants, on the 22d of March, 1772, before daylight, being Sunday morning, he [John Munro] proceeded to the house of Remember Baker in Arlington for the purpose of arresting him. Baker was awakened by the breaking open of his door, and the entrance of a number of men armed with swords and pistols. The intruders rushed upon him with

---

[4] Thompson, *History of Vermont*, pp. 22–23.

savage fury, wounding him by a cut across the head, and also on the arm, with a sword. His wife too was barbarously wounded by a sword cut across the head and neck, and one of his boys also, then about 12 years old. Baker being overpowered and bound was thrown into a sleigh and conveyed off with the greatest speed towards Albany. The news of this transaction being sent by express to Bennington, ten men immediately mounted their horses for the purpose of intercepting the banditti and rescuing Baker. They came upon Munro and his party just before they reached the Hudson River, who on the first appearance of their pursuers abandoned their prisoner and fled. Baker was found nearly exhausted by his sufferings and the loss of blood. Having refreshed him and dressed his wounds, they carried him home to the no small joy of his friends and the whole settlement.

Not surprisingly, the new governor of New York, Sir William Tryon, issued a proclamation outlawing Ethan Allen and eight of his men, and offering a bounty of £60 for the capture of their leader. Allen responded by offering a bounty of £25 for any of the officials involved.

George Clinton, Governor of New York, who tried to keep Vermont within the state of New York. From O'Callaghan, *The Documentary History of the State of New-York*, Volume IV, frontispiece.

At a convention in Westminster on January 15, 1777, Vermont was born. The delegates proclaimed that "the district or territory comprehending, and usually known by the name and description of the New Hampshire grants, of right ought to be, and is hereby declared forever hereafter to be, a free and independent jurisdiction, or state; to be forever hereafter called, known, and distinguished by the name of New Connecticut, alias Vermont." At the time Massachusetts, Connecticut, and New Hampshire were all willing to admit Vermont into the nascent United States, which was then involved in the Revolutionary War. New York was not. The Continental Congress dismissed Vermont's petition to send delegates, and Vermont replied by drafting its constitution. Had New York been less intransigent, there would have been fourteen original colonies instead of thirteen.

Perhaps even at this stage New York might have won the day. In 1782, Governor George Clinton released a proclamation repealing the acts of outlawry and confirming the settlers in their land if they would stay in New York. However, Ethan Allen, newly released from British prison during the war, had the last word in his opposing proclamation:

> The overtures in the proclamation set forth are either romantic or calculated to deceive woods people, who, in general may not be supposed to understand law, or the power of a legislative authority. . . . You have experienced every species of suppression, which the old government of New York, with a Tryon at its head, could invent and inflict; and it is manifest that the new government are minded to follow nearly in their steps. Happy is it for you that you are fitted for the severest trials! You have been wonderfully supported and carried through thus far in your opposition to that government. Formerly you had every thing to fear from it, but now little; for your public character is established and your cause known to be just. In your early struggles with that government, you acquired a reputation for bravery; this gave you a relish for martial glory, and the British invasion opened an ample field for its

display, and you have gone on conquering and to conquer until tall grenadiers are dismayed and tremble at your approach.[5]

New York's attempt at reconciliation was seen as too little too late. In 1783, when the United States signed a peace treaty with Great Britain, Vermont was an independent republic. It coined its own money, naturalized citizens, set up its own post office, etc. It was not until 1791 that the dispute with New York was finally settled and Vermont became the first state added to the original thirteen colonies.

[5] Ibid., p. 53.

New York Counties

County/ Date Formed	County Seat	Parent County/ Counties	Daughter County/ Counties	Part Annexed from/ Ceded to
Albany Nov. 1, 1683	Albany	Original county	Cumberland, *defunct* (1766) Gloucester, *defunct* (1770) Tryon, *now Mont-* *gomery* (1772) Charlotte, *now* *Washington* (1772) Rensselaer (1791) Saratoga (1791) Schenectady (1809)	*Part ceded to* Schoharie (1795) Greene (1800)
Allegany Apr. 7, 1806	Belmont	Genesee		*Part annexed from* Steuben (1808) *Part ceded to* Genesee (1811) Wyoming (1846) Livingston (1846)
Bronx 1914	Bronx Borough, NYC	New York		
Broome Mar. 28, 1806	Binghamton		Tioga	*Part ceded to* Tioga (1822)
Cattaraugus Mar. 11, 1808	Ellicottville (1808–60) Little Valley (1860–pres.)	Genesee		
Cayuga Mar. 8, 1799	Auburn	Onondaga	Seneca (1804) Tompkins (1817)	

continued on next page

County/ Date Formed	County Seat	Parent County/ Counties	Daughter County/ Counties	Part Annexed from/ Ceded to
Charlotte *see* Washington				
Chautauqua (Chautauque) Mar. 11, 1808	Mayville	Genesee		
Chemung Mar. 29, 1836	Elmira	Tioga	Schuyler (1854)	
Chenango Mar. 15, 1798	Norwich	Herkimer, Tioga	Madison (1804)	*Part ceded to* Oneida (1804)
Clinton Mar. 7, 1788	Plattsburgh	Washington, St. Lawrence (annexed 1801)	Essex (1799) St. Lawrence (1802) Franklin (1808)	
Columbia Apr. 4, 1786	Hudson	Albany		
Cortland Apr. 8, 1808	Cortland	Onondaga		
Cumberland July 3, 1766 *defunct*		Albany		*Ceded to* Vermont (1777)
Delaware Mar. 10, 1797	Delhi	Ulster Otsego		
Dutchess Nov. 1, 1683	Poughkeepsie	Original county	Putnam (1812)	*Part ceded to* Albany (1717)
Erie Apr. 2, 1821	Buffalo	Niagara		
Essex Mar. 1, 1799	Elizabeth- town	Clinton	Franklin (1808)	
Franklin Mar. 11, 1808	Malone	Clinton Essex		*Part ceded to* Essex (1822)
Fulton Apr. 18, 1838	Johnstown	Montgomery		

County/ Date Formed	County Seat	Parent County/ Counties	Daughter County/ Counties	Part Annexed from/ Ceded to
Genesee Mar. 30, 1802	Batavia	Ontario	Allegany (1806) Cattaraugus (1808) Chautauqua (1808) Niagara (1808) Livingston (1821) Monroe (1821) Orleans (1824) Wyoming (1841)	*Part ceded to* Livingston (1823) Orleans (1825)
Gloucester Mar. 16, 1770 *defunct*		Albany		*Ceded to* Vermont (1777)
Greene Mar. 25, 1800	Catskill	Albany, Ulster		*Part ceded to* Ulster (1812)
Hamilton Feb. 12, 1816	Sageville Lake Pleasant	Montgomery		
Herkimer Feb. 16, 1791	Herkimer	Montgomery	Onandaga (1794) Oneida (1798) Chenango (1798) St Lawrence (1802)	*Part annexed from* Montgomery (1817) Otsego (1816) Plainfield (1816) Richfield (1816) *Part ceded to* Montgomery (1797)
Jefferson Mar. 28, 1805	Watertown	Oneida		*Part annexed from* Lewis (1813) *Part ceded to* Lewis (1809)
Kings Nov. 1, 1683	Brooklyn Borough, NYC	Original county		
Lewis Mar. 28, 1805	Lowville	Oneida		
Livingston Feb. 23, 1821	Geneseo	Genesee Ontario		*Part annexed from* Allegany (1846, 1856)

continued on next page

289

County/ Date Formed	County Seat	Parent County/ Counties	Daughter County/ Counties	Part Annexed from/ Ceded to
Madison Mar. 21, 1806	Wampsville	Madison		*Part annexed from* Oneida (1836)
Monroe Feb. 23, 1821		Genesee Ontario		
Montgomery (founded as Tryon Mar. 12, 1772; name changed Apr. 2, 1784)	Fonda	Albany	Ontario (1789) Herkimer (1791) Otsego (1791) Tioga (1791) St. Lawrence (1802) Hamilton (1816) Fulton (1838)	
Nassau Jan. 1, 1899	Mineola	Queens		
New York Nov. 1, 1683	Manhattan Borough, NYC	Original county	Westchester (1874)	
Niagara Mar. 11, 1808	Lockport	Genesee	Erie (1821)	
Oneida Mar. 15, 1798	Utica	Herkimer	Lewis (1805) Jefferson (1805) Oswego (1816)	*Part annexed from* Chenango (1804) *Part ceded to* Clinton (1801) Madison (1836)
Onondaga Mar. 5, 1794	Syracuse	Herkimer	Cayuga (1799) Cortland (1808) Oswego (1816)	
Ontario Jan. 27, 1789	Canandaigua	Montgomery	Steuben (1796) Genesee (1802) Livingston (1821) Monroe (1821) Wayne (1823) Yates (1823)	*Part annexed from* Montgomery (1791) Steuben (1814)
Orange Nov. 1, 1683	Goshen	Original county	Rockland (1798)	*Part annexed from* Ulster (1798)

County/ Date Formed	County Seat	Parent County/ Counties	Daughter County/ Counties	Part Annexed from/ Ceded to
Orleans Nov. 11, 1824	Albion	Genesee		*Part annexed from* Genesee (1825)
Oswego Mar. 1, 1816	Oswego Pulaski	Oneida Onondaga		
Otsego Feb. 16, 1791	Cooperstown	Montgomery	Schoharie (1795) Delaware (1797)	
Putnam June 12, 1812	Carmel	Dutchess		
Queens Nov. 1, 1683	Queens Borough, NYC	Original county		
Rensselaer Feb. 7, 1791	Troy	Albany		
Richmond Nov. 1, 1683	Staten Island Borough, NYC	Original county		
Rockland Feb. 23, 1798	New City	Orange		
St. Lawrence Mar. 3, 1802	Ogdensburgh (1802–28) Canton (1828–pres.)	Clinton Montgomery Herkimer		
Saratoga Feb. 7, 1791	Ballston Spa	Albany		
Schenectady Mar. 7, 1809	Schenectady	Albany		
Schoharie Apr. 6, 1795	Schoharie	Albany Otsego		*Part annexed from* Greene (1836)
Schuyler Apr. 17, 1854	Watkins Glen	Chemung Steuben Tompkins		
Seneca Mar. 29, 1804	Ovid Waterloo	Cayuga	Tompkins (1817) Wayne (1823)	*Part annexed from* Tompkins (1819)

continued on next page

291

County/ Date Formed	County Seat	Parent County/ Counties	Daughter County/ Counties	Part Annexed from/ Ceded to
Steuben Mar. 18, 1796	Bath	Ontario	Yates (1823) Schuyler (1854)	*Part annexed from* Allegany (1808) Livingston (1821)
Suffolk Nov. 1, 1683	Riverhead	Original county		
Sullivan Mar. 27, 1809	Monticello	Ulster	Ulster (1809)	
Tioga Feb. 16, 1791	Owego	Montgomery	Chenango (1798) Broome (1806) Tompkins (1822) Chemung (1836)	
Tompkins Apr. 17, 1817	Ithaca	Cayuga Seneca	Schuyler (1854)	
Tryon *see* Montgomery				
Ulster Nov. 1, 1683	Kingston	Original county	Delaware (1798) Greene (1808) Sullivan (1809)	
Warren Mar. 12, 1813	Lake George	Washington		
Washington Mar. 12, 1772 (name change Apr. 2, 1784)	Hudson Falls (until 1994) Ft. Edward (1994–pres.)	Albany	Clinton (1788) Warren (1813)	*Part annexed from* Albany (1791) *Part ceded to* State of Vt. (1790)
Wayne Apr. 11, 1823	Lyons	Ontario Seneca		
Westchester Nov. 1, 1683	White Plains	Original county		*Part ceded to* New York County (1874, 1895)
Wyoming May 14, 1841	Warsaw	Genesee		*Part annexed from* Allegany (1846)
Yates Feb. 5, 1823	Penn Yan	Ontario		*Part annexed from* Steuben (1824)

INDEX